*Grub Street Irregular*

By the same author

*Playing for Time*
*Kindred Spirits*

*Cyril Connolly: A Life*
*Tobias Smollett*
*Penguin Special: The Life and Times of Allen Lane*

*Love Among the Filing Cabinets:*
*The Chatto Book of Office Life*

JEREMY LEWIS

*Grub Street Irregular*

Harper
Press

HarperPress
An imprint of HarperCollins*Publishers*
77–85 Fulham Palace Road,
Hammersmith, London W6 8JB
www.harpercollins.co.uk

Published by HarperPress in 2008

1

A catalogue record for this book
is available from the British Library

ISBN 978–0–00–255906–5

Set in Minion by
Newgen Imaging Systems (P) Ltd, Chennai, India

Printed and bound in Great Britain by Clays Ltd, St Ives plc

**Mixed Sources**
Product group from well-managed
forests and other controlled sources
www.fsc.org  Cert no. SW-COC-1806
© 1996 Forest Stewardship Council
FSC

FSC is a non-profit international organisation established to promote the
responsible management of the world's forests. Products carrying the FSC
label are independently certified to assure consumers that they come
from forests that are managed to meet the social, economic and
ecological needs of present and future generations.

Find out more about HarperCollins and the environment at
www.harpercollins.co.uk/green

*To*
*Amy Freston*
*(soprano supreme)*
*and*
*my sons-in-law*
*Tom Deards and Henry Dimbleby*
*(inessential background reading)*

# CONTENTS

## Contents

# An Explanation,
# and Acknowledgements

Many books come into being by accident rather than design, and when, one evening in the early Eighties, I began to write an account of how some twenty years earlier I had clambered on board the boat train at Euston Station, *en route* for Holyhead, the Irish ferry and a new life as an undergraduate at Trinity College, Dublin, I had no idea that I was embarking on an autobiography, let alone a multi-volume memoir; nor can I remember why I wanted to write such a thing, or what had inspired this sudden spasm of nostalgia. We had recently moved back to London after six years of exile in Oxford, and were living in a rubble of possessions, as yet unsorted and unpacked. I typed at a table in our bedroom, hemmed in by teetering mounds of books and clothes and children's toys, but as I inched my way slowly down the page, the years and my surroundings dropped away and, as though in a trance, I found myself reliving, in the minutest and most vivid detail, that heady moment when I first spotted ffiona, the great passion of my early student life, striding about the deck of the Dun Laoghaire ferry, the wind lashing her auburn hair and her magnificent bosom jutting out like the prow of a Nelsonian warship; or the anticlimactic misery in which, the following morning, I dragged myself round the grey, granitic squares of Trinity, bleary-eyed from lack of sleep and ruinously indigested from a diet of draught Guinness and stale pork pies.

So immersed was I in the minutiae of my vanished youth, and so overwhelmed by the long-forgotten details bubbling to the surface, that I felt I had written a full-length book by the end of that first evening, and was disappointed to discover that I had notched up 400 words at most. Over the next week I produced some 4,000 words in all, and as they seemed to make a satisfying, self-contained item, I posted them off to Alan Ross at the *London Magazine*, since I knew he had a soft spot for memoirs and was often prepared to publish pieces which, for reasons of length or authorial obscurity, were unlikely to find homes in more conventional outlets. Prompt as always, he sent me by return one of his familiar postcards, written on a sticky label pasted down onto a card which he had himself received, the original sender's message plainly legible under Alan's large and widely-spaced handwriting. To my relief, he liked ffiona very much, and would be printing her in the next issue of the magazine; he longed to know what happened next, and hoped I would keep his readers informed.

Dutiful as ever, I produced a second instalment, and then a third in which I described how, to my eternal regret, I had been too shy and embarrassed to take advantage of the situation while sharing a prison cell with my beloved on the Greco–Turkish border in the summer of 1962. This might have been the end of the story had Carol O'Brien from Collins not written to say that she had greatly enjoyed my pieces, and hoped they might form the germ of a book. Nothing had been further from my thoughts, but the opportunity was too good, and too flattering, to pass up, and before long I had signed up to write a slice of autobiography based on my time at Trinity. I have always enjoyed notions of circularity, of ending up pretty much where one started out, and since I had worked, unhappily, for an advertising agency before going up to university, and went into publishing once it was all over, I decided that I would begin and end the book in an office, wondering quite what I was doing there and how soon I could make my escape. I would suspend my Irish adventures between these two poles of office life, like a literary washing line with autobiographical escapades pinned along its length. The fact that Collins were publishing my book seemed appropriate, since theirs were the unnamed offices in which my story ended: in those days it was still a patrician family firm, ruled by a hyperactive and heavily tweeded old gentleman with eyebrows like bolts of carbonated lightning, and both Rupert Murdoch and the Harper prefix lay in the unimaginable future.

Most writers are avid recyclers of their own work, and writing *Playing for Time* was made a good deal easier by the fact that a year or two earlier the poet Derek Mahon, an old friend from Trinity, had offered me a monthly column on the *New Statesman*, where he was then working. Many of the pieces I had written for him were essentially autobiographical, and I eagerly pressed them into service. In due course the book was finished, and was published in 1987. Apart from a couple of stinkers, the reviews couldn't have been kinder, and since publishers always enjoy the mixture as before, Carol O'Brien's successor, Michael Fishwick, commissioned a second volume, *Kindred Spirits*, which dealt with my unsuccessful career in publishing, and was eventually published in 1995. Once again I employed both the circular and the washing-line techniques, and once again the reviews were mercifully kind.

Writing one's autobiography in one volume, let alone two, is a presumptuous undertaking at the best of times, and every so often I was asked how I could remember the past in such detail without having kept a diary, how much of it was made up, and why anyone should want to read about the experiences of someone who has led a pretty humdrum life and is completely unknown to the world at large. I mentioned earlier how things I had entirely forgotten came bubbling to the surface if

I concentrated hard enough, as though everything one had ever experienced had been somehow recorded on a giant tape or DVD, only fragments of which could ever be retrieved. Making things up is rather more problematic. Woefully lacking in imagination, I am quite incapable of inventing stories; I like to think that everything recorded in those two books actually occurred, but, like most writers, I tend to burnish and embellish. Autobiographers and travel writers inevitably concentrate their fire on unusual or memorable occurrences at the expense of the everyday, thereby suggesting that they live more colourful lives than is generally the case.

Every now and then one comes to believe one's own version of events, however far it may have strayed from the truth. In *Kindred Spirits* I described how, when I was working for the Oxford University Press, I went to see John Sparrow, then the Warden of All Souls, and how, after much ringing of the bell and hammering on the knocker, he eventually came to the door of his Lodgings in the High looking distraught and ashen-featured, with a black cowlick of hair falling down across his forehead. When I offered to come back another day, he seized me by the arm and begged me to come in. He was, he said, having the most frightful afternoon: a busload of Japanese academics, all of them admirers of A.E. Housman, had come to talk to him about their hero, about whom he was known to be a world authority; they were very charming, but he couldn't understand a word they said. Would I be an angel and somehow help him out? I explained that I knew next to nothing about Housman, but that, he assured me, was neither here nor there. He escorted me into his sitting room, where nine Japanese scholars sat in a circle, smiling, drinking cups of tea and wearing rimless spectacles. 'Here is my friend Mr Lewis,' Sparrow explained by way of introduction, although we had met for the first time only seconds before. 'He is a leading authority on Housman, and has come to join our discussions.' He then took a seat at the back of the room, smiling broadly, and left me to speak to the Japanese, whose English consisted of a series of impenetrable barks.

Some years later I wrote up this incident for the *London Magazine*; Alan Ross enjoyed it, both for its own sake and because, back in the Fifties, he used to go to football matches with Sparrow and Goronwy Rees, the erstwhile Bursar of All Souls. The proofs arrived, and my wife Petra looked them through. 'But this is all wrong,' she said. 'There weren't nine Japanese Housman experts. There was only one: I remember your telling me so when you got home that evening.' Since Petra is a reliable witness and has an excellent memory, this was a distressing revelation: I was quite convinced that there had been a small army of Japanese in attendance, and still am; it made a far better story that way, and to boil them down to one would involve extensive rewriting on proof. I rang Alan Ross and asked him what I should do. 'For goodness sake keep them at nine,' he said. 'No one will ever know.' And so the nine Japanese Housman experts made their way into the *London Magazine*, and then into *Kindred Spirits*, and eventually into a biography of John Sparrow (not written, I hasten to say, by me). And shortly after the first of my ffiona pieces had appeared, my old Trinity friend Charles Sprawson pointed out that although I had my heroine clutching a copy of Gunter Grass's *The Tin Drum* in the face of a Force Eight gale, its English translation had not yet been published in 1961, and my memory must have been at fault. I thought hard and long about correcting this in *Playing for Time*, but finally decided against: I liked to think that if a perceptive reader gave this loose end a tweak, the entire garment might begin to unravel. Besides, none of us is infallible. But sometimes I have to admit the error of my ways. I got it into my head that Ernest Hecht of the Souvenir Press had once invited the notoriously workaholic André Deutsch to watch Arsenal play at Highbury, and that no sooner had they taken their places than his guest whipped out a fountain pen and the galley proofs of his forthcoming spring list, and never looked up till the final whistle blew. Ernest assures me that there is not a shred of truth to it, and I have reluctantly withdrawn it from the canon.

I was in my early forties when I began to write *Playing for Time*: on the cusp of middle age, I wanted to celebrate and exorcise a vanished youth, to get it out of my system and move on to other things, at work and with my family. My motives were both familiar and prosaic – which may be why, provided they're well enough written, the memoirs of nonentities some-times ring more bells with readers than those of the famous or distinguished. Publishers long to commission the memoirs of celebrities, whether ghostwritten or hand-crafted, yet all too often they are blighted by pomposity, self-importance, discretion in all the wrong places, and even more blatant name-dropping than that on display in the pages of this book.

A few years after the publication of *Playing for Time* I was commissioned to write the authorised biography of the writer and critic Cyril Connolly, and although I wanted, at times, to give him a sharp retrospective kick, I found his prose and his cast of mind entirely sympathetic. Everything he wrote, including the most humdrum book reviews, was essentially autobiographical, and I share to the full his autobiographical bias; for all his snobbery and greed and cowardice and indolence – or, more probably, because of them – he wrote better than anyone else about feelings and failings common to us all. One's reading of Connolly is punctuated by starts of recognition and disconcerting glimpses of oneself; and it is this ability to empathise with and articulate the familiar as well as the unexpected that distinguishes the autobiographies I admire, and not the quantity of famous names or important events that litter the page. Autobiography is an art at which the English excel, and the best memoirs of the last half-century – John Gale's *Clean Young Englishman*, James Lees-Milne's *Another Self*, Julian Maclaren-Ross's *Memoirs of the Forties*, Gerald Durrell's *My Family and Other Animals*, the two-decker memoirs of Alan Ross and Michael Wharton, the various volumes of Richard Cobb and, more recently, the autobiographical writings of Simon Gray and Julia Blackburn – combine comicality with a sense of the sad absurdity of life, a delight in the oddities of human behaviour with a deceptive authorial modesty; and *Playing for Time* and *Kindred Spirits* were written in conscious emulation of a tradition I admire and long to be part of.

Not long after my Connolly biography had been published, George Weidenfeld suggested that I should write a history or survey of English literary life since the war. I was very flattered by his proposal, but never followed it up: quite apart from other obligations, I wasn't at all sure how one might set about it, and instinctively preferred to cover some of the ground through biographies and memoirs rather than attempt a more abstract or generalised survey. But I've always been fascinated by the interaction between the mechanics of literary life – the activities of publishers, literary agents, literary editors and the rest – and what the world at large comes to read and admire. It's an elusive and neglected area, not least because of the great gulf set between theorists and practitioners: academics who interest themselves in 'the book' are strong on economic, social and cultural trends, but tend to deal in broad abstractions and lack practical experience of the trades they set out to diagnose and knowledge of the people involved; publishers pride themselves on using 'hunch' or 'a nose for a book' to interpret the *Zeitgeist*, and have neither the time, the inclination nor the ability to relate their activities to trends in society at large, far preferring Garrick or Groucho Club gossip and the minutiae of trade politics to the broad sociological sweep. Combining the scholarly and the anecdotal, the theoretical and the practical, is easier said than done, and the waters are muddied by the oblique and elusive nature of the publishing business. Apart from rare examples like Victor Gollancz with his Left Book Club, publishers – unlike newspaper proprietors – exert such influence as they have behind the scenes, moulding taste and the climate of opinion indirectly and at second hand: the pre-eminence of Julian Barnes, Ian McEwan and Martin Amis among their contemporaries could, to some extent, reflect the fact that, as young writers, they were brilliantly promoted and publicised by Tom Maschler at Cape, and some agents have an equally electric effect, but such influences are hard to prove or pin down.

Ten years after Lord Weidenfeld took me to lunch at the Garrick, I have produced a book which is part memoir, part potted biography, part rumination on the vanishing world in which I've spent my working life: it is an unashamed ragbag of pieces, written at various times and with no chronological thread, freestanding in themselves yet interconnected by subject matter and recurrent *personae* and motifs. My only qualification for writing such a book is that having been sacked three times and spent nearly twenty years as a freelance writer and editor, I have a varied experience of Grub Street life: apart from writing my own books, I have, over the past forty years, worked for six publishers, two literary agents and three magazines, and written reviews, articles and obituaries for more newspapers and magazines than I can begin to remember.

My biographies have covered some of the same ground, albeit at a more elevated level. Cyril Connolly was the quintessential literary man, agonising over the books he never got round to writing, envying others their success, famously idle yet scrupulous about delivering his reviews on time and written to length, relishing the *réclame* that goes with founding and editing an influential and much-admired literary magazine. Tobias Smollett was Grub Street incarnate, working all hours as novelist, editor, translator, historian and literary jack-of-all-trades at a time when writers were coming to look to the market rather than the aristocratic patron for support, and publishing was assuming a recognisable *modus operandi*: he also provided an opportunity to attempt an old-fashioned Hesketh Pearson type of biography, dependent entirely on secondary sources and without an iota of original research. Allen Lane, the founder of Penguin Books, was the greatest publisher of his time, a hard-headed but idealistic businessman who was both mercenary and missionary, passionate about making the best available to the many, a hugely important and influential figure in the business in which I spent so much of my adult life. I'm now working on a book about the Greene family: Graham Greene himself worked as a journalist, a literary editor, and a publisher with Eyre & Spottiswoode and The Bodley Head, and several other members of his family distinguished themselves as writers and publishers.

I've tried to arrange my vignettes of literary life thematically if not chronologically: the first section touches on aspects of editorial and publishing life, the second describes how I became an inadvertent biographer, the third deals with my infrequent visits overseas, and the last is given over to absent friends. The recurrence of certain names – Alan Ross, André Deutsch and Dennis Enright among them – reflects a tendency to hero-worship which flowered in middle age but was entirely absent when I should have been collecting the autographs of Len Hutton and Stanley Matthews.

Publishing this book with HarperCollins has been like a reunion with old friends. The ever-patient Michael Fishwick has moved on to Bloomsbury, but Richard Johnson, who inherited my book after Mike's departure, is my oldest friend in publishing: we worked together in the publicity department at Collins in St James's Place in 1967, and have remained chums ever since. Richard is one of the great gossips in a trade addicted to the art, and his subversive and disrespectful stories make lunch in The Dove in Hammersmith a high point of the freelance life. Robert Lacey is a fellow survivor from Chatto in the 1980s, and has proved, once again, to be a precise and painstaking editor of the kind we authors dream of. Helen Ellis is a welcome and familiar presence at publishers' parties; she too worked for André Deutsch, albeit after my time, and within minutes of meeting one another we find ourselves fondly reminiscing about those long-departed days in Great Russell Street.

Spouses are notoriously stern critics; I dread showing Petra my typescripts and withhold them from her until the last possible moment, since she has an eagle eye for pomposity, flatulence and those passages or turns of phrase which one feels uneasy about without knowing how to put them right, but hopes to get away with. She put me through the Inquisition, and I feel a better man for it. I'm also extremely grateful to my friend and kindred spirit Lucy Lethbridge for her enthusiasm and encouragement. My agent, Gillon Aitken, has a longer experience of the book business than anyone I can think of with the exception of Lord Weidenfeld and Ernest Hecht, distinguishing himself as a publisher, a literary agent and a mellifluous translator of Pushkin; once again he has been a source of sound and humorous advice. My daughter Jemima has written so entertainingly about Lewis family life in her columns in the *Sunday Telegraph* and the *Independent* that I have felt no need to cover the ground in these pages.

Parts of this book have appeared in the *London Magazine*, the *Oldie*, *Slightly Foxed*, the *Literary Review*, *Logos*, *The Reluctant Biographer* (Slightly Foxed, 2006), *Lives for Sale: Biographers' Tales* edited by Mark Bostridge (Continuum, 2004) and the most recent reprint of *Another Self* by James Lees-Milne (John Murray, 1998). Extracts from the Diaries of James Lees-Milne, published by John Murray, are reproduced by permission of David Higham Ltd.

# SCENES FROM LITERARY LIFE

# ONE

# A Foot in the Door

As a child, I excelled at nothing, and little has changed since then. I was academically average, but no more; cowardice, short-sightedness, physical ineptitude and a total absence of team spirit ruled me out as a games player; I had no artistic leanings whatsoever, and never had the slightest desire to paint, sculpt or play a musical instrument. I was far too self-conscious to sing or dance: so much so that when, in my unself-conscious, music-loving sixties, I am overcome by a bacchanalian yearning to give voice to my deep bass tones, or to hurl myself into a frenzied tribal dance, or to seize Petra in my arms and whirl her round the kitchen when the New Year's Day concert of waltzes and polkas comes over the air from Vienna, I know, to my terrible frustration, that I shall never be able to do so, and have to content myself with humming along in my head and a convulsive twitching of the limbs.

Although I have never suffered since, except in the company of women talking interminably about other people's kitchens, I remember being stupefied by boredom for much of my childhood, and hard-pressed to know how to fill in the long hours, many of which seem to have been given over to watching the rain drumming against the sash windows or being taken for long walks in Battersea Park, where the leaves of the plane trees were coated with the same black soot that left a ring round a forefinger thrust up my nose. I played games of cricket with my teddies in the nursery of our gloomy, rambling, first-floor flat in Prince of Wales Drive, conducted church services when they were not on the games field, and – until I realised that it would never grow back – occasionally trimmed their hair. I pored over maps of imaginary islands, and in order to link them to the mainland I drew red-funnelled Cunard liners, all of which were mounted on castors and trundled along the bottom of the ocean (that being the way I briefly assumed boats moved about the world). I was good at making people laugh: still more so since I was, and remain, superhumanly flatulent, and adept at snarling farts that sent my sister, and later my school friends, into paroxysms of mirth.

When not farting or consorting with my teddies – one of whom I took with me on my first term at public school, hastily hiding him away in my tuckbox when I realised that the other boys were more interested in cigarettes and cider – I greatly enjoyed making lists: a commonplace juvenile obsession shared, in later life, with Cyril Connolly and his father, a bibulous major who was also a world authority on snails and potted meats. Making lists seems, in retrospect, a particularly sterile activity, but it was all-absorbing at the time. I began with Mammals of the World, and to satisfy my craving I asked my parents and family friends to give me books on the subject for Christmas and my birthday. I read these carefully, and every time I came across the name of a mammal I had never heard of before, I entered it in a red-covered exercise book. I tried at first to arrange them in descending order, with apes and monkeys in the front, the egg-laying echidna and duck-billed platypus bringing up the rear, and dogs, cats, cows, deer, whales and the rest ranged in between: but there seemed to be so many mammals demanding entry that before long they began to leap the barriers, and I had to paste in extra pages to accommodate the overflow. To enliven the proceedings, I added a few stamp-sized illustrations: these were either cut out of magazines like *Illustrated* or *Picture Post*, or my own splodgy watercolours, which bore little resemblance to their subjects.

From mammals I moved on, at about the age of twelve, to Classical Composers: these were listed, plus dates, on sheets of blue Basildon Bond notepaper, and arranged in alphabetical order. The Composers never gripped me quite as much as Mammals of the World, partly because I had other distractions: we were preparing to emigrate to Canada at the time, and I spent a lot of time reading and dreaming about the Canadian Pacific Railway which, in a few weeks' time, would be taking us to our new home on the prairies. But when we came back from Canada some six months later I resumed my list-making activities – with, once again, a musical theme. Although I was far too buttoned-up to tap my foot or snap my fingers in time to the music, I became a passionate devotee of traditional jazz, and an expert on the subject.

By now we were in the mid-1950s, and like most trad. jazz addicts of the time I took an austere and restrictive approach to the matter. Our gods were King Oliver, the early Louis Armstrong, Bunk Johnson, Jelly Roll Morton and Kid Ory; we took a dim view of saxophones, Sidney Bechet excluded, and listened to nothing later than Fats Waller and the early Duke Ellington. I read every book I could find on the subject, and collected records of varying speeds: in a fit of fashion-induced madness, I pushed out the middle of my 45s to make them look more like jukebox records, so making it impossible to play them ever again. I persuaded the jazz-loving father of my oldest friend, Tom Pomeroy, to take us to Humphrey Lyttelton's club at 100 Oxford Street; for a short time Penguin Books sold DIY kits with which one could convert one's paperbacks into home-bound hardbacks, and with trembling hands I subjected my Pelican of Rex Harris's *Jazz* to the treatment, pasting in some illustrations at the same time. And, of course, I went on making lists, some of which I still find

tucked into my copies of Rudi Blesh's *All That Jazz* and Mezz
Mezzrow's autobiography: interminable names of long-forgotten
cornet players and drummers and clarinettists, written in
fountain pen in a careful copperplate hand on the same blue
sheets of Basildon Bond.

But my list-making days were almost over. At about the same
time as I became a jazz addict, I decided, for no good reason, to
support Leyton Orient Football Club. I had never been to Leyton
in my life, and the East End in those days was thought of as a
dangerous *terra incognita*; I had no interest in football and little
understanding of the rules, even though I ended my school days
as a qualified referee, a man in a brown blazer travelling down
from Wolverhampton to present me with a certificate and
express the hope that one day he would see me in action at
Wembley Stadium; and Leyton Orient had an undistinguished
record, forever lurking at the bottom of the Third Division
(South). I expect I decided to feign an interest in football to
ingratiate myself with the hearties who ruled the roost in the
most games-mad house in a games-mad school, and chose
Leyton Orient because I liked the name, and the tigerish striped
shirts worn by the players: either way, I dutifully snipped out the
details of that week's defeat from the sports pages of the *Sunday
Express* and pasted them into a notebook, along with the rare
reports of the matches themselves. But this was not, strictly
speaking, list-making as we know it; more the decadent remnant
of a fading childhood addiction.

My literary ambitions as a child were equally modest, and
easily satisfied: so much so that when I read about writers who
have scribbled incessantly since they could first hold a pen, and
are never happy except when seated behind their desks, I know
myself to be a fake, or the literary equivalent of a Sunday painter,
a dabbler who would probably never write another word if
suddenly endowed with a large private income. Like thousands
of my contemporaries, I was adept at knocking out jocular

imitations of Belloc's *Cautionary Verses*; like thousands more, I edited miniature newspapers, made by folding sheets of blank white paper again and again until it became impossible to bend them any more, and then filling the inch-high pages with tiny writing and drawings of pin men in action, arranged in columnar form. When I was at prep school I wrote, but soon discontinued, a story about two Romans, named – unwittingly, and to my parents' amusement – Testiculus and Constipides; I don't remember writing a word at my public school, and it was only when I went to Trinity College, Dublin, in the early 1960s that I began, very tentatively, to write poems and articles for the college magazines, two of which I eventually edited.

A few years later I took to reading my handful of poems out loud in London pubs, once in tandem with Jon Stallworthy; but I knew myself to be a hopeless dilettante, and soon abandoned both writing and performing. Despite my propensity for embellishing the truth, I have never had any desire to write fiction. When, in due course, I found myself poring over Cyril Connolly's abortive attempts to write novels and short stories, and noted how this most eloquent of autobiographical writers became wooden and self-conscious in the process, I recognised, once again, a kindred spirit. (Connolly longed to be a novelist like Evelyn Waugh, but *The Rock Pool*, his only completed novel, is wretchedly stiff and unconvincing.)

When I left university I thought, in some vague way, that I might become a writer, but it never occurred to me that the only way to do so was to put pen to paper. I liked the *idea* of being a writer, but my approach was entirely passive: I assumed that, rather like the truths of Christianity or the existence of God, all would be revealed if I waited long enough. I never gave a moment's thought to becoming a lawyer or an accountant, or going into business of any kind: partly because I suspected, rightly, that I would be no good at such things, lacking as I did both team spirit and the competitive urge, and partly from an arrogant and unjustified sense that I was cut out for better things. Had I done so, and had I survived the course, I would now be looking forward to an easy retirement and a reasonable pension rather than worrying where and how I can earn the next penny. But if my life has been short on both incident and material rewards – writers' lives are famously dull affairs, and for the most part badly paid – at least it has been a continuum: editing and writing for the magazines at university had given me a taste for Grub Street existence, and I have gone on doing much the same ever since. But forty years ago, when I started out on the literary life, I had no idea where I was going, or what I wanted to achieve.

Cyril Connolly was always fascinated by the ways in which writers scraped a living. Shortly after the end of the war he sent a questionnaire to various eminent authors asking them what jobs or means of earning money were most compatible with the literary life, and published their answers in *Horizon*. Connolly himself recommended a rich wife; a common ideal among his less worldly contributors was a job, preferably manual, which wasn't too exhausting, left the mind free, and didn't compete with the business of writing. Wood-turning and vegetable-growing were among those mentioned by his correspondents. None suggested a job in publishing, so confirming Connolly's own belief that the enemy of promise was not so much the pram in the hall as work in what he termed 'cultural diffusion' – publishing, journalism, broadcasting, the British Council and other agreeable, convivial and literate activities which brought one into contact with writers and the literary world, and could all too easily become a substitute for writing itself.

Despite such warnings, publishing houses inevitably include among their staff an above-average number of would-be writers, part-time writers and writers *manqués*. Every now and then one of them moves to the other side of the desk, and becomes a full-time writer. Most of them, no doubt, had gone into publishing for reasons which Cyril Connolly would have found deeply suspect. For my part, I assumed that all publishers were rather like the late Colin Haycraft of Duckworth – bespectacled, articulate, immensely well-read characters with double firsts from Oxford and a good line in corduroy jackets and colourful bow-ties – and that the life of a publisher's editor (for such I assumed I would be) consisted of a little light editing in the morning, an afternoon spent reading the typescript of some new masterpiece, and the early evening given over to dry sherry and waggish repartee with eminent authors.

I eventually landed a very junior job in the publicity department at Collins, and I soon realised how misconceived my notions had been. There were plenty of literate, well-read individuals working there as editors, Philip Ziegler and Richard Ollard among them, but the salesmen ruled the roost; and although the formidable boss, Billy Collins, was a product of Harrow and Magdalen, he was, I'm sure, far happier haranguing the reps or moving Collins titles to the front of the pile in bookshops than discussing new trends in poetry with John Lehmann or lit. crit. with F.R. Leavis. The best publishers, I soon realised, were neither literary nor academic, but were an intriguing and forceful combination of the businessman and the impresario. Although the period between the wars had seen the rise of the gentleman publisher who went into the business after public school and Oxbridge – some as members of publishing dynasties, like Billy Collins or Jock Murray, others as new arrivals, like Rupert Hart-Davis, Hamish Hamilton, Fredric Warburg or Ian Parsons of Chatto – the traditional publisher had tended to come from a lower-middle-class, non-conformist, rather Wellsian background, starting from the bottom after leaving school and learning every aspect of the trade as he worked his way up. Stanley Unwin and Allen Lane had begun in this way; and many of those who dominated the trade in my youth – Tom Maschler, Tony Godwin, Paul Hamlyn, Charles Pick of Heinemann – had followed in their footsteps, with both Godwin and Hamlyn selling books off barrows in their early days.

From Collins I moved on to André Deutsch, where more salutary lessons were learned. Like all the best publishers, Deutsch himself was shrewd, quick-witted and parsimonious, adept at picking other people's brains and possessed of an almost intuitive 'nose' or 'hunch' for a book or an author, and an equally strong sense of what books would or would not suit his list. The literary side of publishing – reading and assessing works offered to the firm, and then knocking them into shape – he could safely leave to Diana Athill in particular; and it formed only part of his job, competing for his time with the demands of printers, binders, papermakers, literary agents, booksellers, wholesalers, librarians, libel lawyers and literary editors. He was workaholic, monomaniacal and possessed of just the right amount of tunnel vision – all qualities that distinguish the publisher proper from the mere editor.

The great publisher has to have something of the actor about him, able to simulate (and yet at the same time genuinely feel, if for an instant only) overpowering enthusiasm, excitement, rage and disappointment, as the occasion demands. 'This is the most amazing book I have taken on in my entire publishing career,' he will declare *à propos* a particular favourite on that season's list, and he will believe it for the next six months at least; he will become almost apoplectic about some modish new novel on offer to the firm, and prophesy doom and destruction if he fails to take it on, but it will be instantly forgotten if it goes to another publisher – unless, of course, it proves to be a disaster in terms of sales, in which case a degree of *schadenfreude* and retrospective wisdom may be in order. What made Tom Maschler the most brilliant publisher of our time, apart from stylishness, charisma and a feeling for the spirit of the age, was his ability to persuade his colleagues, and then his salesmen, and then the world at large, that all his geese were swans, and that

Cape books were synonymous with both excitement and distinction.

However much the editor-cum-writer *manqué* may enjoy his work, he almost always has one eye on the clock and one foot in the door; and however much he may admire the authors whose books he edits, he is hard-pressed to indulge in the wholehearted suspensions of disbelief that distinguish the genuine publisher from his more apathetic and less driven colleagues. Asked out of hours about the modish new novel, assuming his firm has taken it on, he will probably concede that it's 'all right', but no more, and recommend instead a rereading of Trollope or Turgenev. The most extreme example of the editor as Doubting Thomas was the poet and critic D.J. Enright, my colleague at Chatto for many years. Dennis thought that only a handful of books deserved to be published in any one year, and since he completely lacked the competitive spirit so essential to the successful publisher, he didn't mind whether we or Faber or Secker or Cape published the few titles he thought worth taking on. A firm run by Enrights would soon die from inanition, publishing far too few books to cover the overheads, let alone make a profit; and since literary men employed by publishers tend to steer clear of the business side of things, this might not occur to them until it was too late.

T.S. Eliot of Faber was the most famous writer-publisher still active in my lifetime; others included C. Day Lewis, Dennis Enright and Andrew Motion at Chatto, Graham Greene and J.B. Priestley at The Bodley Head, Nigel Nicolson at Weidenfeld, and Diana Athill and Nicolas Bentley at Deutsch. They provided useful contacts, they looked good on the notepaper in the days when directors' names were still listed there, and they could be invoked to impress or overawe recalcitrant authors. 'I would like you to meet Professor Enright,' Norah Smallwood of Chatto would declare, summoning the sage from his lair with a peremptory blast on the internal telephone. Dennis, who was almost certainly tamping his pipe or trying to recover from a long lunch in The Marquis of Granby when she rang, would shuffle down the bare, lino-floored institutional corridor, grumbling *sotto voce* to himself, deliver his views while simultaneously scratching the back of his head and standing to attention, and shuffle back to his office once his services were no longer required ('You may go now, Dennis').

Although some of the most interesting books of the last century were published by part-time writer-publishers like Leonard Woolf, John Lehmann and Alan Ross, publishing and writing call for very different attitudes and abilities, not easily combined in a single individual. Ernest Hecht of the Souvenir Press, who has remained in business longer than most, likes to quote Sir Stanley Unwin's dictum that a publisher's overriding duty to his authors is to remain solvent; effective publishers like Ernest, are, in the last resort, hard-headed if idealistic business-men, and as such they are far removed from most authors and editors. As I discovered when researching my biography of Allen Lane, and as Tom Maschler's ill-advised memoirs make plain, publishers are more interesting for what they do than for what they say or think; whereas writers and academics are prone to, and delight in, indecisiveness and ambiguity, priding themselves on their ability to see all sides of a question and to hold contradictory views at once, the businessman-publisher is, by comparison, uncomplicated, decisive and single-minded.

But I knew nothing of this at the age of twenty-five. What I did know was that working as a minion in publicity depart-ments, and then as a junior editor, was wretchedly badly paid, and that in order to keep afloat – and, in due course, to support a wife, two daughters and an endless procession of cats – I would have to supplement my earnings somehow; still more so since, unlike many of my contemporaries in publishing, I had no private means. I had only been working in publishing for a year when Petra and I got married, and shortly afterwards I began my double life as a reviewer, writing short, anonymous, hundred-word reviews for Michael Ratcliffe on *The Times*. I acquired my first byline when his successor, Ion Trewin, allowed me to give Peter Greave's marvellous autobiography *The Seventh Gate* a full-length review after I had urged him to allot it more than a mere hundred words, and from then on I combined work as a publisher's editor with as much reviewing as I could manage and acquire; and every month or so, feeling like a dealer in rubber goods or some kind of shady salesman, I would make my way to Gaston's remainder shop off Chancery Lane with an overnight bag crammed with review copies, and take whatever he gave me with due deference and gratitude. When times were bad I wrote reports for paperback publishers and entries on molluscs and the countries of Eastern Europe for Reader's Digest Books: a severe discipline in my case, since not only did the facts have to be checked and double-checked, but long sentences, parentheses and subordinate clauses were strictly taboo. I was becoming, perforce, a writer of a kind, and finding my way about the alleys and pubs of Grub Street; but I had no idea what, if anything, I wanted to achieve, and I felt almost claustrophobic with envy and admiration when I read (or read about) those authors who combined reviewing and articles with full-length books as well. Writing books was altogether different, and something I could never aspire to.

# TWO

# Rogues' Gallery

One of the disadvantages of having been to a rather humdrum public school is the occasional embarrassment of explaining where one went. Charles Sprawson is the only person I know who quizzes complete strangers on their schooldays, but every now and then a beaming Old Etonian of my own age will pop the question, hoping for the best and momentarily deceived by my fruity tones and superficial familiarity with his *alma mater*, gleaned from my researches into the life of Cyril Connolly, that most nostalgic and agonised of Old Etonians.

'You won't have heard of it,' I reply, lowering my voice to a confidential whisper in case I am overheard and exposed to the world at large, 'but I went to a place called Malvern.'

'Marlborough?' my questioner booms. 'But that's a splendid school. What house were you in? Did you happen to know . . . ?'

'No, *Malvern*,' I say, making my voice as quiet but as clear as possible; at which a half-pitying, half-baffled look flits across his kindly features, and the conversation is swiftly hurried in a more wholesome direction.

Part of the problem with being an Old Malvernian is that one's fellows are a fairly undistinguished crew. Like Malvern, Marlborough in the old days seems to have been a fairly brutal, philistine school, but at least its more literary pupils had the consolation of knowing that John Betjeman, Siegfried Sassoon and Louis MacNeice had also suffered and survived. Malvern, by comparison, offered cold comfort. During my time at the school, the Old Malvernian most admired by the Governors, and held up as a model for us all, was an angry-looking cove called Sir Godfrey Huggins, who boasted bulging blue eyes, scarlet cheeks and a bristling grey moustache. (I have taken some liberties with the colour scheme, since the photograph of Huggins which hung in the place of honour in one of the school corridors was, of course, in black and white.) Huggins had risen to become the Prime Minister of Rhodesia, and when in due course he was made a peer, he assumed the title of Lord Malvern, in gratitude to his *alma mater*. One of the trains that ran between Paddington and Malvern, and points beyond, was named after him, and bore on either side of its boiler a curved metal plaque to that effect. A photograph of the train's engine, some five feet wide, had been presented to the school in a handsome wooden frame and nailed up alongside that of the former Prime Minister, rubbing shoulders with former headmasters in gowns and mortar boards, and cricketing elevens dating back to the 1860s.

Altogether more interesting, but less widely advertised within the grounds of the school, were James Jesus Angleton, the CIA's paranoid master-spy, and Aleister Crowley, the bald, pop-eyed black magician who liked to be acclaimed 'the wickedest man in the world' or 'the Great Beast', and spent much of his time frolicking with naked handmaidens and sacrificing goats in a deserted monastery in Sicily. C.S. Lewis was a balding sage of a more reputable variety, but although he was an old Oxford friend of Mr Sayer, the Senior English Master, he had blotted his copybook by ridiculing Malvern (referred to as 'Wyvern') in his autobiography, *Summoned by Joy*.

Curiously, for such a philistine and sports-mad school, minor literary men loom larger than games players among the old boys of interest. Raymond Mortimer, a most unlikely Malvernian, hated the place and moved on as quickly as possible to Balliol,

Bloomsbury and the *Sunday Times*; John Moore, an affable old countryman who looked as though he should have worn a tweed fisherman's hat, smoked a pipe and spoke with an *Archers* accent, was much admired in my childhood for his novels set in a country town based on nearby Tewkesbury, and was involved in setting up the Cheltenham Literary Festival; Sir John Wheeler Bennett was well known in his day as an urbane and well-connected historian, diplomat and, no doubt, secret service agent; Humphry Berkeley, a former Tory MP, wrote *The Life and Death of Rochester Sneath*, which must be one the funniest books ever published, with the bonus of drawings by Nicolas Bentley. Younger Old Malvernians, or so I'm told, include Jeremy Paxman, James Delingpole, Giles Foden and the historian Dominic Sandbrook.

But the one who intrigued me most was a shady-sounding Irishman called Derek Verschoyle, who like me was not only a Malvernian but had then gone on to Trinity College, Dublin: he had also had dealings with André Deutsch, and had been a friend of Alan Ross. I first heard of Verschoyle nearly thirty years after I had left school, when I began to contribute to the *London Magazine*, and what Alan Ross told me about him tickled my interest in long-forgotten publishers and minor literary men. Like all the best anecdotalists, Alan liked to tell the same stories, suitably embellished, over and over again; and Verschoyle was one of the figures who regularly resurfaced. I don't think Alan knew much about his background, but I later learned that the Verschoyles were of Dutch origin, and had settled in Ireland in the seventeenth century. Hamilton Verschoyle had given up the Bar for the Church, eventually becoming the Bishop of Kilmore, and had been admired by Queen Victoria who, spotting him riding in Rotten Row, declared him to be the best-looking man she had ever seen; his son, Frederick, spent most of his life in the west of Ireland, dreaming of his undergraduate years at Cambridge and recalling how he had once played cricket for the Gentlemen of Kent.

One of three children, Derek Verschoyle was born in 1911. His father, an engineer, wrote scientific books and was the inventor of a hand-operated lathe known as the Verschoyle Patent Mandrel, and the family divided its time between London and Tanrago House in Co. Sligo. Derek Verschoyle's fifth and final wife, Moira, remembered meeting him on a family holiday in Kilkee, on the west coast of Ireland. 'I had noticed him before,' she wrote in a memoir, *So Long to Wait*, 'because I always noticed colours that were pretty and that looked satisfying when put together, and he was always dressed in lovely mixtures – pale green shirts and dark green trousers, or two shades of blue, and I had seen him once in a primrose shirt that looked simply beautiful with his red curly hair.' She noticed too that he was 'very, very neat and tidy and wore a tie, and his shirt had a proper collar like a man's with a pin in it. He had a nice square face with freckles and he smiled at me, but I didn't think he could be much fun to play with if he was always going to be so tidy.' Years later she would have ample opportunities to discover whether or not he was fun to play with, but in the meantime his mother told her that 'He has been delicate, and he needs a little rough treatment.'

No doubt rough treatment was in plentiful supply when he was sent to Arnold House prep school in north Wales, where he ended his days as head boy. Evelyn Waugh was then briefly employed at the school, and outraged the more conventional masters by turning up for work in baggy plus-fours, an ancient tweed jacket and a rollneck sweater. Verschoyle later claimed that Waugh taught him to play the organ, despite having no knowledge of the instrument himself, and some say that the head boy provided a model for the precocious and worldly Peter Best-Chetwynde in *Decline and Fall*: in later years he employed Waugh as a reviewer for the *Spectator*, and lent him his flat in St James's Place in the summer of 1943. After leaving the model for Llanabba Castle, Verschoyle went on to Malvern: he reached the Classical VI, became a house prefect and a lance-corporal in the

Corps and, according to the Old Boys' Register, was 'prox. acc. of the English Essay Prize' before leaving for Trinity College, Dublin in 1929.

Not long after leaving Trinity he resurfaced as the theatre critic of the *Spectator*. A year later, in 1933, he was made the magazine's literary editor. According to Diana Athill, who had it from her father, he kept a .22 rifle in the office in Gower Street, and would occasionally fling open his window and, his feet propped up on the desk, take potshots at stray cats lurking in the garden or on the black-bricked wall beyond; but however unpopular he may have been with Bloomsbury cats, his convivial, heavy-drinking ways recommended him to his colleagues. He became particularly friendly with Peter Fleming, who was also on the staff, and beginning to make his name as a glamorous and fashionable travel writer, and with Graham Greene. With Fleming he co-edited *Spectator's Gallery*, an anthology of essays, stories and poems from the magazine, published by Jonathan Cape in 1933, and through him he got to know the publisher and man of letters Rupert Hart-Davis. When, some years ago, I wrote to Hart-Davis to ask what he remembered of Verschoyle, he replied that he could recall absolutely nothing about him even though he had been the best man at Verschoyle's second wedding; he told his son Duff that Verschoyle had been 'an absolute shit', but Duff's biography of Peter Fleming includes a pre-war photograph of a white-clad bounder waiting his turn to bat for a team that included Fleming, Edmund Blunden and Rupert Hart-Davis, then an energetic editor at Cape.

Like Fleming before him, Verschoyle employed Graham Greene as a fiction reviewer, and then as a film critic. Greene, who eventually succeeded Verschoyle as the *Spectator*'s literary editor, commissioned him to write the essay on Malvern in *The Old School*, a collection of essays he edited for Cape in 1934 in which Auden, Greene, Stephen Spender, Harold Nicolson, Antonia White, L.P. Hartley, William Plomer, Elizabeth Bowen and others looked back on their schooldays with varying degrees of affection, ridicule, amusement and disdain; maddeningly, Verschoyle's contribution sheds no light on the school itself or his time there, and although I have read it several times, I have no idea what – if anything – he was trying to say: it is even less revealing than the photograph in the Fleming biography, which gives one little impression of what he looked like.

Verschoyle is said to have published a book of poems in 1931, but I can find no record of it in the British Library Catalogue. Like many of the best literary editors – and all the best publishers – Verschoyle was no writer himself: his literary ambitions may have included editing and introducing *The English Novelists: A Survey of the Novel by Twenty Contemporary Novelists*, published by Chatto in 1936 and including Greene, Louis MacNeice, V.S. Pritchett, Edwin Muir, H.E. Bates, Peter Quennell and Elizabeth Bowen among its contributors, but that was about as far as it went. According to Alan Ross, he was 'an impresario rather than a journalist by nature': he was forever pondering the plays, poems and memoirs he planned to write, but 'the gin bottle used to come out at an early hour, so I imagine Derek belonged to the company of those who took the wish for the deed'. But if he failed to advance his own career as a writer during his time at the *Spectator*, he may well have made contacts that would prove useful to him as a spy or double agent: the magazine's editor, Wilson Harris, was an old-fashioned Tory, but those writing for the *Spectator* included Graham Greene, Goronwy Rees, later to be implicated in the flight to Soviet Russia of his friends Guy Burgess and Donald Maclean, and Anthony Blunt, whom Verschoyle enlisted as the art critic.

Shortly before war broke out, Verschoyle married the willowy, elegant Anne Scott-James, who went on to become a well-known journalist, the mother of Max Hastings, and the wife of Osbert Lancaster. He had taken a cottage in Aldworth, the village in the

Chilterns in which Richard Ingrams now lives, and used to invite her down for weekends. 'In that summer of 1939 there was a fair amount of false emotion in the air,' she wrote in her auto-biography: Verschoyle left almost immediately to join the RAF, working in Intelligence, and 'later, when we were divorced, it was as though it had never happened'. When I asked her to elaborate, she said she would rather not: 'although Derek caused me a lot of anxiety one way and another,' she bore him no ill will after all these years; marrying him had been a 'big mistake,' but she hadn't had the nerve to back out of it. He had, she went on, 'made a lot of mischief in his time,' but when, years later, they met occasionally, 'all his spark had gone, and it was quite heavy going'.

I have no idea what Verschoyle's war record amounted to, though he is said to have risen to the rank of wing commander; he was also enlisted by MI6, along with Graham Greene and Malcolm Muggeridge. In *Coastwise Lights*, the second volume of his autobiography, Alan Ross suggests that Verschoyle was somehow involved with a Partisan unit in Rome as the Allies fought their way up the spine of Italy. As such he was forever requesting his superiors in London to send out large sums of money to fund a particularly useful and well-informed secret agent. The information supplied by this mysterious agent was so valuable that it was decided to send out a senior officer to inves-tigate: the senior officer chosen was Verschoyle's old colleague and drinking companion Goronwy Rees, who soon realised that the secret agent didn't exist, and that all the information being fed back to London was guesswork on the part of Verschoyle. Alan, who was a good friend of both men, reckoned it was a case of putting a thief to catch a thief, and that once the matter had been sorted out they felt free to spend their time carousing. Bald and with a 'pinkish complexion,' Verschoyle was, Alan recalled, 'dapper in appearance, though slightly moist and shifty about the eyes', and 'an entertaining fantasist with as little concern for the truth as his friend and contemporary Goronwy Rees'.

The war over, Verschoyle stayed on in Rome, and was the First Secretary to the British Embassy from 1947 to 1950. Theodora FitzGibbon, a colourful chronicler of post-war bohemian life in Chelsea, met him at the time, and remembered in her memoir *Love Lies at a Loss* how he invariably brought with him a bottle of wine or gin provided by Saccone & Speed, the wine merchants who in those days supplied British embassies with their every need. He was, she recalled, 'very mondaine and charming, with an unusual face of regular features, a very attractive face and smile. His manners were impeccable, putting people at ease immediately.' He spoke without seeming to open his mouth, and 'talked in a lightly muffled voice on a variety of subjects – sometimes, as I was to find out later, Irish-fashion; that is, he tended to please rather than be factually correct. His walk was quick, but with a gliding motion; one almost felt he could disappear at will. His manner too was sometimes guarded, to cause one to think that his life held many secrets.' He was always very secretive about his work, but one day he asked her if she would do a 'job' for him: she was to go to a particular café, carrying with her a walking stick as a means of identification. She went along to the café every day for a week, walking stick in hand, but no one ever approached her or contacted her in any way. At the end of the week she reported back to Verschoyle, who nodded in an appreciative way, told her she had done very good work, and paid her as agreed.

According to the spy writer Nigel West, Verschoyle's activities as a secret agent took a more dramatic and sinister turn in 1947, when he was involved in an MI6 plan to blow up ships carrying concentration camp survivors to Palestine. Ernest Bevin, as Foreign Secretary, was determined to reduce the flow of Jewish refugees for fear of aggravating Arab sensibilities, and Count Frederick van der Heuvel, the head of MI6's Rome station, was ordered to set the plan in motion. The man in immediate charge of the operation was Colonel Harold Perkins ('Perks'), a legendary figure who had worked in the Polish section of SOE during the war, and would, the following year, work closely with David Smiley in an abortive scheme to land anti-Communist Albanians in their homeland as part of an attempt to subvert the regime of Enver Hoxha: all of them were rounded up and shot within hours of their landing after Kim Philby, then working for the Foreign Office in Washington, had tipped off the Russians, who had in turn alerted the Albanian authorities. Among those enlisted by Perks to prevent the Jewish refugees from reaching Palestine was, West claims, Derek Verschoyle. Posing as Adriatic cigarette smugglers, he and another MI6 operative were told to attach limpet mines to the hulls of the rusting and overloaded ships bound for Haifa from Trieste. The whole wretched story eventually inspired Leon Uris's bestselling novel *Exodus*: and, in retrospect at least, Verschoyle seemed an improbable figure to find in a frogman's uniform.

In the early fifties Theodora FitzGibbon and her husband Constantine set up house in Hertfordshire, where they gave weekend house parties famed for their drunkenness and riotous living. Michael Wharton, a regular visitor, described these massive debauches in *A Dubious Codicil*, the second volume of his funny, melancholic memoirs, and other participants included John Davenport, Nigel Dennis and, in due course, Derek Verschoyle. Every now and then Theodora FitzGibbon would cook a meal to soak up the booze, and so delicious were they that Verschoyle urged her to write a cookery book: he had just set up in business as a publisher, so she need look no further. After leaving the diplomatic service, he had gone to work for Michael Joseph as a literary adviser, and had persuaded the Duchess of Windsor to be published by the firm; he had also commissioned Alan Ross's travel book about Sardinia, *The Bandit on the Billiard Table*, and when he decided to set up on his own this was one of the books he took with him, together with Theodora FitzGibbon's proposed cookery book.

'Derek's ideas tended to run ahead of his capacity to deal with them,' Alan Ross later observed, and Derek Verschoyle Ltd was no exception to the rule. Verschoyle's partner in the firm, albeit of the sleeping variety, was Graham Eyres-Monsell, a rich and well-connected homosexual whose sister Joan was married to Patrick Leigh Fermor; and their offices were in an elegant, rickety Georgian house in Park Place, a cul-de-sac off St James's Street. Although the firm lasted for little more than a year, and although most of the titles under contract were eventually published by other companies, the list of authors was extremely distinguished, and included Patrick Leigh Fermor, Alan Ross, Lawrence Durrell, Roy Fuller, James Hanley, Bea Howe, G.S. Fraser, Vernon Bartlett and Christopher Sykes. The firm's colophon was a bristly boar's head which looked as though it was about to be served up at a medieval banquet. The staff, many of them part-time, included Francis Wyndham, who joined the firm in April 1953 and remained with it until its collapse at the end of the following year, working as a reader and blurb-writer; John Willett, later to become an authority on East Germany and the works of Bertolt Brecht, who toiled in the attic; and Mamaine Paget, one of the Paget twins, famous beauties of their day, and much admired by Cyril Connolly and his friends. She came in for mornings only: she had been in love with both George Orwell and Arthur Koestler, who had recently left her for his last wife, and she died of asthma while working for the firm. The office manager was Verschoyle's wife, Moira. Beautiful and given to wearing stylish dresses pinched at the waist with a black patent leather belt, she had previously been married to Humphrey Slater, a seedy and heavy-drinking inhabitant of bohemia who had once edited *Polemic*, a short-lived but much admired literary magazine. The Verschoyles' married life was a tempestuous affair, and he would occasionally reel into the office swathed in bandages or sporting a black eye. 'You've been in the wars, I see,' Mamaine would remark, and he would mutter something about having been hit by a door.

Business life was equally tumultuous and unpredictable: according to Francis Wyndham, the bailiffs would arrive just as he was in the middle of typing a letter, hand over writs to him or to Moira, and whisk away the typewriters, office furniture and any other items of value, leaving any letters to be completed once the outstanding debts had been settled. Verschoyle was a generous employer who couldn't bear to sack anyone, so the staff, such as it was, survived these turbulent comings and goings: these were the days of long publishing lunches, and Verschoyle enjoyed lengthy sessions at the Travellers or the Garrick with Patrick Kinross or Patrick Leigh Fermor, returning to the office rather red in the face but still in control. Francis Wyndham remembers him as a dandified, plummy-toned, manicured figure, given to wearing dubious Edwardian suits with tight trousers, waisted jackets with double vents at the back and fancy waistcoats; he found him cold, snobbish, conceited and keen on showing off, and was repelled by his pretensions and a whiff of crookedness. Alan Ross was more forgiving and more amused. 'He was a considerate, genial, generous host, always delighted to purvey information of a kind not ordinarily come by. In this sense he was the reverse of a spy, but with similar instincts for elaborate fabrication,' he wrote in *Coastwise Lights*.

Every now and then Verschoyle would invite Alan to lunch at the Garrick, but would sit there in silence, perhaps because 'his general deviousness or marital problems were weighing heavily'. On other occasions, 'possibly as a result of an excess of gin, he sometimes looked as if he might explode, his face getting pinker and pinker, his eyes smaller'. Roy Fuller, whose novels were recommended to the firm by Alan Ross, noted how 'from Verschoyle's reddish visage, somewhat watery eyes, one might have guessed he had no distaste for the bottle'; and after the collapse of the firm, his drinking reached epic proportions.

Like many small literary publishers of the time – John Lehmann or MacGibbon & Kee, for instance – Verschoyle did his best to pull off the admirable but impossibly hard double act of publishing worthwhile books he believed in while at the same time making a sufficient profit to remain in business. He failed, and had to sell out to André Deutsch, a similar practitioner who managed to keep afloat by a combination of parsimony, shrewdness, monomania and sound literary advice. Deutsch took over Verschoyle's new offices in Carlisle Street, bang opposite the building that would later house *Private Eye*. In her publishing memoir, *Stet*, Diana Athill remembers Verschoyle as 'a raffish figure, vaguely well-connected and vaguely literary', and very much the kind of dubiously upper-class Englishman with whom, to her dismay, André tended to become involved. When they moved in, she remembers, the offices had been stripped bare: the only evidence of their previous occupants was an RAF dress uniform, hanging in a cupboard in an upstairs room. For some time afterwards, wine merchants' and tailors' bills continued to be delivered to Carlisle Street: more usefully, André inherited Ludwig Bemelmans' bestselling children's books about Madeline, Roy Fuller's undervalued novels, Lawrence Durrell's *Pope Joan*, Theodora FitzGibbon's cookery books, which formed the basis for a list briefly edited for the firm by Elizabeth David, and Patrick Leigh Fermor's *The Violins of Saint-Jacques*, published jointly with John Murray. Francis Wyndham moved too, and with Diana he was responsible for discovering V.S. Naipaul, and rediscovering Jean Rhys. When Deutsch moved on to Great Russell Street, where I went to work in the late Sixties, the Carlisle Street offices were taken over by Secker & Warburg.

Verschoyle's later years make for melancholy reading. He spent some time in the early Sixties as the managing director of Grower Publications, and edited *The Grower*, a magazine for vegetable enthusiasts. Even more improbably, he went into partnership making prefabricated doors with the equally bibulous Goronwy Rees, his former colleague on the *Spectator*, then living in penury in Essex: the business was not a success. By now Verschoyle had left London for East Anglia. He and Moira moved into a large and handsome Georgian house near Framlingham and, with a hard-drinking ex-SOE man who lived in the same village, he set up the Deben Bookshop in Woodbridge; Collins the publishers then backed him when he established the Ancient House Bookshop in Ipswich, later the scene of a mysterious fire. He died in 1973.

'I am rather surprised that you should consider Derek for a biography, because he is forgotten now except for a very few old people like myself who knew him,' Anne Scott-James replied after I had written for information about him. He deserves a brief life at best: he is one of those characters who flit through the footnotes of other people's diaries, letters and biographies, adding colour and comicality to the proceedings; and he was the antithesis of the average Old Malvernian.

A few years ago I thought of writing a literary rogues' gallery featuring bibulous, rather raffish characters like Verschoyle and based on the post-war years: Julian Maclaren-Ross and Patrick Hamilton, my particular heroes, weren't minor enough, and had already been written about at length, but possible candidates might have included hardened literary journalists like Maurice Richardson, John Davenport and John Raymond, all of whom fell victim to the enemies of promise. At some stage in the proceedings I went to Bryanston Square to have a drink with Charles Pick, a shrewd old publisher who had started life in the 1930s as one of Victor Gollancz's reps, moved on to Michael Joseph in its heyday, and ended his publishing career as the managing director of Heinemann. Charles had come across Verschoyle at Michael Joseph, thought him a snob and a poseur, and couldn't quite understand why I wanted to waste my time on him.

Towards the end of our session, when the gin-and-tonics had begun to take their toll, and a certain exhaustion had set in, I asked Charles who was the worst rogue he'd met in publishing. 'John Holroyd-Reece,' he answered, without a moment's pause. 'Now there's a man you ought to include in your rogues' gallery. *Far* more interesting than Derek Verschoyle.' I had never heard of John Holroyd-Reece, and although, over the next twenty minutes, Charles gave a detailed account of his career and his publishing crimes, I was too tired to take it in. I wish I had. A few years later I suggested to Penguin that I should write a biography of their founder, Allen Lane, and during my researches I discovered that Lane had been a friend of Holroyd-Reece, *né* Hermann Riess, and that part of the inspiration for Penguins had come from Albatross Verlag, a much-admired firm of English-language paperback reprint publishers, originally based in Germany, of which Holroyd-Reece was a founder member: Albatross titles were only available on the Continent, and their plain lettering covers, colour-coded jackets, bird motif and elegant typography were among the qualities shared by Albatross and Penguin.

A pallid, monocled figure clad in a black cloak, Holroyd-Reece had, I discovered, been expelled from Repton after being cited as a co-respondent in a divorce case, had been appointed Governor of Zable and Malloake in the Sudan after World War I, and had taken over the publication of Radclyffe Hall's *The Well of Loneliness* after Jonathan Cape had been threatened with prosecution for obscene libel by Sir William Joynson-Hicks, a famously censorious Home Secretary. A rabid pursuer of other men's wives, Holroyd-Reece sounded a perfect candidate for a rogues' gallery. Charles Pick, who had done work for Albatross in the thirties, was one of the very few people around who had known him well: but he had recently died, and now it was too late. My biography of Allen Lane would have been that much better-informed if I'd paid more attention over the gin-and-tonics. As for the rogues, I'd have to look elsewhere.

Back in the mid-sixties, towards the end of my time as an undergraduate at Trinity College, Dublin, I got to know through his daughter Deborah the Irish writer and man of letters Terence de Vere White, who had recently abandoned life as a Dublin solicitor for the literary editorship of the *Irish Times*. A sociable, eloquent and kindly character, with a leonine mane of thick grey hair, a distinguished cast of feature and a penchant for lovat three-piece suits fashioned from Donegal tweed, he enjoyed his sporadic forays into London literary life, numbering among his particular cronies Compton Mackenzie, John Betjeman and the publisher Martin Secker. When I told him, in a vague, hesitant way, that I was interested in a career in publishing, he hurried to pull some strings on my behalf. Letters were written to various luminaries of the book trade, all of whom I promised to visit when the summer vacation came round.

Like many undergraduates with publishing pretensions, I had very grand and romantic ideas of what the trade involved. When Leonard Cutts of Hodder & Stoughton, widely revered as the inventor of Teach Yourself Books, suggested that I might like to start work in the Hodder warehouse near Sevenoaks, I was duly outraged. My ardour was dashed by the prospect of trading in my new moss-coloured corduroy suit for a brown cotton over-garment, as worn by ironmongers and middle-aged grocers. I made no effort to conceal my disappointment, and another two years were to pass before I started at the foot of the publishing ladder.

Among the publishers whom I condescended to visit that summer was the old-fashioned firm of B.T. Batsford Ltd, best known for its distinctive and elegantly produced books on English churches, English counties, English inns and the like, and for steady-selling lines devoted to chess and handicrafts.

It didn't sound my cup of tea, but Terence had spoken with particular warmth of its managing director, Sam Carr, a fellow Irishman, so I dutifully arranged an appointment. I made my way to Fitzhardinge Street, off Manchester Square, where Batsford was housed in a black-bricked eighteenth-century house, with a royal coat of arms nailed above the fanlight. Quite why they were entitled to flaunt such a crest I never discovered, but the inside of the office was equally gracious and awe-inspiring. Wider than most, with elaborate plasterwork overhead and a black-and-white marble chessboard underfoot, the hall had been painted in the glowing terracotta fashionable at the time; apart from the familiar publisher's litter of brown paper parcels, recently arrived from the printers, and battered-looking cardboard showcards, I was left with an impression of gilt and polished wood, with the firm's recent publications suitably on display. A curving staircase with a gleaming wooden balustrade led to the first-floor landing, off which, I was told, Mr Carr had his lair.

I remember very little about Sam Carr, and nothing whatso-ever about my interview. I like to think that he was a short, eager, friendly Ulsterman, akin to a bright-eyed wire-haired terrier in looks and demeanour. No doubt he recommended a spell in the warehouse, or in a bookshop, or in a printing works, and no doubt my crestfallen look and the lack of enthusiasm with which I greeted his kindly suggestions soon made it obvious that I was yet another undergraduate with ideas above his station. I heard no more from him; nor did I give Batsford another moment's thought during the long years I spent in the book trade. Only once did their name crop up, and then for a lunchtime only.

In the early Seventies I found myself working as a literary agent with the venerable firm of A.P. Watt & Son. I spent much of my time working out how much we should charge textbook publishers to quote lines of Yeats or Kipling, and invoicing them accordingly, but one morning Hilary Rubinstein, a senior partner in the firm, bustled into my office and told me that we were to have lunch with the new and dynamic editorial director of Batsford. We had never done any business with the firm – hardly surprising, given the specialised nature of their list – and this was a chance to put things right and nip in ahead of rival agencies like A.D. Peters, David Higham and Curtis Brown. An hour or so later we set out for Soho, where our host had booked a table at Bianchi's, an upstairs restaurant much patronised by trend-setting publishers and agents. He was already installed when we got there, and had made hefty inroads on a bottle of house red. He rose, unsteadily, from behind the table, shook us both warmly by the hand, and waved us to our seats. A shock-haired character in his late thirties, he was clad in jeans, corduroy jacket, open-necked shirt and slip-on shoes, a style of dress pioneered by whiz-kids like Tom Maschler of Jonathan Cape which, though *de rigueur* nowadays, seemed bold and unconventional at the time, a deliberate gesture of defiance aimed at the tweeds and chalk stripes then favoured by the panjandrums of the trade – including, no doubt, Sir Brian Batsford MP and his fellow directors.

As he poured us a drink, refilled his own and ordered a second bottle, our host explained that he had been working until recently at Penguin, initially under Tony Godwin, another legendary whiz-kid, keen on open-necked shirts and four-letter words, who had eventually been sacked by Allen Lane after publishing a book of cartoons by the French cartoonist Siné of which Lane deeply disapproved – so much so that, to Godwin's extreme annoyance, he and some fellow conspirators stole into the Penguin warehouse in Harmondsworth in the middle of the night, removed the entire stock of Siné books, and burned them in Lane's farmyard nearby. Batsford, our new friend disloyally explained, hastily draining his glass, was run by a load of old farts – kindred spirits to Sir Allen Lane, no doubt – not one of whom had even heard of modish American novelists like John Barth or Thomas Pynchon. His mission as he saw it – here he banged his glass on the table with such ferocity that the stem snapped in two, the contents sprayed across the table, and his diatribe was briefly interrupted while Elena, the *maîtresse d'* of Bianchi's, hurried forward with a cloth and a replacement glass – was to be shot of all those f****** awful books on chess and country churches and make a pre-emptive bid for Norman Mailer's next! Batsford was awash with cash, he assured us – earned, no doubt, by *Scottish Castles*, *The Cathedrals of England* and *Embroidery for Beginners* – and was in a position to make giant offers such as Tony Godwin (now installed as George Weidenfeld's right-hand man, and known for his extravagant advances) could only dream of. Yet the old farts were so half-asleep, so unaware of what was going on in the *real* world of publishing, that not one of them had ever met a literary agent or a paperback publisher, let alone had lunch at Bianchi's! He was going to make Batsford the leading literary publisher in London, far outstripping Jonathan Cape . . .

As he raged on, his spaghetti congealing on his plate before him, a fresh glass of wine brimming by his right hand, Hilary and I raised eyebrows at one another and then, when the torrent began to ebb, tried to introduce a note of realism into the proceedings. Had it not occurred to him, we wondered, that although publishing books on bridge and English Alehouses was less newsworthy and less glamorous than publishing Eldridge Cleaver or Kurt Vonnegut, it was also, if well done, more dependable as far as the market was concerned, less expensive in terms of authorial advances, and almost certainly much more profitable? Nor was it possible to change a firm's reputation overnight. The book trade functioned on the basis of a kind of shorthand: authors, booksellers, literary editors, literary agents, journalists and even a few members of the reading public associated particular publishers with particular types of book, and for Batsford suddenly to lash out and publish *Portnoy's Complaint* or Brian Aldiss's *The Hand-Reared Boy* would cause the system to short-circuit, as well as inducing apoplexies among senior members of staff, including Sir Brian Batsford. He looked thoughtful for a moment, ordered a third bottle, and resumed his diatribe. As we walked back in the direction of our offices in Bedford Row, Hilary and I shook our heads and predicted the worst. A few weeks later we learned that our excitable new friend had been sacked. I have never heard mention of him since, and Batsford continued to publish books on chess and country churches.

Some twenty years later my interest in Batsford was unexpectedly revived. I became gripped by a demonic character called Charles Fry, who popped up every now and then in James Lees-Milne's diaries, emitting whiffs of sulphur, while in charge of editorial matters at Batsford in the Thirties and Forties. Described by John Betjeman as 'a phallus with a business sense' and by James Lees-Milne as a 'terrible man, the worst and most depraved I know', Fry was – if the great diarist is to be believed – a drunk and a lecher of satanic proportions. Like Betjeman, Sacheverell Sitwell, Peter Quennell, Cecil Beaton, Raymond Mortimer, Oliver Messell, Rex Whistler, Dick Wyndham and Christopher Hobhouse, Lees-Milne was one of the bright young artists and writers whom Fry persuaded onto the Batsford list. The two young men were united in their love of English country houses, and during the 1940s, when Lees-Milne was trundling round England in his baby Austin on behalf of the National Trust, his publisher sometimes joined him on his tours of inspection of run-down ancestral homes and their often demented proprietors. 'I really think Charles is Satan,' Lees-Milne noted after an uneasy encounter with the Duchess of Richmond. En route to their appointment, Fry insisted on 'gin or whisky at every stop', on top of which he 'chain smokes, splutters and coughs with every breath' and 'loses his temper with waitresses at luncheon and in the tobacconist's shop'. Although the Duchess turned out to be 'a very sweet, simple old lady', Fry quickly turned the conversation from her house to less wholesome matters. 'He makes me say the most outrageous things,' Lees-Milne went on, 'and even makes a dear old duchess talk about brutish indelicacies.'

Not only was 'that horror Charles Fry – it is the only word for him – drunken, dissolute and destructive', but he was prone to sexual boasting as well. He informed the bookseller Heywood Hill's wife Anne (unasked) that he had slept with three of her cousins, two male and one female; when Lees-Milne met him on his return from one of his frequent publishing trips to New York, he tossed back seven whisky-and-sodas before announcing that he had slept with forty people during his time away; towards the end of the war Lees-Milne remembered how

> I had lunch with Charles Fry at the Park Lane Hotel. He was late, having just got up from some orgy *à trois* with whips, etc. He related every detail, not questioning whether I wanted to listen. In the middle of the narration I simply said 'Stop! Stop!' At the next table an officer was eating, and imbibing every word. I thought he gave me a very crooked look for having spoilt his fun.

I longed to learn more, but suspected that, like Derek Verschoyle, Fry survived only as a footnote in the memoirs of better-known friends and acquaintances. And then, poking about in a second-hand bookshop, I came across a handsomely produced book, edited by Hector Bolitho and published in 1943 to celebrate the centenary of B.T. Batsford Ltd. Not only did it contain a full-length photograph of the young Fry – a chinless, moon-faced character with thinning hair, leaning pensively against some bookshelves, an open book in one hand and a cigarette dangling from the other – but from it I learned that he was a member of the well-known Quaker family, and was a great-nephew of Admiral 'Jackie' Fisher of Jutland fame. He had himself started out in the Navy, but decided to try his hand at publishing instead, and joined the firm in 1924 as the assistant to its Chairman, Harry Batsford. Cecil Beaton met him at about this time, and thought him 'frightfully nice-looking, all very fine and smooth and pale – a gorgeous complexion, and very pale yellow hair brushed right back'. On another occasion, Beaton joined Fry, Brian Howard, Raymond Mortimer and Eddie Gathorne-Hardy for dinner and noted how, after the meal was over, his companions suddenly whipped out powder-puffs and set out to 'find a man'.

'Pink and plump, hatless and without a waistcoat' – or so his new employer described him – Fry presented himself for work at the Batsford offices in April 1924. He made his way to a large Georgian house, long since bombed or demolished, on the north side of Holborn, overlooking Red Lion Square. After he had rung the doorbell three times, a wicket door opened and 'I was confronted by an elderly crone,' Fry remembered, 'whose sparse wisp of grey hair haloed a lined and battered face. A ruined mouth produced an unholy leer. "Come in, ducks," said a cracked, hoarse voice, "Mr Arry's not ere yet." ' Such was his introduction to the firm: Mrs Murphy, the housekeeper, very occasionally 'bestowed a whack with her duster on a book or a chair', and liked to buy the staff their cigarettes. Every now and then the stubs from Fry's ashtray were passed on to her 'for the old man to fill his pipe with'.

Like other old-fashioned publishers, Batsford continued the eighteenth-century tradition whereby publishing and book-selling were combined under one roof. The firm specialised in producing hefty, ornate and handsomely illustrated volumes on architectural history and interior decoration. These were edited and designed from the first floor up, while the ground floor was occupied by a bookshop selling their own and other firms' new publications as well as second-hand books. The directors' office was on the first floor, a dark, dusty room crammed with yellowing first editions, the removal of any one of which left a patina of black dust on the fingers.

Mr Harry, Fry's new boss, had succeeded a brace of uncles as the man in charge. A jovial, scholarly bachelor with a bald pate, he was, in Lees-Milne's opinion, 'the dirtiest, yet the sweetest old person I ever saw. He smokes, and coughs, and shakes incessantly, while the cigarette ash spills down his front, and not only ash. Saliva also. His eccentricities are Dickensian. He adores cats, and fills his coat pockets with the heads, tails and entrails of fish. As he stumbles down the pavement he distributes these remnants to the congregating cats. The smell of his clothes is overpowering. Charles is devoted to him.'

Hector Bolitho was equally fond of Mr Harry, but 'the chaos of his office quickens my blood into real temper, for I cannot abide the idea of my manuscripts joining such a muddle'. Apart from the mounds of paper on his desk, the clutter in his office included a family of stuffed hedgehogs in a case, a cat basket for the use of passing strays, a huge West Indian knobkerry, referred to as the Authors' Welcome, a thick coating of dust, and a broken thermos flask brimming over with cigarette ends. 'And here sits my friend Harry Batsford,' Bolitho recorded, 'drinking tea, shouting *Hell! Damn and Blast!* – yet slowly forming with his authors such friendships that calling upon him becomes a delight. He never ceases to be surprising. The last time I called on him he lifted a copy of "Way Down in Old Kentucky" from the table and asked me to sing. I obliged, in a bronchial voice, and he listened with polite delight.'

'Once one realised the "point" of what one was doing, one's working hours were gay, unconventional and wildly interesting,' Fry later wrote, adding that 'we all let ourselves go and, when working under high pressure, we have had some tremendous tiffs, with explosions of highly coloured language all round.' Fry's desk became, in due course, as chaotic and heavily piled as Mr Harry's, with two telephones into which he shouted rather than spoke, and a brimming-over ashtray. According to Bolitho, 'Charles's praise for an author is guarded, so that the slightest compliment from him is to be treasured. His scorn is like a hive of bees let loose.'

In the late Twenties the firm moved from Holborn to a late-eighteenth-century house in North Audley Street. Sir Albert Richardson, an architect and historian of eighteenth-century England, and the man responsible for the post-war efflorescence of 'Post Office Georgian' buildings, designed an elegant shopfront, the coat of arms was nailed up over the door, and – on the surface at least – life went on as before. But the Depression of the early Thirties took its toll on a firm rooted in the Edwardian era, so to save money Mr Harry decided that they should dispense with the services of writers and illustrators, and do the work themselves: he and Charles Fry would write and edit the books they needed, while his nephew Brian Cook would provide line-drawing illustrations and the jacket artwork. The three men took to touring the British Isles in Mr Harry's cube-shaped Morris. In the evenings, their researches done, Fry and Cook would search out a suitable pub and install themselves in the bar, while Mr Harry, suitably clad in trilby, plus-fours and rustic tweeds, went on making notes and inspecting buildings until nightfall drove him indoors.

Of the three, Brian Cook was the quietest and, in terms of what he achieved, the most interesting. A slim young man with a domed forehead and a widow's peak, he had enjoyed the benefits, while at Repton, of a remarkable art teacher named Arthur Norris, whose other Reptonian protégés included Anthony Gross and Anthony Devas. After school, Cook joined the family firm, simultaneously studying at the Central School of Art. The line drawings he provided for the insides of the firm's books were pleasantly old-fashioned, very much in keeping with its dusty image, but the jackets he produced in the thirties were very different – dazzling and audacious works of art, as redolent of the period as the Chrysler Building or a Bugatti, Peter Jones or a silver cocktail-shaker.

As the Depression lifted, and with it the need for the editorial staff to write as well as publish their books, Fry persuaded Mr Harry that Batsford should extend their architectural and topographical interests to embrace a less specialised and scholarly kind of reader; the books should be shorter, less freighted with academic paraphernalia, and more dashingly presented. By taking a gamble and printing 8,500 or even 10,000 copies of new titles, they could afford full-colour jackets; by having one artist responsible for all the books in a series, it should be possible to create a distinctive 'Batsford' look, of a kind that appealed to collectors, in much the same way as Allen Lane and Victor Gollancz were creating distinctive 'looks' for their firms. (Although we tend to think of 'branding' as a modern phenomenon, it found nimble practitioners in the Thirties, from huge corporations like Guinness and Shell to publishers like Lane and Gollancz, who sold and promoted the image and reputations of their firms quite as keenly as those of their authors: novices and famous names alike were expected to don the magenta, black and tulip-yellow lettering jackets designed by Stanley Morison for the Gollancz list, and the same egalitarian approach applied to Penguin's bird and famous horizontal bands, designed originally by Edward Young, later to become the bestselling author of *One of Our Submarines*, and refined by the great Swiss typographer Jan Tschichold: nowadays Penguins only differ from other conglomerate publishers by the persistence of Penguin Classics, and an elegance of design that harks back to the days when Lane employed men like Tschichold and Hans Schmoller.) It was here that the youthful Brian Cook came into his own. Now collectors' items, the jackets he painted for the British Heritage and the Face of Britain series must be among the most beautiful ever commissioned by a London publisher, rivalled only by Berthold Wolpe's lettering jackets for Faber in the Fifties and

Sixties, and they were revolutionary in the way the painting carried round onto the spine and the back panel, and were bled to the edge of the paper. They were printed in four or even five colours by the Jean Berthe method, using water- rather than oil-based inks. His silhouette shapes and bright, flat, often unexpected colours – trees might be mauve, a church tower royal blue – were reminiscent of the great railway or steamship posters of the time. As Hugh Casson remarked in his introduction to *The Britain of Brian Cook*, 'you could spot them a mile off'.

Whereas Charles Fry, for all his liking for country houses, was irremediably urban, decorating his office with Rex Whistlers and a drawing by Walt Disney in preference to a family of stuffed hedgehogs, Mr Harry pined for country life; and after the Munich Crisis he decided to move the main body of the firm to Malvern Wells in Worcestershire, leaving Fry to run a rump in London. It was in Malvern Wells that, at many removes, I came across Sam Carr's name once again. At the fag end of the Thirties, Cyril Connolly's marriage to his American first wife, Jeannie, began to unravel. Both parties had become overweight and over-fond of the good life: Jeannie drank too much, while Connolly had become involved with a young art student and, unfairly, blamed Jeannie's addiction to 'footling' and nightlife for his own failure to get down to the writing of books. Shortly before she finally returned to America, Jeannie went on a tour of the West Country, and in March 1939 she found herself taking the waters at Malvern Wells with two sulphurous prima donnas: Denham Fouts, a drug addict from the Deep South and, according to Christopher Isherwood, 'the most expensive male prostitute in the world', whose lovers had included Prince Paul of Greece and the margarine millionaire Peter Watson, soon to put up the money for Connolly's *Horizon*; and Charles Fry, whom Mr Harry associated with 'a pair of spectacles worn awry, a gift for fiery anger which trumpets through the house, a chirping sort of wit, and great knowledge of the business', though Jeannie remembered him becoming 'pedantic, irrational and sentimental' after the first drink of the day. Later they were joined by Sam Carr and Brian Cook. They discussed the possibility of Jeannie getting a job with Batsford, but instead she and Fouts borrowed a fiver off Sam Carr, hired some bicycles, and headed off to the Brecon Beacons.

And with that, it could be, the great days of Batsford were over. Brian Cook succeeded Mr Harry as Chairman in 1952, and changed his name to Brian Batsford; in due course he became Tory MP for Ealing South, was knighted, retired to live in Lamb House, Rye, once the home of Henry James, and incurred the short-lived animosity of my overcharged lunching companion. As for Charles Fry, he seems to have gone from bad to worse, with James Lees-Milne cast in the role of recording angel. 'God help him!' Lees-Milne exclaimed when he learned that 'Sachie' Sitwell was planning a month-long tour of the Netherlands with Fry and Mr Harry; as for Fry's suggestion that they should visit New York together, 'I would sooner die than do such a thing.' 'Lunched with that fiend Charles Fry at the Ritz,' Lees-Milne noted in July 1948. 'He launched into a paean of praise of himself and his business successes. Conversation then lapsed into his drink and sex prowess, which disgusts and bores. During the hour and a half I was with him he consumed five gins and tonics.'

A year later, even Mr Harry had had enough. He had once compared 'Charles's deep and abiding attachment to the firm with that of Ulster to the British Crown and Empire', and claimed that 'it is impossible to imagine a time when he was not one of the vital, integral parts of the firm', but in June 1949 Sam Carr told Lees-Milne that Fry had become 'quite impossible' and was being sacked. Sent out to open a New York branch of the firm, he had – or so it was rumoured – bought a house off Fifth Avenue, crammed it with Aubusson carpets, and sent his London HQ a bill for £57,000. Enough was enough. For all Fry's awfulness, Lees-Milne couldn't help but feel 'sorry for this clever and deplorable man, losing his livelihood in middle age'.

Four years earlier, a young Hungarian named André Deutsch had set up as a publisher under the name of Allan Wingate (he worried that the name Deutsch might excite anti-German prejudice so soon after the end of the war). Unwisely, as it turned out, he offered Fry a job, and in due course they were joined by a rich young man named Anthony Gibbs, the son of the middlebrow novelist Sir Philip Gibbs, and himself the author of novels about men in sports cars. He was also a useful source of funds – too useful, in fact, since he ended up effectively owning the firm. When I asked André about Fry, he said that he could remember nothing about him except that he was permanently in tears. Diana Athill remembered the tears, but added that, like Gibbs, he was 'absolutely useless'. In *Stet*, Diana recalls that Fry – whom she refers to as 'Roger' – was often drunk in the afternoons, and that 'occasionally he came in with a black eye, having been roughed up by an ill-chosen boyfriend'. It may be, she continues, 'he had thought he would work gently, between hangovers, on elegant books about eighteenth-century chinoiserie or Strawberry Hill Gothick, but he never got round to signing up any such work and made no contribution to what we had on the stocks'.

Then as always the workaholic all-round publisher, André, when not designing display ads or delivering copies in the back of his car, signed up Norman Mailer's *The Naked and the Dead*, which no other publisher dared to touch, the works of his compatriot George Mikes, and the wartime stories of Julian Maclaren-Ross, who, being permanently broke, sometimes chased his diminutive publisher round his desk in search of funds, waving his silver-topped cane. But André was eventually pushed out of the firm by Messrs Fry and Gibbs, and set up a new business, this time under his own name, once again with Diana and Nicolas Bentley as his partners.

By the time Gibbs got to know him, Fry was a 'confirmed alcoholic'; he was also 'the most civilised man I have ever known', with a vast knowledge of architecture, painting, food and 'royal bastardy' and a huge range of first-name friendships ranging from 'Willy Maugham to Tom Eliot, John Betjeman, Bob Boothby, Dylan Thomas, Gerald Hamilton and Gerry [the Duke of] Wellington'. He had 'flaming red hair', and was given to sudden rages: 'When he began to rap on the table at a mounting tempo, which meant that an explosion was imminent, people ran at the double to execute his lightest request.' After André, Diana and Nicolas Bentley had left, Allan Wingate limped along somehow without its energetic and enterprising founder. Its offices were in Beauchamp Place, opposite a pub called The Grove: by ten in the morning, according to Gibbs, Fry had begun to tremble so much that 'the ash tray would set up in sympathetic vibration', and as soon as The Grove opened, at 11.30, the thirsty publisher hurried over the road, drained three double gins in a matter of moments, and returned to the office in a mellower mood. Lunch at The Belfry, off Belgrave Square, was lubricated by martinis, wine and Armagnac, and by half-past five in the afternoon, when the pubs reopened, Fry was standing impatiently outside The Grove, peering in through the windows and angrily rattling the letterbox. Once installed – and joined by Dylan Thomas, René Cutforth, Peter de Pollnay or Lord Killanin – he might down twenty whiskies before hailing a taxi home to his flat in Nell Gwynn House in Chelsea. After one lunchtime session, Fry is said to have reeled back to the office and announced that he had offered Dylan Thomas £1,000 for what became *Under Milk Wood*. Gibbs was horrified by this display of extravagance, and cancelled the offer at once.

Apart from commissioning *Persona Grata*, an anthology by Kenneth Tynan and Cecil Beaton of one hundred living people whom they jointly admired as 'unique human beings', Fry's most dramatic contribution – or non-contribution – to the fortunes of Allan Wingate allegedly involved an elaborate and suitably shady scheme to smuggle his old friend Guy Burgess back from Moscow. Other participants included the writer James Pope-Hennessy, later murdered by a rent boy, an Italian-American Mafia man, and the editor of the *People*, who promised large sums for serial rights if a book eventually emerged. It never did; and despite the success of Leon Uris's *Exodus* and a cheap reprint of *The Naked and the Dead*, run off by Hector Bolitho on the presses of the *Jersey Morning News*, the firm began to lose money heavily – so much so that towards the end of the Fifties Gibbs had to lay off members of staff, Charles Fry among them.

He took it like a man, but the reprobate's spirit was broken at last. Michael Wharton records in his memoirs how a sozzled Fry tried to pick him up in a Fleet Street pub; and late one afternoon Gibbs was rung at the office to be told that Fry was dead. His body had been found in a house off the Fulham Palace Road, and beside it were two empty bottles of gin, a bottle of whisky and an empty box of phenobarbitone. A note nearby suggested that 'if you wish to enquire further into the reasons for my action, I suggest you get in touch with Brian Cook-Batsford and Mr Anthony Gibbs'. Gibbs went down to identify the body. 'He was unrecognisable,' he wrote later. 'He lay with his face turned sideways. He was bloated and blotched and three little runnels of dried blood ran from his nostrils and one corner of his lips,' and his hair was now 'snow white'. With any luck he was already happily ensconced in one of the loucher wings of Heavenly Mansions, W1, every now and then whipping out his powder-puff before setting out to 'find a man'.

# THREE

# No More Long Lunches

Forty years ago, when I started out at the bottom of the pile, publishers were public figures, known to the world at large. They have long ago been elbowed aside by celebrity chefs, footballers' wives, telly personalities and the other heroes of a less literate age, but in those days George Weidenfeld, André Deutsch, Tom Maschler and Tony Godwin were profiled in the colour supplements, and their activities recorded by Atticus, Pendennis, Peterborough and other pseudonymous gossip columnists; Allen Lane's death in 1970 was front-page news, and not just in the upmarket papers, as had been his very public sacking of Tony Godwin three years before. Peter Mayer, the onetime ruler of Penguin, and Carmen Callil of Virago and Chatto were the last newsworthy publishers, hogging the column inches back in the 1980s, but although bestselling books and their authors attract more attention than ever, the men and women behind the scenes have become objects of indifference, except to their authors. The odd literary agent sticks his head above the parapet, but beyond the trade papers publishers receive about as much attention as actuaries or quantity surveyors.

This reflects, in part, the competition of rival media and, some would say, a general dumbing-down and shortening of attention spans – and the fact that publishing is a less colourful, individualistic business than it once was. Familiar names, once run by their founders or family members, have been swallowed up by American, French or German conglomerates. John Murray has exchanged its Albemarle Street home for a tower block in the Euston Road, Cape has traded in Bedford Square for the anonymity of the Vauxhall Bridge Road, and the traditional publishing office in a ramshackle Georgian house in Bloomsbury or Covent Garden – the entrance hall clogged with brown paper printers' parcels, every square inch brimming over with teetering mounds of books, files, press cuttings, proof copies, photographs, letters waiting to be signed, discarded display material and recently emptied wine glasses – has become a relic of times past, to be recollected with rose-tinted nostalgia by watery-eyed old hands reminiscing over the whisky bottle. In working hours, though not thereafter, it is a more sober, less bibulous business than it was. Twenty years ago the long, boozy publishing lunch became the object of widespread disapproval, and steak and kidney pudding washed down with two bottles of claret was dropped in favour of smoked salmon, a lettuce leaf and Perrier water, while the long, rambling, after-lunch dictating of letters has given way to emails fired off left and right.

In those days the top echelons of the trade were white-haired, elderly and male, as often as not rather red in the face and prone to wearing tweed or chalk-striped suits. 'Billy' Collins, my first boss, and Hamish Hamilton were in their late sixties when I started out, 'Fred' Warburg and Victor Gollancz were even older, and judging by the photographs in the trade papers, Sir Stanley Unwin looked as old as the hills with his Colonel Sanders goatee beard, wire-rimmed specs and Shavian knicker-bockers. Nowadays women predominate, both numerically and in terms of power exercised within the trade, but in the old days they were limited to being secretaries and receptionists, with a small band of heroic spinsters looking after children's books or acting as underpaid and overworked editorial dogsbodies, devoted to their often tyrannical masters, lugging bags of proofs and typescripts home in the evenings and at weekends, and holding the fort while the menfolk moved on to the brandy at the Garrick or the Gay Hussar. Eunice Frost at Penguin and Norah Smallwood at Chatto were the first to reach the top in an all-male trade, followed shortly after by Diana Athill and Livia Gollancz. Reviewing my biography of Allen Lane, Carmen Callil reproved me for applying the word 'formidable' to Eunice Frost and Norah Smallwood, somehow suggesting that only an unreformed male chauvinist would instinctively employ such a word to clever and successful women: but my use of it was descriptive rather than mocking or pejorative, since those two in particular had to be tough, determined and seemingly thick-skinned to get where they did.

In the days of my youth, publishers ruled the roost, not only within their firms but in the trade at large. Booksellers were regarded as humble, impoverished, rather impractical folk who wore moth-eaten maroon cardigans, lettuce-green shirts, baggy cords and Pirelli slippers, and were grateful to be offered a discount of one third off the published price. Salesmen were there to obey, and wore nylon shirts with vests visible beneath, well-ironed grey suits and highly polished black shoes, which they burnished on the calves of each trouser-leg when summoned to report to the sales manager. Accountants were black-clad figures who announced their arrival with a deferential cough ('Ahem') and stood dutifully to attention behind their masters, pointing out items in the handwritten ledger with marbled endpapers as and when required; I like to think they came equipped with thin grey moustaches, Homburg hats and the kind of glasses worn by Reginald Maudling, the frames of which were tortoiseshell around the top half of each lens and transparent plastic below. Those working in production and design might get away with a black shirt with a red knitted tie, while corduroy and slip-on shoes were making inroads among the younger editors.

Publishers alone decided what should be published. The idea of consulting salesmen, let alone booksellers, about what to publish and what kind of jacket a book should wear would have seemed pernicious nonsense to the old guard, and close to *lèse majesté*. Books were costed, and memos written, on the backs of envelopes; deals were famously sealed over post-prandial glasses of port; meetings and paperwork were kept to a minimum, partly because the publishers saw no need to consult anyone other than their editorial advisers – the rest were told what to do, most particularly at the six-monthly sales conferences – and partly because computers, photocopiers and pocket calculators were either waiting to be invented or were great lumbering machines with wheels juddering and rotating in all directions, fed by spools of punctured paper, tended by men in white coats and emitting the occasional puff of smoke. For all the talk about 'paperless offices', technology is productive of bumph, and bumph is productive of meetings and the exhalation of hot air, and publishers of the old school would have been baffled and irritated by both.

All this began to change in the 1970s. For some inexplicable reason, the City began to show an interest in publishing – and not just in the less glamorous areas of publishing like legal, medical or academic textbooks, where advances to authors were unknown, discounts to the trade were minimal, the market was assured and quantifiable, price was no object to potential purchasers, and profits were large and dependable, but in the altogether more risky realm of 'trade' or 'general' publishing. There was much excited talk, seldom translated into action, about 'synergy': no one seemed to know what it meant, but it was thought to involve the interdependence of books and other media, and cooperation between the New York and London arms of multinational empires. Family firms, from the mighty Collins to the venerable John Murray, gradually sold out to conglomerates, as did all but a handful of independents. The grand old men of publishing died or retired or were put out to grass, and life continued much as before.

It was generally agreed that publishing had fallen into the hands of accountants and sales managers, and that 'mid-list' titles – books that got well reviewed but only sold a handful of copies – were in imminent danger as a result of the Philistines taking command, but firms like Chatto, Cape, Weidenfeld, Allen Lane and Hamish Hamilton continued (and still continue) to publish risky and worthwhile books, but with greater resources at their command.

Towards the end of my time in publishing, in the late 1980s, something very curious happened. The big publishing groups were becoming ever larger and more musclebound, swallowing up firms to left and right; and yet, in what seemed like an act of self-immolation, they and their fellow publishers wilfully abdicated their position as the ringmasters of the literary circus. Far from ruling the roost, they became, in effect, supplicants, seemingly at the mercy of people whom, in days gone by, they had regarded as inherently inferior, namely booksellers and literary agents. Far from resisting or resenting their conquerors, they warmly welcomed them in, like decadent emperors confronted by virile barbarian tribes.

To begin with, dusty old backstreet bookshops were steam-rollered aside by the new chains, headed by Waterstone's. Publishers and their sales managers were carried away by this, happily envisioning American-style shops in which customers were served hot drinks and cake and sat about reading in armchairs without spilling crumbs or coffee into the books they might or might not buy. The new shops were bright and smart, often in prime sites, and were said to be staffed by enthusiastic and well-informed graduates, but they ordered as many (or as few) copies of most books as the much-maligned men in cardigans, only at a far higher discount and on a sale-or-return basis. (In the dim and distant past bookshops had tended to buy firm, and were allowed to return copies only in exceptional circumstances.) Not only were publishers giving away a larger slice of the cake, but all too often they were so carried away by the huge orders from the chains that they foolishly reprinted – only to have all the sale-or-return copies flood back, leaving them with warehouses full of unsaleable stock, and converting what might have been a modest profit into a thumping loss.

Life became even more hazardous after the abolition in 1997 of the Net Book Agreement, which had legally prohibited the sale of books below the published price for two years after publication. Before long the chains were joined by supermarkets and online booksellers, all demanding ever larger discounts. Chains and supermarkets fought to undercut each other, offering bestsellers to the public at a fraction of the recommended published price, to the benefit of no one: the publishers were giving away their most valuable assets, the booksellers were making little or no profit on their bestselling titles, the authors were paid the derisory royalties that apply on high-discount sales, and the traditional balancing act whereby the occasional bestseller and boring but dependable books on gardening and bridge fund first novels and books of poetry was thrown into jeopardy.

Conceding higher discounts and more favourable terms to the retail trade coincided with a surge in the level of advances paid to authors. In the bad old days, authors without private means or a job teaching in a school or university were expected to live in a garret on a diet of baked beans. Despite the enormous earnings of a tiny handful of writers, which mislead the world at large into thinking authorship a lucrative profession, most writers still earn far less than the minimum wage, but can now wash down their beans with a glass or two of supermarket red. Nor is their loyalty to publishers what it once was. H.G. Wells used to be quoted as a dreadful warning because his readiness to move from one publisher to another with each new book meant that none of them had an interest in promoting his backlist or keeping his works in print. With editors forever on the move, the life expectancy of the average book put at weeks rather than years, and the chains concentrating their energies on short-lived, highly promoted bestsellers, backlists are no longer as prized as they were: authors shop around, and exploit other media in order to survive.

Better terms for writers reflected the increased power of literary agents. A.P. Watt, where I spent six unhappy years in the 1970s – unhappy due to my own incompetence and unsuitability for the job – is generally thought to have been the world's first literary agent, setting up shop some time in the 1880s, and going on to represent Kipling, Yeats, Conan Doyle, Buchan and other great figures of the time. Watt's near-contemporary J.B. Pinker had an equally impressive cast of authors, but his reputation for shady dealing blighted the trade. Agents came to be regarded as parasitic, slightly dodgy figures, literature's equivalent of the used-car salesmen played by George Cole in post-war British comedies. Although he ended his career as an agent, Charles Pick of Heinemann was among the last publishers to make no bones about disliking and distrusting literary agents. More often than not they retained American, translation and serial rights, all of which he regarded as part of the publisher's inheritance, and because he was nimble at selling such rights himself, to the benefit of his firm as well as his authors, he resented agents all the more. As a publisher, Charles Pick dealt fairly with his authors, but in the early years agents had their work cut out. Whenever possible, publishers would fail or refuse to pay royalties, and buy the copyright in an author's work for a modest outright fee; in more recent times, Paul Hamlyn founded his fortune on paying flat fees to unworldly authors of highly illustrated books about seashells or macramé, which were then sold in huge numbers around the world in risk-free co-editions.

A.D. Peters is generally credited with converting literary agency into an honest and reputable profession. A former journalist, he founded his business in 1924, and included Hilaire Belloc, Evelyn Waugh, Edmund Blunden, J.B. Priestley, Storm Jameson, Stephen Spender, Hugh Trevor-Roper, Arthur Koestler, Rebecca West, C. Day Lewis, Frank O'Connor, Eric Linklater, V.S. Pritchett, Nancy Mitford and C.S. Forester among his clients. Petra worked there towards the end of his life, and I spotted him once or twice when I called in there to pick her up after work. The firm then inhabited an elegant eighteenth-century house in Buckingham Street, with a three-sided bow window overlooking the street, creaking floorboards, and barleysugar banister rails up the staircase. Peters was a sturdy, red-faced, blue-eyed man, clad in immaculate suits and highly polished hand-made shoes, a shy and benevolent Mr Toad who looked as though he should have had a large cigar in one hand and a brandy glass in the other.

Agents are, by definition, pullers of strings who work behind the scenes, and Peters was the ultimate *éminence grise*. A keen cricketer and a friend of J.C. Squire and Alec Waugh, he was part of the world immortalised between the wars by A.G. Macdonell in *England, Their England*. During the war he worked for both the Ministry of Information and the Ministry of Food, while simultaneously running his business; in 1940 he joined Harold Macmillan, Hugh Walpole and others in a successful campaign to dissuade the Chancellor of the Exchequer from imposing purchase tax on books; a year later he was a moving spirit in the influential 1941 Committee which drew up blueprints for a more egalitarian and socialist post-war Britain, and included among its luminaries Victor Gollancz, David Astor, Kingsley Martin, H.G. Wells, Ritchie Calder, Douglas Jay and Tommy Balogh. In later life his liberal instincts manifested themselves in campaigning for the abolition of the death penalty, and on behalf of prisoners and refugee writers. He was one of the founders of Associated

Television, together with Lew Grade and his author Norman Collins, the author of the bestselling *London Belongs to Me* and a former director of Victor Gollancz. He backed new plays in the West End, launching the theatrical careers of Terence Rattigan and J.B. Priestley, and produced films, among them *An Inspector Calls*. With A.P. Herbert, Billy Collins, V.S. Pritchett, Roy Jenkins and others he campaigned for reform of the obscenity laws, culminating in Roy Jenkins's Obscene Publications Act of 1959. Yet if most publishers are forgotten within their lifetimes, agents are even more ephemeral. Peters may be remembered by the world at large as an occasional recipient in the published letters of Evelyn Waugh – his contemporary David Higham occupies a similar role in those of Dylan Thomas – but influence and celebrity don't always coincide.

Relative anonymity is more than made up for by material success, and successful agents can make a good deal of money for themselves as well as for their more saleable authors; and never more so than over the past twenty years. The sums paid for serial rights by Sunday newspapers are not what they were back in the Sixties, but for the lucky few the sale of film and television rights more than makes up for this; and, more importantly for the average author, the advances paid for even modest-selling books far exceed those on offer in the past. Agents, or so it is said, have replaced publishers' editors as the lynchpins in authorial lives, doling out editorial words of wisdom, advising on publicity, giving their views on jackets and typography and acting the part of manager-cum-nursemaid, as well as performing their traditional roles of haggling over terms, drawing up contracts and checking royalty statements. Vulnerable and footloose, publishing editors are no longer fixed points in the literary solar system; and whereas publishing houses are labour- and capital-intensive businesses, with money tied up in advances, work-in-progress, stock and backlists, as well as in the salaries of those who work there, literary agencies rely entirely on the skills of the agents themselves, without whom they are empty shells. Because they are their firms' most precious assets, successful agents tend to be far longer-lived than their publishing coevals: very few of my publishing contemporaries are still in the business, but many of the agents who loomed large in my youth – Michael Sissons, Gillon Aitken, Deborah Rogers, Pat Kavanagh, Bruce Hunter – loom as large as ever, providing welcome continuity in an increasingly unfamiliar landscape.

There is, and always has been, a great gulf set between how much money an author needs to research and write a book, and what a publisher should sensibly pay for it by way of an advance. I haven't looked at *The Truth About Publishing* for nearly forty years, but I suspect it was Stanley Unwin who decreed that, ideally, advances to authors should be based on 40 per cent of the royalties likely to be earned from the first printing of a book, and that on no account should the author's share of any subsidiary rights income be included: that way there could be no question of a book failing to earn or cover its advance – which, it was emphasised, was in essence a loan from the publisher against future earnings.

I spent much of my life working for famously parsimonious publishers – André Deutsch, and Chatto under the *ancien régime* – who were more than happy to go along with Sir Stanley's recommendations, but during my time in publishing these were steadily eroded. Pressed by agents acting on behalf of full-time writers who needed every penny they could earn, publishers began to pay advances equivalent to all the likely royalties on the first impression, and then to include the author's share of subsidiary rights income as well. In the late Eighties the publishers lost control. Panicked by the thought of losing their bestselling authors to predatory rivals, and boosted by the seemingly illimitable coffers of their new corporate owners, they regularly paid advances that bore no relation to likely earnings. We were told that paying over the odds was essential to keep authors or build up a list, and publishers' accountants happily provided Jesuitical justifications for their masters' excesses. I'm easily baffled by figures, but when, in a spirit of enquiry, I sometimes asked whether – to take a very modest example – paying an advance of £5,000 for a collection of stories which would earn £2,000 in royalties didn't leave us with a deficit of £3,000, I was greeted with a condescending sigh. Did I not realise that advances, like stock, were written down in the accounts, and that all these unearned advances somehow evaporated into the ether? Years later I asked a numerate publisher to explain: he said that an economist would agree with me, but not an accountant; and, in the short term at least, the accountants' view prevailed.

Over the past few years, publishers have begun to pay most authors more 'realistic' advances, and new publishers continue to try their luck, making good use of computer technology and colonising markets ignored or overlooked by the conglomerates; but the combination of huge discounts and unreal advances has undermined the ecology of trade publishing, prompting agonised debates about the future of 'midlist' titles and the over-dependence of the trade on celebrity bestsellers which continue to attract enormous advances and are then sold on to whole-salers, retailers and the general public at discounts so huge as to erode any profits that might be made *en route*. Towards the end of my time in publishing I often felt I was working in a lunatic asylum, but although the vestigial publisher in me deeply disapproves of what has happened, as a writer I'm happy to benefit from an altered balance of power.

Shortly after I'd been commissioned to write my Connolly biography, I bumped into the publisher Tom Rosenthal outside the old André Deutsch office in Great Russell Street.

'Forgive my raising this, dear boy,' he said, 'but do you mind my asking how much Cape have paid you to write about Cyril?'

I didn't mind in the least, and when I told him he flinched back like a boxer evading a blow, and drew in his breath between his teeth. 'Tell me,' he went on, 'how much would *you* have paid for your book if you were still at Chatto?' I suggested about a quarter of what I'd been offered. We both agreed that seemed a sensible amount, but had the old rules prevailed I could never have written my book.

# FOUR

# Wielding the Blue Pencil

'At Chatto we don't publish authors who need *editing*,' Norah Smallwood once told me, in withering tones, after I had suggested that although a new novel by one of the firm's long-established authors wasn't a masterpiece, it would pass muster if cut and rewritten in places. Years earlier, the author in question had produced a bestseller, and although she had never repeated her early success, she had a loyal following and steadily outsold most of the more literary writers on the list; but Norah had never cared for her, in print or in person, and ever since Ian Parsons's retirement she had longed to get rid of his middlebrow protégée. In the end we persuaded Norah that it made commercial sense to continue with her, and I was authorised to get out my hacksaw and shears: but her days with the firm were numbered all the same, since Norah's successor felt the same about her work and had no hesitation about turning down her next.

Writers, reviewers, literary agents and other denizens of the literary jungle spend a fair amount of time grumbling about the decline – or even extinction – of editing in even the most literary publishing houses, but I'm not sure they're right to do so. Before the war Norah Smallwood had worked as a secretary on the elegant but short-lived magazine *Night and Day*, jointly edited by Graham Greene and published by Chatto, and she had clambered to the top of the publishing tree while her male colleagues were away at the war; she had grown up in a world in which writers and their editors had a better grasp of grammar than their modern descendants, and a stronger sense of a shared culture based on the Bible, the classics and general knowledge of British and European history, all of which reduced (but by no means obliterated: Cyril Connolly, for example, always spelt the possessive of 'it' as 'it's') the likelihood of spelling, grammatical and historical howlers, and lent force to Norah's claim *vis-à-vis* the kind of books published by a distinguished literary firm like Chatto. But what she didn't mention – and what those who look back with yearning to an imaginary golden age conveniently forget – is the dependence of old-fashioned publishers on their typesetters. 'Make it look like the last,' Ian Parsons would scribble on the typescript of the latest Aldous Huxley or Margaret Irwin, and the typesetters would be expected not only to design the page, but to pick up spelling mistakes, factual errors and the fact that 'Jim' had inexplicably become 'Joe' halfway through, or the colour of his eyes had switched from green to brown: in other words, to do the kind of detailed editorial work nowadays expected of the editor, or copy-editor. Some of these typesetters had legendary powers, and were said to be able to compose and correct in Arabic, Greek, Urdu, Cyrillic and other languages and scripts, none of which they could read or understand. Every now and then, at OUP, I would spot a huge, baffled-looking man with enormous Spam-coloured legs shambling down the corridor wearing a pair of tiny khaki shorts even in mid-winter, and was told, in a reverential whisper, that he had spent his working life as a compositor in the University Press, and that he could set the most obscure languages and typefaces known to man, working from the feel and weight of the lead in his hand as well as from the look of what was on the page before him.

Not even the most brilliant typesetter would presume, or dare, to suggest that the author should cut or rewrite: that kind of strategic editing was the preserve of the publisher or the commissioning editor. Norah may have been correct in suggesting that Chatto authors didn't need editing in that way – though the correspondence between her predecessor, Charles Prentice, and T.F. Powys suggests that she may have romanticised the past in order to make her point – but in her days, and mine, there was a difference between firms like Chatto, where an editor was expected to look after every aspect of a book's editorial well-being, and those like Cape or OUP, where a raft of sub- or copy-editors would take over. At Chatto a commissioning editor would be expected to agree and negotiate terms with the author's agent, vet the contract, edit the typescript at both strategic and tactical levels, sort out any libel or copyright problems, write the blurb and publicity material, choose and caption any photographs, deal with the jacket and jacket copy, correct the proofs and liaise with the sales and publicity departments, while at the same time reading new books on offer to the firm, keeping up to date with developments in the trade at large, attending meetings, most of them unnecessary, going out for long lunches and the occasional publishing party, and somehow finding time to read and edit A's new book while at the same time writing Advance Information Sheets for B's, C's and E's, hosing down F after he'd received a drubbing in the Sunday papers, and collating G's corrections to his proofs with those of our outside reader. The obvious answer was to work in the evenings or at weekends, but somehow I never had the time or the inclination; and it may well be that the overall standard of editing in small firms like Chatto wasn't as high as it was in firms like Cape, where the commissioning editor would discuss and suggest strategic cuts or changes with the author before passing the approved typescript on to the copy-editors, while such matters as vetting contracts or writing blurbs were hived off to specialist departments.

All of us live in periods of transition, and the forty-odd years I've spent in and around the book trade have been more fast-moving than most: it seems a long haul from the days when some books were still bound in cloth and printed in hot metal to print-on-demand, e-books and blogging on the internet. New technologies have affected the ways in which editors go about their business, in that books are now delivered by email, edited on screen, and, in effect, typeset by their authors; and with well over 100,000 new titles being published every year, authors are more numerous and more varied than they were in the past, while assumptions of a common culture can no longer be taken for granted. Editors in even the most literary firms may find themselves heavily editing, or even rewriting, works written, or ghostwritten, by celebrities, sportsmen, spin doctors, chefs, politicians and tycoons, many of whom are barely literate: all of which makes the editor's work a good deal more demanding and time-consuming than it was in those halcyon days when most books were written by scholars or professional writers, and eagle-eyed typesetters were there to save us from ourselves. American publishers have traditionally dismissed English editors as indolent, lightweight and insufficiently professional, while those in London claimed that their equivalents in New York were intrusive, prescriptive, over-reliant on fact-checkers and style books, and immune to the finer shades of irony, ambivalence and acceptable hyperbole. Given the changing nature of both writers and readers, British editors have become closer to their American contemporaries than they were in the past, in that they positively rework books rather than looking out for the occasional spelling mistake or wrong date before passing them on to the printer.

The collapse of a common culture, of shared knowledge and assumptions taken for granted by author, publisher and reader, is reflected in the competitive world of classics publishing. E.V. Rieu started the Penguin Classics list in 1946. Each book came equipped with a brief introduction and no more, and so it remained throughout my time at school and university. It was assumed that readers knew about names, places or subjects mentioned in the text, and that reference notes – printed at the back, and referred to in the text via an asterisk or numeral – were intrusive and unnecessary. Over the years I've greatly enjoyed writing introductions to paperback reissues, starting with Bulldog Drummond and E.W. Hornung's Raffles stories for Everyman paperbacks and moving on to *Three Men in a Boat, The Diary of a Nobody, The Prisoner of Zenda, Love and Mr Lewisham* and Surtees's *Mr Facey Romford's Hounds*: it's rather like writing obituaries, in that one becomes an instant expert on the life and times of one's chosen author, and forgets every word of it within a matter of weeks. Twenty-five years ago one was expected to write an introduction and no more, but before long we introducers had to provide, in addition, a chronology setting the author's career in the context of contemporary events, a bibliography, and increasingly detailed reference notes. My reference notes to the Penguin Classics *Three Men in a Boat*, for instance, explain the value of a guinea, give a pair of dates and a potted c.v. to Ethelred the Unready, provide an etymology for a 'scold's bridle', and account for the introduction of the banjo into this country, as well as well as explaining the siting and history of Runnymede, Hampton Court and Moulsey Lock. The retired colonel in me wonders why readers can't look these things up for themselves, as I had just done, but I'm told that university students expect this kind of service, and that we mustn't forget the all-important export market, for which Anglo-Saxon monarchs or the geography of the Thames Valley are a closed book. I don't imagine *Three Men in a Boat* or *Mr Facey Romford's Hounds* often feature as set books, or are widely read overseas, but it's the thought that counts.

After I'd delivered my introduction and notes to a Penguin Classics reissue of Smollett's last novel, *Humphry Clinker*, my then editor asked me (in vain) to refer to Fanny Burney as Frances Burney, and queried the word 'Hottentot' as pejorative and racially offensive: I had to explain that, apart from anything else,

I was quoting Smollett himself, and that to censor him all these years later wasn't on even in an age of retroactive guilt. And yet, for all its absurdities, the editorial baggage has its uses, and becomes curiously addictive: reading a selection of D.H. Lawrence's letters published by Penguin in the 1950s, I was irritated by the complete absence of explanatory notes, and found myself thinking what an idle and incompetent piece of work it seemed by modern standards – reluctantly so, given my admiration for Allen Lane, an exemplary publisher who prided himself on making the best available to the many without any element of condescension or dumbing down.

Some authors, of course, are amenable to editing; others resist even the removal of a comma, and none more so than Iris Murdoch. Dennis Enright was her editor when I arrived at Chatto, and although he liked her very much in person, as we all did, he found her later novels implausible and over-long. Petra and I first met her at a dinner party given by Brian and Margaret Aldiss. These were, invariably, convivial and hard-drinking affairs, and the wine was never in short supply, but every time our host and hostess left the room to clear away a course or bring in the next, Iris's husband, John Bayley, would spring from his chair, rush to the sideboard, seize a bottle and replenish our already brimming glasses, while Iris, spluttering with laughter, would mutter, '*Really*, John, it's *too* bad.'

Iris had been Norah Smallwood's great discovery, back in the early 1950s, when her novels were short, made sense and needed no editing. Dennis and I may have grumbled about them behind the scenes, but she continued to get far better reviews than we thought she deserved, was revered by the literary world at large, and was, by the time I went to work at Chatto, far and away the most famous and esteemed writer on the list. She also made the firm a great deal of money, still more so after *The Sea, the Sea* won the Booker Prize in 1978, and the fact that other publishers would happily have lured her away put her in a very strong position. I always felt that Chatto had done her a great disservice by not insisting on editing her later books, but by then it was too late. Her novels were treated as Holy Writ; a reverential hush would fall over the Chatto building when we learned that a new novel had been delivered, handwritten in blue ink and ready for the typist. As Dennis soon discovered, she was not prepared to be edited in any way. He used to tell us how, feeling he ought to earn his keep, he pointed out that a word used in her latest novel didn't appear to exist, in that it couldn't be located in *The Complete Oxford Dictionary*. 'It does now, Dennis,' Iris shot back – very reasonably, it seemed to me. When Dennis retired, I took over the 'editing' of Iris's books. My contributions were purely topographical. She was poor on the geography of London, so I would write to point out that the Circle Line doesn't call at Hyde Park Corner, or that Charlotte Street runs north–south rather than east–west. 'Thank you *so* much for all your help. I'm most grateful,' Iris would reply in navy blue ink on a sheet of royal blue Basildon Bond. My editorial labours were over, and I could turn to other things.

# FIVE

# A Cautionary Tale

One of the minor irritations of being a writer is the widespread assumption that writing is an easy business, to be undertaken if and when the prospective author has nothing better to do. All writers must be familiar with the bluff, red-faced man at a party who says, 'So you write books, do you? I've often thought of writing one myself, and may give it a whirl one of these days . . .' No one would say to a composer, 'So you write string quartets, do you? I've often thought of writing one myself, and may give it a whirl one of these days,' but we all know that being able to play an oboe or a violin requires a modicum of training and talent, while the mere sight of a musician's score is guaranteed to induce a reverential hush. Painters and sculptors are more vulnerable, but writers are the easiest game of all: writing is, in theory, the most democratic of the arts, since even the most boring and monosyllabic among us use words and sentences, the common currency of writers and non-writers alike. And the internet has made writers of us all: in the age of the blog we are all equal, or so they would have us believe.

But the printed page, and the book in particular, still retains its magic and its *réclame*, and every now and then one is bullied or browbeaten into reading something written by the red-faced man at a party – egged on by his friends, who assume, quite wrongly, that jocular, articulate and entertaining anecdotalists must, by definition, be equally effective in print, and fail to realise that good writers are often tongue-tied and unforthcoming in company, only coming to life when seated at a keyboard. These good-hearted friends would never dream of asking solicitors, accountants or dentists for free advice, but writers, most of whom earn well below the minimum wage, are expected to devote long hours to reading and reporting on such works free of charge. They are thought to be unworldly, generous-minded characters, holy fools far removed from sordid financial considerations, while the publicity attracted by that tiny minority who receive huge advances misleads people into thinking that authorship is a lucrative profession.

'He's *such* a character, and has led *such* an interesting life,' the good-hearted friends assure one, and the heart sinks as they speak. Those of us who have spent long hours trawling through publishers' slush piles, carefully removing the stray hairs or tiny strips of Sellotape planted to ambush the professional reader ('You can't have read to the end, since the hair is exactly where I left it'), will recognise at once the telltale phrases which betray the man who might well be the life and soul of the party, but is hopelessly adrift once he tries to put it all down in print. 'I'll never forget old So-and-so. What an amazing character he was,' we read, but when – if forced to discuss the work with its author – we ask how and why old So-and-so was such an amazing character, a bruised and baffled silence falls. 'The times we had . . . how we all roared . . . I'll always remember . . . ' : the rhetoric is there, but missing are the details, the minutiae, the observations that bring abstractions to life. Writers notice and remember trivia which may seem unimportant to the world at large, but are touching and revealing when put to good effect. If I stop to ask directions, I am far more likely to remember my informant's bottle nose or the colour of his tie than how to get from x to y, which is why – unlike the red-faced raconteurs – authors sometimes seem half-dazed, and are widely believed to live in worlds of their own.

'There's a book in all of us' is one of those benign, well-meaning phrases which offer hope to the many while keeping the few firmly in their place. I have never believed it, but just occasionally the old cliché comes true – sometimes with unhappy and unintended consequences. I must be the least public-spirited of men, never involving myself in good works or the local community, and the only way in which I redeem myself – apart from being kind to cats and my daughters – is by encouraging potential writers, both professionally and in my private life. On one occasion I wish I hadn't: not because the book was no good, but because of the effect it had on the author and his family.

Early on in my time at Chatto, we were sent a dog-eared, battered-looking typescript which looked so unpromising that, if I hadn't been less busy than usual, I might well have turned it down after sampling a couple of pages at most. I started reading, and, to my amazement, found myself hooked. It described how, back in the 1930s, the author had been a pupil on board HMS *Mercury*, a training ship for boys moored in Southampton Water and run on despotic lines by Beattie, the sadistic wife of C.B. Fry, the cricketer and athlete who had once been offered the throne of Albania. The book was mercifully short – it needed heavy editing, and rewriting in places – but the story was so fascinating, and the interlacing of the author's own experiences with the bizarre Fry *ménage* so tantalising, that I urged my colleagues to take it on. I had, I soon remembered, read it some years before, while I was at OUP, but had been easily outvoted when I suggested that we should take it on; later I learned from the author that it had been turned down by at least twenty publishers before it found its way to Chatto's offices in William IV Street. Carmen Callil, by now in charge at Chatto, was happy to go ahead, but told me – not unreasonably – to make a very modest offer. We were unlikely to sell American or even paperback rights, so the book would have to pay its way through hardback sales alone. I don't remember the terms we offered, but the advance was in the hundreds rather than the thousands, and it may well be that, as the author later claimed, we paid a starting royalty of 7½ per cent rather than the standard 10 per cent. But it had found its way into print at last, and I was determined to do everything I could to help it along.

Soon after the contract had been signed, the author called in at Chatto for the first of several lunches in an Italian restaurant in St Martin's Lane. He was a bustling, stocky schoolmaster in his late fifties, with a mane of gleaming white hair, a Wellingtonian beak and a gait so upright that I expected him to topple over backwards at any moment: I liked him well enough, but he had the pomposity and the assumption of omniscience that goes with a lifetime spent ordering small children around. He had never published anything before, and had no knowledge of publishing or the literary life: he referred every suggestion I made to the local librarian of his home town in Nottinghamshire, and since she knew as little about publishing as he did, I fought to master my irritation when, at our next meeting, he quoted her views back to me in reverential tones.

Editing his book was the kind of work I enjoyed, and was good at. Sentences were reordered, entire paragraphs rewritten, and – this was long before the days of desktop computers – whole chunks were scissored out and pasted down elsewhere, with notes in the margin that read 'Take in (A)' or 'Move to p.75 (B)'. But my tinkerings were only skin-deep: he had written a good and interesting book, and I was happy to do what I could to make it even better. I wrote a flamboyant and entertaining blurb, though he blenched momentarily when I referred to Beattie's habit of inspecting the boys' pyjama bottoms every morning for evidence of beastliness. We agreed to eight pages of black-and-white photographs; for reasons of cost, we could only afford a two-colour jacket, but the overall effect looked pretty good, and since there were no full-colour pictures of the *Mercury* in the late 1930s, our jacket had the virtue of verisimilitude. When the proofs came in, I sent copies to well-disposed authors like Richard Cobb and Alan Ross, both of whom wrote admiring letters. The reviews could not have been better, and William Boyd's rhapsodic account was the lead review in the *TLS*. As expected, American publishers thought it far too English for their market, and the paperback publishers wouldn't bite; but we sold out our modest hardback printing and made an equally modest profit, and both book and author received the acclaim they deserved.

All this was well and good – until I discovered that the reviews had gone to my author's head. Over lunch one day, he told me that he had decided to give up his job as a schoolmaster in order to write full time. This was most alarming news, and I urged him to reconsider. Very few authors, I told him, could live off writing books alone, and it would be madness to take this step at his stage of life. Although I didn't say so, I sensed that he was a 'one-book author', the living embodiment of the notion that 'there's a book in everyone', but the fact that his book had been so well received had stirred up expectations that could never be satisfied. I begged him, in vain, to think again: pension time was only round the corner, he could perfectly well combine another book with teaching, and the literary life was a notoriously perilous business. In due course he produced an outline and a sample chapter of the next book he wanted to write. It was, as I had dreaded, utterly unpublishable. We turned it down and, as discarded authors will, he vanished from view.

Some fifteen years later I wrote a piece in the *Author* about the hazards of the literary life, at the bottom of which a potted biography mentioned that I had switched from publishing to writing, and had written two volumes of autobiography and a life of Cyril Connolly. Not long after it appeared, the Society of Authors forwarded to me a letter from my old author. He sounded very cross indeed. Well, he said, you seem to have done very well for yourself, as one might expect from someone who was part of the London literary scene, prone as it was to back-scratching and mutual self-regard. His own life had been a good deal less happy since the publication of his book, and it was entirely my fault. I had made no effort to sell or publicise his book; his wife's health had suffered as a result of his decision to go freelance, and penury was looming; no one had published the book we'd turned down; the local librarian had been outraged by my reference in the blurb to Beattie's inspecting the boys' pyjama bottoms, and was convinced that by doing so I had alienated innumerable readers and ruined the book's hopes of bestsellerdom; I had disgraced the name of publisher by paying him a royalty which, or so he had learned, was below the going rate.

Most of us drift through life on the vague if misguided assumption that most people like us well enough for most of the time. To be suddenly confronted with such raw hatred, and to be blamed for ruining someone else's life, was a disconcerting business, and for a couple of days I felt shaken and depressed by this blast from the past. And then, quite suddenly, contrition gave way to anger, and I wrote him a furious letter in return. He had written, I told him, a very good book, but I now felt I had done him a great disservice by rescuing it from the slush pile, for although the reading public would have been the poorer without it, the price had been too high. I reminded him of how I had begged him not to give up his job, and told him that, sorry as I was to hear about his wife, he had only himself to blame. I recalled the time and attention I had happily devoted to editing his book, and told him how, without my enthusiasm, William Boyd and the others might never have reviewed it. I couldn't remember the contractual terms, but was ready to plead guilty, bearing in mind that, with the costings as tight as they were, we may well have had no alternative. And if he and the Nottinghamshire librarian felt so strongly about the pyjama bottoms, then maybe he should have removed them from the text itself.

A few days later I received a placatory, apologetic letter from my old author. I wrote a friendly letter in return, wished him the best of luck, and have never heard from him since. His book, for all its faults, had been one of those rare oddities that brighten the publisher's life, making a welcome change from the slick, often rather conventional offerings of sophisticated London literary types, and it seemed terrible that its publication, so exciting at the time, and so well-meant, should have brought such misery in its wake. A writer's books are like his children, to be loved and worried over like their flesh-and-blood equivalents, and my author's anxiety and irritation were understandable if, to my mind, misplaced: but one of the perks of a writer's life is the ability to talk to family, friends and complete strangers *in absentia* and from beyond the grave, and he can draw comfort from the fact that his book will still be available, in the copyright libraries at least, long after his tribulations have been entirely forgotten.

# SIX

# Ghostly Presence

Ghostwriting is a lucrative business nowadays, as publishers compete to publish the maunderings of illiterate celebrities, self-important politicians and sportsmen with nothing to say for themselves. Very often the resulting books sell in derisory quantities, and the enormous advances have to be written off. But that is neither here nor there to the ghostwriters, who have already received a sizeable slice of the advance, and – provided they do their work well, and deliver on time and at the right length – can be fairly sure that more pop singers, celebrity chefs, footballers and television personalities are waiting eagerly in line to spill the non-existent beans. Yet until fairly recently ghostwriters were badly paid and poorly regarded, seedy and faintly disreputable denizens of the literary underworld who got drunk by day and toiled all night in a garret.

I've never been tempted to become a ghost, partly because I suspect it could very easily take over one's life, and partly because – for good or for bad – I have too distinctive a tone of voice, which I would find it almost impossible to repress. Sometimes, as an editor, I rewrote and reworked a book to such an extent that I almost crossed the line between heavy editing and ghostwriting. I've written elsewhere how, thirty years ago, I helped Tam Dalyell write his prescient but disregarded diatribe against Scottish devolution, in which he spelt out the constitutional anomalies embodied in the West Lothian question, named after his own constituency, and forecast that devolution would introduce yet another layer of bureaucracy and would lead, in due course, to Scottish independence. Because time was so short – Cape, his publisher, wanted to get it out in time for that year's Labour Party Conference – I ended up writing about half the book, pounding away on an old manual typewriter in an empty attic room in his ancestral home near Edinburgh while Tam strode up and down behind me, pontificating as he went and tearing articles out of newspapers and magazines. But I regarded myself as, essentially, his editor, and would never claim to have ghostwritten his book. Some years later Tam wrote to say that he had been brooding on the matter, and had decided that, like the nail in the horse's shoe, I had single-handedly held the United Kingdom together, since without his book Jim Callaghan might well have pressed ahead with devolution. Alas, he had reckoned without Tony Blair, never the man to ponder the consequences of ill-thought-out actions.

I have ghostwritten one book, however, and that was towards the end of my time at Chatto. I first came across its author when my colleague Rupert Lancaster commissioned him to write an account of his celebrated cricketing career. Rupert was bug-ridden or out of the office when the typescript arrived, and it was agreed that someone else should take a first look at it, and come up with reactions and suggestions. The obvious man for the job was my colleague John Charlton, who had played cricket for Winchester and for his college at Cambridge, and had once bowled out Alan Ross with a slow lob which, much to Alan's irritation, had somehow dive-bombed his wicket from a great height, rather like a kamikaze pilot. For some reason John was unable to take the job on, and it was passed to me instead – most unsuitably, since I know nothing about cricket and have no idea how a longstop differs from a silly mid-on. I read our author's book, and although I was sure it would be of interest to his admirers, I felt it was too functional for its own good, and lacked the human touch. 'I went in to bat,' he would write of some important match. 'I scored 200 runs. I was bowled out. I walked back to the pavilion,' and so on and on.

'This is very interesting stuff,' I told him as we sat together in my tiny office in Bedford Square, 'but I think it would be even better if you put more of yourself into the story. How did you feel, for example, when you were first chosen to play for your county, or when you scored your first century?'

'Feel? What do you mean "feel"?' he wondered, a puzzled frown wrinkling his handsome brow.

'Well,' I asked, 'were you nervous, or elated, or immensely excited? What did it feel like when you went out to bat in a Test match for the first time?'

'It felt all right,' he replied, and that was the end of the matter. Luckily Rupert returned to the office a few days later, and I was able to pass the whole thing back to him.

But that was not the end of my involvement with the great man. Shortly afterwards he was commissioned to write a book about his native land. It was to be a large-format, heavily illustrated book, with colour photographs specially taken by a well-known practitioner, and our author providing a text of some 20,000 words, taking us on a journey from one end of the country to the other, and interlacing topography and history with snatches of autobiography. A handsome advance was agreed with his agent. A great deal of money would be tied up in production costs and monies paid to the author and the photographer, and because the book was expected to make a sizeable contribution to turnover in the season in which it was due to appear, much emphasis was laid on getting the typescript and the photographs delivered bang on time.

Once again, for some reason Rupert was out of the office at the critical moment. At one of our editorial meetings Carmen Callil pointed out that our man was due to deliver his book any moment – the photographs had long since been taken – and that since I was the only person other than Rupert who had had any dealings with the great cricketer, she told me to find out at once what was going on. I rang him at home, and we agreed that I should pay him a visit the following day.

Next morning, instead of heading for Bedford Square, I made my way to the top end of Sloane Avenue, and rang the bell of his flat. There was no answer. 'He's a lazy bugger, that one,' said a man selling flowers on the pavement outside. 'Never gets out of bed, if you ask me. Keep ringing, you'll get him in the end.' Eventually a buzzer let me in, and I made my way up to the first floor. Clad in flowing white garments, our author waved me towards a low sofa, covered with large, soft cushions. He was not a man for small talk, so within seconds of my arrival I had asked him when we could expect delivery, and reminded him that its timing was all-important. At this he handed me a leatherbound notebook or diary containing a few jottings and autobiographical snippets. It took me, at most, five minutes to read them; and that, it soon became apparent, was all we had to go on. I took the notebook with me, and reported back to the office.

'Darling,' Carmen said, 'we've got far too much money tied up in this book, and we can't afford to carry it over for another season. There's only one solution: you must drop everything else, and write it.' And that's exactly what I did. I had never been to the author's country in my life, and knew nothing about its peoples, its rivers or its mountain ranges. But that afternoon I went round to the London Library, took out a pile of books, and began my researches. I read histories and travel books and memoirs; I spent long hours in the London Library. I remember nothing about it now, but for a very short time I was a world expert on the subject. After three weeks or so I felt I had done enough, and Chatto's production department was agitating in the wings. I wrote the entire book over a long weekend, interlacing the author's modest contributions with great slabs of descriptive prose, and brought it to a conclusion reminiscent of the travel documentaries shown in the cinema when I was young. 'And so our journey comes to a close, in a very different world from that in which we set out,' I wrote, before ending on a note that was both uplifting and admonitory: 'If my book helps to persuade my country's government to do all it can to preserve so rich and unique a heritage, I shall feel I have not written it in vain.'

The photographs were rather more genuine than my prose, and the finished book looked very handsome indeed. With luck, it not only contributed to Chatto's overheads – rent, rates, salaries, lighting, heating, warehousing and all those humdrum expenses which have to be deducted from the publisher's share of the monies received from copies sold – but made a modest profit as well. The author's agent very generously offered to pay me a share of the advance due on delivery, so I was more than happy; but – foolishly perhaps – I have never been tempted since to resume the ghostwriter's mantle.

# SEVEN

# Muscular Prose

Cyril Connolly's *Enemies of Promise* was published in 1938, and in it he famously contrasted the elaborate Mandarin prose favoured by the writers of an older generation with the terse, unadorned vernacular favoured by younger writers like Hemingway, Isherwood and Orwell. For as long as I can remember, the plain style of English prose has been in the ascendant. Clarity, simplicity and brevity are extolled as the supreme virtues, to the exclusion of all others. Interminable parentheses, sectioned off by colons, semi-colons, dashes and brackets, are regarded as redundant and irrelevant, quaint survivals of a more verbose and leisurely age. Linguistic balancing acts, with sentence piled upon sentence, have gone the way of aquatints or Morris dancing; flat, inanimate prose is *de rigueur* for our buttoned-down practitioners, who see themselves as the heirs of Isherwood and Orwell, but lack their ability to both simplify and intensify the language. A few reactionary figures have held out against the tide. Patrick Leigh Fermor continues to write an elaborate, baroque prose, glittering with words that are both exotic and exact; following their great Victorian precursors, Evelyn Waugh and Hugh Trevor-Roper interlaced long rolling periods with short, sharp sentences, like cooks contrasting sweet and sour, or painters counterpointing light and shade. Although long sentences and elaborate constructions of clause and sub-clause are equated nowadays with obscurity, pretentiousness, whimsicality and general windbaggery, the great masters of the art – Trollope or Stevenson, for example – combined prolixity with an almost luminous clarity of mind and style: few things give more intellectual and aesthetic pleasure than following a thread, unbroken, through some enormous nineteenth-century sentence, often a paragraph long in itself.

I have a very soft spot for the long sentence and the parenthetical aside, yet some of the best and most effective prose of the twentieth century comes from the opposite camp – and was written, not by literary men, but by soldiers and men of action. Soldiers' prose tends to be strong, direct and succinct, like a musclebound version of *Goodbye to Berlin* or *To Have or Have Not*. When these rather prosaic virtues are combined with vigorous turns of phrase and the ability to evoke character and tell a good story, the effect can be overwhelming. I once asked Tom Rosenthal why, at their best, soldiers write such effective and efficient prose, and – speaking as a former National Service man to someone who had, much to his relief, escaped the net by a couple of years – he came up with an instant solution. 'My dear fellow,' he said, 'the answer is obvious. When soldiers communicate with one another they have to be clear, simple and unambiguous: they can't afford not to be. It could, after all, be a matter of life or death.'

One of the best examples of the genre came my way in the early eighties, when I was working at Chatto. An agent sent me the typescript of a book called *Albanian Assignment*, by one David Smiley. It was very short – well under 200 pages – so I decided to take it home with me for the weekend. Most of the typescripts I took home for the weekend remained in my briefcase, and travelled back to the office on Monday morning in the same condition as they left it, having made the journey in order to make me feel virtuous and dynamic; but this was a rare exception, in that I took it out of my briefcase, settled down with it in a deckchair, and couldn't stop reading. It described how, as a young professional soldier, David Smiley had been parachuted into wartime Albania to ginger up the resistance to the Italian and German occupying forces, working alongside Julian Amery, Billy McLean, Peter Kemp and other members of SOE; and how, like their equivalents in Yugoslavia, they had found themselves caught up in a civil war between the Communists, led by Enver Hoxha, and an uneasy coalition of monarchists and right-wingers. Smiley was less interested in politics than were his companions – what he really enjoyed was blowing up bridges, much to Hoxha's irritation – but he shared their romantic attachment to the old order and their loathing for the Communist partisans, and enjoyed being able to go to war wearing jodhpurs, sandals and a white fez, all of which outraged more orthodox army officers. Written in the spare, no-nonsense style of the quintessential military man, his story rattled along with such speed and energy that I must have finished it within four hours at most; it was also suffused by a tremendous anger at what he considered to be the betrayal of the non-Communist parties in Albania by the Allies – who, as in Yugoslavia, had decided to back the Communist partisans to the exclusion of all others.

Although it wasn't at all her sort of book, Carmen Callil allowed me to take it on, and after agreeing terms with the agent, we arranged for Colonel Smiley to come into the office. He was, and still is, a stocky, muscular figure, with fair hair faded to white, bright blue eyes, a broken nose, hands like root vegetables and an iron handshake. He had, I soon discovered, led a more adventurous life than most: before being parachuted into Albania he had fought in Abyssinia and North Africa, and afterwards he caught the tail end of the war in Indo-China, again working for SOE. After the war he had served as a military attaché in Poland, and, while based in Malta, had been deeply involved in a doomed Anglo-American plan to destabilise Hoxha's Stalinist dictatorship, involving some of his old non-Communist friends from Albania: the authorities in Tirana were said to have been tipped off by Kim Philby, then working for MI6 in Washington, who alerted his masters in Moscow. The Colonel then spent many years in the Middle East, running the armies of the Sultan of Oman and others.

I took to him at once, and was even more impressed when he revealed that his old friend Patrick Leigh Fermor had agreed to write a Foreword. During the war they and various other dashing young blades had shared a house in Cairo. Always referred to as Tara, it was run by a lively Polish lady, had a resident mongoose, and was the scene of bacchanalian carousings whenever Leigh Fermor and Xan Fielding found themselves on leave from capturing German generals in the mountains of Crete, or Smiley, Billy McClean and Julian Amery returned from their guerrilla exploits among the Ghegs and the Tosks of Albania.

A few days after our first meeting the Colonel asked if he could have the typescript back, since 'Paddy' was in London and wanted to have another read of it before writing his Foreword. Some weeks went by before I saw it again, and it was no longer the book it had been. Paddy, the Colonel explained, had decided to edit and rewrite the book. The Colonel's terse, staccato sentences had been stitched together; colons and semi-colons had supplanted innumerable full stops, like exotic plants invading an arid terrain; functional, straightforward verbs and adjectives had been elbowed aside by more obscure and efflorescent synonyms. It was magnificent, but it was no longer the Colonel's book, nor was it written in his tone of voice. When I pointed this out, the Colonel was suitably dismayed, but not on his own account: Paddy was not only an old and dear friend who had gone to great trouble to help his book along, but was generally regarded as one of the great writers of his time; we couldn't just ignore his changes. No one admired Paddy's prose more than I did, I told him – which was true – but he had a very different style and tone of voice, and since David Smiley's account worked so well as it stood, it seemed pointless to go ahead with the new version. The only answer was to unstitch the whole thing, and restore the old order.

The Colonel was appalled at the idea: Paddy would be dreadfully wounded if he learned that his hard work and his selfless suggestions had been entirely ignored. I told him not to worry: the chances were that Paddy would never read the book again, and would never know. Everything was put back as it had been before; Paddy sent in a flamboyant and affectionate Foreword, written out by hand in royal-blue ink on large sheets of maths paper, each the size of a pillowcase; maps and a jacket were commissioned, the pictures collected up, and *Albanian Assignment* inched its way into production. The whole episode was, in a way, a cautionary tale: as an editor, I tended to impose my own tone of voice at the expense of the author's, and it was only when I went to work with Alan Ross at the *London Magazine* that I learned the value of leaving well alone.

All that is well over twenty years ago, but although I lost touch with Colonel Smiley, I was haunted by the memory of his book. I loved the idea of those tough, romantic, upper-class young men, like John Buchan heroes, living like bandits among the wild mountains of Albania; I was overawed by their nerve and their insouciance, by the way in which McClean and Julian Amery, still only in their twenties, not only performed deeds of derring-do, but consorted as equals with Anthony Eden and even Churchill himself, and I contrasted their courage and self-confidence with my own timorous and tentative existence. Like many men of my age, I suspect, I half-envied my father's generation for having fought in the war, while at the same time harbouring the conviction that, had I been put to the test, I would have proved both cowardly and inadequate, suffering endless attacks of fear-induced diarrhoea, failing to show any signs of initiative or leadership, skulking at the back when the time came to make a bold advance, and hiding behind other people if bullets or bayonets headed my way, in much the same way as I step nimbly behind Petra if I see a drunk with a bottle weaving towards us.

The war in the Balkans had proved a divisive business, and old suspicions and dislikes still smouldered on. Smiley and his friends were convinced that they and their non-Communist allies in Albania had been betrayed by Communist moles in SOE's headquarters in Bari, and sacrificed to the demands of *realpolitik* and the wartime alliance with Russia. A future Ambassador in Paris was, I soon discovered, a particular *bête noire*. I longed to learn more about the activities and influence, in SOE's Cairo office, of the brilliant, openly Communist James Klugmann, a Cambridge contemporary of Burgess, Maclean, Philby and Blunt, and a lifelong member of the Party, and of the intrepid left-wing journalist Basil Davidson, who fought with Tito's Communist Partisans in Yugoslavia, and was later described as the man who invented African history. Among those regarded with some disfavour was the glamorous, kilted figure of Fitzroy Maclean. With Bill Deakin, later the Warden of St Antony's, Oxford, Maclean had been parachuted into Yugoslavia to liaise with Tito's Partisans, and had urged Churchill to abandon the allegedly compromised royalist resistance – led by the bearded and bespectacled Mihailovich, who was eventually executed by firing squad on a golf course near Belgrade – and to back the Communists instead. His *Eastern Approaches* seemed to me to be one of the great books of its time, the very model of the man-of-action memoir I so admired.

Although I couldn't read a word of German, let alone Albanian or Serbo-Croat, I decided to write a book about Smiley and his friends, placing their adventures in the context of the Balkans in particular and the war as a whole, and trying to find out whether there was any truth in their belief that they had been betrayed by, among others, the future Ambassador to France.

I had recently completed my biography of Allen Lane, and although I knew nothing about warfare, or Balkan politics, or the Mediterranean campaign in World War II, I relished the idea of plunging into *terra incognita*, and temporarily exchanging the feline manoeuvrings of literary London for something more robust.

I ploughed through innumerable volumes of Albanian history, read biographies of King Zog and Enver Hoxha and scholarly articles about British policy in the Balkans before and during the war, and tried to work out who exactly was allowed access to Enigma decrypts, how much of Kosovo had been reunited with Albania during the war, and which wild and bearded tribal chieftain supported whom, and why. All this was interesting enough, if baffling at times, but the perk of the job was reading yet more Buchanesque accounts of high adventure, most of them published just after the war: Julian Amery's two volumes of memoirs, too Gibbonian at times but gripping all the same; the autobiography of H.W. Tilman, the black-bearded Himalayan mountaineer and long-distance sailor, who spent any time left over from harrying the Hun walking the mountains of Albania, but finding them too tame for his taste; Anthony Quayle's novel about the time he spent as an SOE officer camping out in a cave on the Adriatic coast; the adventures of Brigadier 'Trotsky' Davies, a portly, moustachioed infantry officer of the old school, who disapproved of the sashes and fezzes sported by Amery and Smiley, tried to introduce some order into the proceedings, and was eventually captured by the Germans. The best writer of them all, perhaps, was my old acquaintance Peter Kemp, whose *No Colours or Crest* must be one of the masterpieces of the Second World War.

But my great discovery, the book which, by itself, would have made all my abortive researches worthwhile, was Christie Lawrence's *Irregular Adventure*, published by Faber in 1946. Lawrence was captured when the Germans invaded Crete, and taken back to the Greek mainland for deportation to a prisoner-of-war camp in Germany. As the train trundled slowly north, he managed to escape from the cattle-truck in which he and other prisoners were held. He made his way through northern Greece and Bulgaria to Serbia, where he joined up with Mihailovic's *cetniks*, heavily bearded monarchists who had yet to be denounced by the Partisans as quislings and collaborators. The book ends with Lawrence being captured by the Gestapo, and resuming his journey north. Barely 200 pages long, it was an extraordinarily vivid evocation of guerrilla warfare and Balkan peasant life. Despite a laudatory foreword by Evelyn Waugh, *Irregular Adventure* defies the comforting old saws about good books never being forgotten, and cream rising to the top. I imagine that Christie Lawrence has been long dead, but he and his book deserve to be better remembered.

At some stage in my researches I wrote to Roderick Bailey, a young man at the Imperial War Museum, who had written an excellent piece about the genial but sinister figure of James Klugmann, taking him from his schooldays at Gresham's School, Holt, and his years at Cambridge to his activities in the Rustum Buildings in Cairo, the headquarters of SOE in the Middle East, and his post-war proselytising on behalf of the Communist Party. We had tea together, during the course of which it became apparent that he had spent the last seven years – as a postgraduate at Cambridge, and at St Antony's in Oxford – working on exactly the book I had in mind. He didn't, as yet, have a publisher, but it seemed madness for me to plod along in his footsteps, duplicating work he had done long before; still more so since he could speak both Albanian and Serbo-Croat, and had made several trips to Albania to interview moustachioed brigands and wizened crones who remembered Smiley, Maclean, Amery, Kemp and my other Buchanesque heroes. I decided to bow out, and introduced him to my agent and to Dan Franklin at Jonathan Cape; and the resulting book, *The Wildest Province*, is far better than anything I could have attempted, though it contains no evidence of a Communist conspiracy in SOE, which would have made a good story even more dramatic.

Even though I'm no longer professionally involved, I still perk up at the mere mention of Albania, terrifying and brutish as it always sounds; and despite my own love of a more convoluted style, I still think that soldiers and men of action write better prose than most literary men – Leigh Fermor, Richard Cobb, Trevor-Roper and a handful of others always excluded. And, along with the naval poems of Alan Ross and Keith Douglas's *From Alamein to Zem-Zem*, memoirs like *Eastern Approaches*, *Irregular Adventure*, *No Colours or Crest* and *Albanian Assignment* give the lie to the notion that, compared with its precursor, World War II produced little prose or poetry of lasting value.

# EIGHT

# The Melon-Shaped Grin

In the early 1950s a pale young man named Ernest Hecht published, in paperback, a biography of Len Hutton. He had recently graduated from Hull University, and his office was the spare bedroom in his parents' home in north London. He had originally planned to publish theatre programmes, but the Ballet Rambert had been his only taker; when the Hutton biography turned in a modest profit, he decided to try his luck in hardback, with the memoirs of Ron Burgess, the captain of Spurs and Wales. In due course he published his first bestseller, *The Password is Courage*, which told the story of an English soldier who broke into Auschwitz, and was later filmed with Dirk Bogarde in the starring role.

Started on savings of £250, the Souvenir Press has gone on to publish Erich von Daniken's *Chariots of the Gods* (fifteen million copies sold in the English-language market), the novels of Knut Hamsun, one of five Nobel Prize-winners on the list, and *Le Petomane*, the story of the flatulent Frenchman who stunned Paris society in the early years of the last century with his displays of public farting: the cover carries a photograph of its moustachioed hero leaning forward in the firing position.

Hecht grew up in Moravia, where his father was in the textile business. He was nine when the Germans marched into Czechoslovakia. Travelling by train with his mother soon afterwards, he was sick all over a Wehrmacht officer's uniform; much to their relief, he mopped up the mess, smiled, and said he had children of his own, and was used to such goings-on. Ernest arrived in England by *Kindertransport* shortly before the war broke out. Now in his mid-seventies, and as cheerful and fast-talking as ever, he is, with George Weidenfeld, the last survivor of that buttonholing, entrepreneurial generation of Jewish immigrants who reinvigorated British publishing after the war, and included André Deutsch, Paul Elek, Walter Neurath of Thames & Hudson and Max Reinhardt of The Bodley Head.

If Robert Maxwell was their rogue elephant, Hecht, with his melon-slice grin and disrespectful views, was the court jester: a dishevelled figure and an erratic shaver, he often looks as though he is wearing pyjamas under his black business suit, with a white T-shirt underneath. He was also, with Paul Hamlyn, the shrewdest businessman of the lot: but whereas Hamlyn ran empires, Hecht has prized his independence above all else, preferring to stay small and travel light. He has made some profit every year since he started, has never run up an overdraft, and his *modus operandi* is reminiscent of that vanished world in which publishers were their own masters, ruled the literary roost, and operated out of ramshackle, paper-strewn offices in Bloomsbury or Covent Garden.

'Anybody can create a high-class literary list of prestige titles,' he claims, so putting more pretentious literary publishers firmly in their place. Hecht embodies the old publishing principle of subsidising the virtuous with the saleable: Charles Berlitz's *The Bermuda Triangle* and Arthur Hailey's *Airport* have happily co-existed with the works of Borges and Pablo Neruda, Cliff Richard's memoirs with those of the incomparable P.Y. Betts, the thoughts of the Dalai Lama and Wilhelm Reich with *Knickers: An Intimate Appraisal* – the author of which, Rosemary Hawthorne, is married to the former vicar of Highgrove, and has since gone on to write *Bras: A Private View*. W.H. Auden,

Einstein, Heidegger and Lord David Cecil are among the unexpected luminaries on the list, sharing warehouse room with *The Rear View: A History of Bottoms* and that evergreen classic of lavatory humour, Charles Sale's *The Specialist*.

The Souvenir Press must be the only publishing firm apart from the two great university presses to boast a Latin motto, printed on the notepaper, and a coat of arms approved by the College of Heralds. The motto, provided by an Eton classics master, is translated as 'Bestsellers are the Best Revenge': the coat of arms incorporates the three great passions of Hecht's life in the form of an open book, an ice-cream cone and a football, all set out in the colours of his favourite teams, Arsenal and Brazil. Hecht won the right to hoist the office flag, incorporating the coat of arms, after a lengthy battle with Camden Council, and flies it at half-mast in the rare event of a book being remaindered. He shuns the Frankfurt Book Fair and trips to New York in favour of football matches in South America, and has sampled ice creams around the world.

Hecht has published Bobby Charlton and Matt Busby, and acted as Pele's literary agent: he was the first to publish the Beatles, and his liking for showbiz has led him to act as an impresario, producing plays in the West End, including Flora Robson in Rodney Ackland's *The Old Ladies* and Warren Mitchell in Simon Gray's *Dutch Uncle*, concerts at the Queen Elizabeth Hall, and one-man shows featuring Michael Foot, Patrick Garland and Alan Bennett (years ago, he published the script of *Beyond the Fringe*). And every year he sponsors a Myra Hess memorial concert in the same room in the National Gallery in which she gave her lunchtime concerts during the war.

Despite a staff of only five – these included, until recently, a long-serving freelance rep who eventually retired at the age of eighty-seven – the Souvenir Press occupies all four floors of a white Italianate building opposite the British Museum. It incorporates the remains of a church, and a gothic arch hovers over the bookshop on the ground floor, where all the books are laid out – among them the works of Ronald Searle, who joined the list with *The Illustrated Winespeak*.

Ernest Hecht happily provides visitors with a guided tour of the premises, limping up the steep stairs on an ebony walking stick, grinning all the while. The chaos on his desk outclasses even that of master practitioners like Richard Ingrams, André Deutsch and Alan Ross. On my last visit he told me how he had been forced to evacuate his last office, driven out by the sheer volume of paper; I peered round its door, and was driven back by a tidal wave of proofs, old letters, playbills, theatre programmes, football memorabilia, sleeveless gramophone records and age-old detritus, included a long-discarded T-shirt. His current office is already silting up, the desk long buried under teetering mounds of bumph and the floor covered with posters, display material, typescripts and Arsenal programmes. 'A tidy desk is proof of an untidy mind,' Ernest claims; if the success of Souvenir is anything to go by, he may well be right.

# NINE

# Trade Secrets

Publishing and money-lending are the two great British businesses which have continued to flourish while all else has crumbled round them. Ship-builders and home-grown car-makers have long vanished from the scene, and few Dinky Toys or items of ironmongery still bear the once-proud legend 'Made in England'; but even though most of the great publishing conglomerates are foreign-owned – the Penguin group is the sole exception – the expertise and the experience and the personnel are still home-grown and, for the most part, London-based. Publishing has been a hugely successful enterprise, exporting half its output and doing business all over the world; but whereas the City – in both its bowler-hatted and hedge-fund incarnations – has presented a bold, confident face to the world at large, publishers until quite recently liked to see themselves as bumbling, absent-minded amateurs, ignorant of cash flow, puzzled by balance sheets and generally adrift in the world of commerce. It was widely assumed that publishing houses were staffed exclusively by absent-minded, impractical literary men and well-heeled chinless wonders who couldn't think of a better way to fill in the long hours.

This was, I think, particularly true of that gentlemanly generation of publishers who ran or founded small, independent firms from between the wars until the 1980s, when they sold out to the conglomerates. 'Tell me, Mr Ryder-Runton,' Norah Smallwood would enquire of the company secretary at Chatto board meetings, 'what *exactly* is a balance sheet?' or 'Remind me of what you mean by overheads.' This was both genuine and disingenuous: she might have been hard pushed to read a profit-and-loss account, but she knew how to combine publishing good books with the cheeseparing virtues of driving hard bargains, running tight ships and all the rest of it, with the result that, for most of her time at the helm, Chatto remained afloat, to the benefit of writers, staff and the reading public.

No one has celebrated the bumbling aspects of the book trade more entertainingly than Leo Cooper. Leo was known for many years in the trade as an affable, convivial figure, a pillar of the Publishers' Publicity Circle and a keen cricketer who once smashed Denis Compton for six with such vigour that he toppled a paraplegic's wheelchair into a nearby pond, so bringing the game to a temporary halt. After doing his National Service in Kenya at the time of the Mau Mau rebellion, he decided to try his luck in publishing. He had connections in the literary world – an uncle had written a life of Surtees, his aunt Lettice was a novelist, published by Gollancz, and his aunt Barbara worked for many years for John Lehmann, a famously tight-fisted and irascible employer – and after his aunts had intervened he was recommended for a job checking invoices at Longman's. 'I am very glad that you take an interest in the books,' Mark Longman told him, 'but whatever you do, don't talk to me about them when there are other people around. You see, I don't actually read them.' Another Longman's only known contribution was to organise the All England Croquet Tournament at Hurlingham; a defrocked clergyman snoozed behind his desk; the Publicity Manager was a poet and ex-boxer who had earlier been the transport manager in a laundry.

After a brief, unhappy spell with André Deutsch, whom he compared, unkindly, to a 'boiled canary', Leo moved a few hundred yards down Great Russell Street to work for Hamish Hamilton, a dapper, broken-nosed Anglo-American Olympic oarsman and aeronaut who had built up one of the best literary lists in London under an oak tree colophon designed by Reynolds Stone: according to Leo, he was a crashing snob who changed the photographs on his piano according to who was coming to dinner that evening. Intent on office business, he once refused to return a call from Sir Malcolm Sargent, who had rung in to say that he was 'slipping away quietly'; by the time 'Jamie' Hamilton had bent his mind to the matter, the great conductor was dead. Leo blotted his copybook with his employer when he confessed that, in an ideal world, he would rather be a game warden than a publisher. Hamish Hamilton was not best pleased when, assuming that Leo was out of London on a business trip, he turned up at the Coopers' house on Putney Common, clutching flowers and champagne and hoping to find Jilly Cooper – my erstwhile colleague in the publicity department at Collins – alone in the house, only to have Leo open the door and usher him in.

While at Hamish Hamilton, Leo had started a series of regimental histories, and in 1968 he set up on his own, specialising in books on military history. Some were written by ex-soldiers like Brigadier 'Honky' Henniker, who embarrassed his publisher by breaking into song at the Athenaeum; others by hard-drinking denizens of the 'publishing undergrowth', one of whom notched up over twenty books a year. Life as a small, independent publisher has always been a hazardous business, with printers and paper merchants demanding payment, authors insisting on advances, and the bookshops taking their time to settle up. Nor were those employed by Leo's firm always first-rate material. At one stage the warehouse was run by an eighty-year-old, one of the packers was blind, and the invoice typist was unable to type. Equally unsatisfactory was a Nigerian accountant recommended by the local Job Centre. 'I know you don't like to drink,

Mr Adamolo, but don't let the others put you off,' the office cleaner told him at the Christmas party. 'I think you are an 'uman bein' and deserve to be treated like one.'

Leo Cooper's autobiography celebrates publishing as we like to remember it; Rayner Unwin's provides a measured, melancholy defence of the old order. His father, Sir Stanley, prided himself on being the ultimate all-round publisher, a master of every aspect of the trade and a guru to lesser practitioners. He was bustling, overbearing, penny-pinching and workaholic, and when, in due course, he vanished from the scene, Allen & Unwin lost both energy and direction. Sir Stanley prided himself on having started at the bottom, and thought a university education irrelevant to a career in publishing; Rayner studied at Oxford and Harvard, and although he was a more cultivated man than his father, he lacked his drive, self-confidence and total immersion in the business. The firm staggered from one false start to another before being sold to Rupert Murdoch's HarperCollins, who retained the Tolkien titles and sold off the rest of the list to academic and specialist publishers. Rayner Unwin evokes a vanished world in which serious publishers, like his father, sought out the best books they could find on particular subjects, paid their authors affordable advances, subsidised worthy if uncommercial works with occasional bestsellers like *The Hobbit* and Thor Heyerdahl's *The Kon-Tiki Expedition* and, having no need to consider outside or institutional shareholders, pocketed for themselves a modest proportion of that year's profits, persuaded other members of the family to do likewise, and ploughed the balance back into the business. Working for Allen & Unwin in Sir Stanley's time must have been a dour and badly paid affair, but both authors and employees knew that they were participating in a worthwhile enterprise run by an instinctive businessman who could be guaranteed to keep it in working order.

Both books are essential items for those of us who like to read and collect all we can in the way of publishing memoirs and biographies. It's a curious appetite, since few publishers are natural writers, and most publishing memoirs are pompous, ill-written affairs, redolent of yellowing press cuttings and dwelling fondly on those moments of glory that once set the Garrick ablaze and loomed large in the pages of the *Bookseller*, but have long been forgotten by those who were not involved. The best books of all tend to be written by amateur or part-time publishers. Richard Kennedy's *A Boy at the Hogarth Press* must be the funniest book ever written about publishing, with Leonard Woolf cast in the role of miser-in-chief, worrying over missing halfpence in the petty cash box and doling out galley proofs for re-use as lavatory paper; the pages of Woolf's own memoirs devoted to his time at the Hogarth Press are a riveting read, with much space given over to the minutiae of profit and loss accounts, as are those of his former employee John Lehmann; Diana Athill has provided vivid accounts of working with André Deutsch in *Stet* and in the last chapter of *Instead of a Letter*, while W.E. Williams's miniature memoir of Allen Lane tells us almost all we need to know about the most influential and innovative publisher of the last hundred years. The memoirs of Fred Warburg, Bob Lusty, Anthony Blond and David Higham are better written than most, but are unlikely to be of great interest to the world at large.

Michael Howard's history of Jonathan Cape is far and away the best firm's history, with Joseph McAleer's scholarly survey of Mills & Boon trailing in second place. Howard's father, Wren Howard, was the co-founder of Cape; Howard himself spent most of his working life with the firm, and bucked the trend by being an exemplary writer as well. Few publishers merit full-length biographies. Allen Lane, or so it seemed to me, was an exception to the rule, and so too was his great contemporary,

Victor Gollancz, best remembered as the founder of the pre-war Left Book Club, and for his orange, magenta and black lettering jackets, designed by Stanley Morison and an early example of publisher's 'branding', soon to be emulated by Allen Lane's equally effective orange and white horizontal bands and portly penguin logo. 'How dare you?' the irascible VG once shouted at a literary agent who had dared to question his judgement. 'I am incapable of error!' He took an equally dim view of the Publishers' Association ('I refuse to be manacled by fools!'); his colleague Norman Collins once wrote that 'Victor exuded a greater dynamism than any man I've ever known. Even to see him coming through the front door was like a tempest coming in. He sat down in a chair; the chair creaked. I remember going in to see him one day. He was sharpening a pencil; it was like a lesser man hewing down an oak tree.' All this can be found in Ruth Dudley Edwards's marvellous biography, plus an account of how the great man, worried that he might have the symptoms of VD, pulled down his trousers to inspect the affected areas while standing in the window of his first-floor office overlooking Henrietta Street, in full view of the houses opposite and passers-by on the other side of the road. That's the kind of publisher we like to remember.

## TEN

# Temporary Postings

In the first year of my freelance life I was offered (and accepted) two part-time jobs: neither lasted more than a few months, but both added to my experience of the literary world, and bridged the gap between the dependability of a full-time occupation, however uncongenial, and the more hazardous role of the self-employed hack who is never quite sure where his next penny will come from, or what lies around the corner.

The first of these was suggested by John Walsh, a breezy, convivial and faintly conspiratorial London Irishman who was then editing the books pages of the *Sunday Times*. I had met him first when he was doing the same job on the *Evening Standard*: I liked him at once, admiring his flamboyant mode of dress – multi-coloured shirts and shoes, gangsters' chalk-striped suits, iridescent ties – and relishing his exuberant delight in publishers' parties and mass carousals. One of his staff had taken a temporary leave of absence, he told me; would I like to stand in for him, and look after the paperback reviews?

I had always wanted to work on the books pages of a newspaper, and here at last was an opportunity. Back in the Seventies I had been a regular reviewer for Duff Hart-Davis on the *Sunday Telegraph*. He had struck me as an exemplary literary editor, in that if he suddenly found himself shorter of space than expected, he trimmed one's reviews so expertly and so imperceptibly that one never noticed the loss; and he never fell into the trap of commissioning more reviews than he could use, which was good for his budget in that he didn't have to pay kill fees for unpublished pieces, and good for his reviewers in that we could be sure that our work would eventually find its way into print. One day he rang me, sounding very cloak-and-daggerish, and asked me if I was a member of the National Union of Journalists. I wasn't, though Petra had often urged me to join its freelance branch, and told him so. He grunted, and said no more; a year or two later he told me that he had wanted to offer me a job on the books pages, but my not being a union member had ruled me out.

Since then the unions had lost their stranglehold over both printers and journalists. Rupert Murdoch's papers had led the assault on the unions, and by the time John Walsh rang me Times Newspapers had moved from their gold-fronted ziggurat in Gray's Inn Road to Wapping. A few years earlier these had been under siege from infuriated printers, but by the time I reported for duty life had calmed down and one no longer had to walk the gauntlet. The *Sunday Times* was housed in what looked like a gigantic Nissen hut, and the offices were disconcertingly bleak, like a modern minimalist home. My notions of a literary editor's office were based on my visits, fifteen years before, to pick up review copies from Duff Hart-Davis, or Ion Trewin at *The Times*, and I expected to be confronted by a tidal wave of bumph, with books and proof copies piled up on every available surface, including the floor, long galley proofs snaking over the desks or spiked on lethal-looking butchers' hooks, and ink-stained fingerprints much in evidence. What I found instead were bare desks and winking computer terminals. Some buffoon – almost certainly a management consultant – had decreed that the computer had rendered paper obsolete, and that the paper-free office represented the way ahead, and the *Sunday Times* was doing its best to put theory into practice. It seemed odd that a newspaper, of all places, should want to inhabit a paper-free universe, but a ruling had gone out and we were expected to obey. Only Penny Perrick defied authority and tapped away on an old manual typewriter; it was almost impossible to find a piece of paper on which to write oneself a reminder, let alone send a postcard to the outside world. (In the old days, reviewers received a handwritten postcard acknowledging safe arrival, followed a day or two later by a grubby-looking proof. The computer has done away with this human touch: more often than not, one emails one's piece into a void and, with Alan Ross no longer with us, Richard Ingrams is the only editor I know who still thanks his contributors with a postcard.)

I had no idea how to use a computer – an instinctive Luddite, I only abandoned my typewriter in 2003, when I belatedly realised that I was doing myself out of work by sending reviews through the post rather than as email attachments – and my colleagues seemed almost as baffled as I was. Despite their historic role in destroying the power of the unions, the *Sunday Times* machines were, I gathered, ancient and slow-moving. The screen was coal-black, the print a lime-green simulacrum of typewriter lettering, and the words materialised in a torpid manner, inching their way across the page from left to right. The paperback reviews were all extremely short, signed with the authors' initials rather than their full names. I typed them out very slowly, editing if necessary as I went; when that was done, I pressed a button, the screen went blank, and I moved on to the next offering. Later in the day I went out of the building and joined a queue of people waiting to collect shiny ozalids of those sections of the paper for which they were responsible. I handed these over to my colleagues, and, greatly relieved to have survived the ordeal by computer, turned my attention to the more congenial business of sending out review copies.

I enjoyed my stint at the *Sunday Times*, but was uneasily aware of inhabiting an alien world, and worried dreadfully about pressing the wrong button on my computer and losing all my contributors' copy or, even worse, somehow short-circuiting the system and blanking out the elderly computer screens throughout the entire newspaper at a critical moment in its weekly cycle. My next part-time job was less nerve-racking, and altogether more familiar. My friend David Burnett rang to ask if I would help out as a part-time editor at Victor Gollancz, and I eagerly accepted. Gollancz was an old-fashioned literary publisher, very similar in size and *modus operandi* to Chatto or André Deutsch. Its offices in Henrietta Street were very like those of Chatto's old building in William IV Street: a warren of tiny rooms and creaking staircases, it had the same blue lino on the floor, the same bare walls, and the same pre-war telephone exchange, with plugs on the end of snake-like wires being pushed into and pulled out of holes in a board as members of staff were connected and disconnected; the typewriters were huge and upright, with spools in red and black, and pink, white and green carbons were taken of every letter and memo, one copy of each to be circulated among the senior staff; and although we were by now in 1990, the only computer was to be found in the sales department.

The firm was still run by Victor Gollancz's daughter Livia, a strong-featured woman with bright blue eyes, an outdoors, scrubbed-looking face and thick white hair pulled back from her face. A keen musician and mountaineer, she was, I suspect, a reluctant publisher, dutifully taking on the job after her formidable father retired. She too was – and still is – a forceful personality, but she was nothing like as alarming as Norah Smallwood or Carmen Callil, and I had always liked her very much. When we moved back from Oxford she tried to persuade us to settle in Highgate, and invited us to inspect her allotment. She was wearing a pair of thick black sandals of the kind I associated with old-fashioned nuns; after our tour of inspection was over she took us back to her house, where she poured me a sherry and Petra a glass of orange juice. The tin of orange juice was so old that the juice was discoloured with rust. 'Oh dear, that will *never* do,' Livia said, fishing out another tin from the kitchen cupboard. She didn't drink, and disapproved of smokers. One day, when I was having lunch with her in Covent Garden, an expansive-looking man at the table next door leaned back in his chair and lit up a post-prandial cigar. I approved of this, since I love the smell of second-hand cigar smoke, but Livia was unamused. 'Would you kindly put that out *at once*,' she asked our fellow luncher, fixing him with her pale blue eyes and leaning purposefully forward – at which he dutifully removed the cigar from his lips and stubbed it out on his side plate. I thought Livia's action a trifle high-handed, but since smokers had not yet become a persecuted minority, I also thought it rather splendid.

David Burnett is one of the publishers I most admire. A dark, sardonic figure, he radiates professional gloom and is much given to a farmer-like shaking of the head and sucking in of the breath when contemplating the state of the trade or the follies of his fellow practitioners. A veteran of Heinemann, Paul Elek and Book Club Associates, he occupied a bunker in the basement of Gollancz, where his desk was hemmed in by fishing tackle and crates of wine: he owned part of a vineyard somewhere in France, and spent much of his spare time on riverbanks, with rod in hand. He looked after the Witherby list, which dated back to the eighteenth century and specialised in books about fishing, dogs, wildlife and country matters: unlike most editors, he was an all-round publisher, busying himself with every aspect of the business and priding himself on having arranged to sell impressive quantities of books on the salmon or fly-fishing to angling shops up and down the country. During my short spell at Gollancz he was particularly excited about a book he had recently published on salmon and women, the gist of which was that because of their sexual allure, women are far more successful salmon-fishers than their male equivalents; the serial rights had been sold, and fishing shops up and down the country were ringing in with repeat orders. Nowadays he operates as a one-man band in Ludlow: every now and then my phone will ring, a lugubrious voice will announce itself with 'DB here,' and he will tell me how he has published an elegant line of hardback cookery book reprints after discovering a tail end of suitable paper in a bindery with spare capacity, and reminisce, with a good deal of laughter, about life at Heinemann under the redoubtable Charles Pick.

I had a drink with DB towards the end of my time at Chatto. We were just about to publish the second volume of a three-volume biography of a heavily bearded Irish sage, and he asked me how many Chatto had sold of Volume I. 'Tell your boss,' he said, 'to print half as many of Volume II, and half again of Volume III.' I never delivered his message, since Volume II had already been printed, and I have no idea whether its sales, and those of Volume III, bore out his suggestion; but I'm sure his instinct was right, since his approach to publishing was based on long experience, attention to detail, great knowledge of every aspect of the trade, and an awareness of what a complicated, difficult and risky business 'trade' or general publishing has always been. Given a steady nerve and an ability to publicise oneself as well as one's authors, it's not that difficult to make a reputation as a go-getting publisher by signing up authors who are already well known, paying advances that bear no relation to sales, and printing too many copies in order to keep the price down, justify an advance or make a demanding author happy; but DB is a true publisher, and every time I talk to him I am reminded of what an endlessly fascinating profession it can sometimes be.

# ELEVEN

# Critical Times

Shortly before publication of my first book, *Playing for Time*, I was invited to lunch at the *Spectator*. I was one of the first to arrive at their Doughty Street offices, and had just poured myself a drink when Jennifer Patterson, the magazine's flamboyant cook and future television personality, sidled up to me with pursed lips and a conspiratorial air.

'How's that daughter of yours?' she barked. 'And have you done anything about her dreadful teeth?' I can't remember where or how Jennifer had met Jemima, who was then about thirteen, but she had immediately remarked on her Bugs Bunny teeth, and accused us of being remiss as parents for not having had them seen to at once. I told her that Mima's teeth were protruding as much as ever. She thwacked me on the arm with the back of one hand and then, looking more serious, drew me aside.

'I must warn you,' she murmured *sotto voce*, 'there's the most *dreadful* review of your book in the next issue. I thought I should tell you in advance, so it isn't too much of a shock.' The news cast rather a dampener over the lunch, though the editorial staff, who must have known what lay in store for me, were their usual jocular selves, and no further mention was made of it.

I haven't looked at it for twenty years, but it was a full-page lead review, and the work of an Irish author called Aidan Higgins, whose name I dimly associated with a well-regarded novel called

*Langrishe Go Down.* I had noticed while at university in Dublin that Irish humour was very different from English, in that it was more abstract, more given to puns and word play, and more concerned with the absurdity of the human situation in a cosmic, Beckett-like sense than with the comical minutiae of class, accent, unsuitable clothing, malapropisms and other manifest-ations of social unease; and the gist of his argument was that humorous writing in England was a fairly debased business, relying as it did on self-deprecation, facetiousness and solecisms, and that my book was a dispiriting example of the genre. Far from reacting with rage and indignation, I had an uneasy feeling that much of what he said was all too true. Nor was I the only one to be singled out for attack, with P.G. Wodehouse in partic-ular coming under the lash; and at least his review wasn't *ad hominem*, unlike that by an Oxford don in the *Sunday Telegraph*, which exuded a very personal loathing, even though we'd never met. But it was something I could have done without.

Some six months later Alan Ross rang me from the *London Magazine* to ask if I'd like to review a new book by Aidan Higgins. This wasn't mischief-making on his part: if he'd read Higgins's review, he'd forgotten all about it. I explained the situation to him, and said that I'd happily read it, but would only review it if I liked it, or was indifferent to it: to write a stinking review would look like petty retaliation. A proof of *Ronda Gorge and Other Precipices* arrived through the post, and I started reading it on the train on my way to work. To my surprise, I loved it. Loose-limbed but cunningly constructed, and beautifully written, it consisted of a series of autobiographical incidents, set partly in Dublin, partly in North London, partly in Africa, and partly in Copenhagen, in which the hard-drinking, amorously inclined anti-hero ruminates on lost love and the passing of time. It was funny and touching, and the author had a genius for evoking feelings and states of mind familiar to us all, ignoble as they often were. I wrote a rave review, and popped it in the post.

After the review had been published, Alan rang me, with some glee, to say that 'Rory of the Hills', as Higgins liked to be known, was duly embarrassed by my review; and when, some nine months later, another Higgins book was published by Secker, Alan immediately asked me to review that as well. I liked *Helsingor Station and Other Departures* quite as much, and said so. The review appeared a month or two later. Alan, who by now was enjoying the whole business, reported that Rory was keen that we should meet next time he was over from his home in Kinsale. Petra and I were eventually summoned to Alan's house for drinks with Higgins and his girlfriend, Alannah Hopkin. I liked her very much, but I don't think Rory and I saw each other as kindred spirits, despite a shared fondness and admiration for Derek Mahon, a fellow inhabitant of Kinsale and another enthusiastic champion of Higgins's work. Keen on the drink and sporting a black spade beard, matted locks, round steel-rimmed specs and an Aran sweater, he looked like a member of the Dubliners band, but altogether more alarming. We made polite conversation over the drinks before going our separate ways, and I have never seen him since.

By now I was working part-time on the *London Magazine*, and every now and then Rory – who signed off his letters with a carefully-drawn glass of red wine – wrote in to congratulate Alan on the latest issue, pausing only to wonder why he allowed such a patently unsuitable character as myself to be involved with the magazine, or to deride something I had written in it. I found this mildly irritating and rather hurtful, but since I knew myself to be, in intellectual and literary terms, irremediably lightweight and frivolous, whereas Rory had the gravitas associated with Irish writers in the line of Joyce and Beckett, I had an uncomfortable feeling that there was much truth in his scornful asides. But 'You'd better do it,' Alan muttered, looking more mischievous than ever, when *Donkey's Years*, the opening volume of Rory's autobiography, arrived in the office, to be followed in due course by *Dog Days*, and I dutifully took them home. By now we were locked in a curious love–hate relationship: I had come to think of him as one of the best and most underrated writers at work, and was one of the very few people on this side of the Irish Sea who bothered to read, let alone review, his books; and, for want of anything else, he had to accept praise from someone he despised.

The breaking point came some time after publication of my Connolly biography. Rory had written Alan such an angry and contemptuous letter after reading my review of his most recent book that I had decided enough was enough, but shortly afterwards he decided that I wasn't such a bad thing after all. In 1972 Connolly had been a Booker Prize judge, together with Elizabeth Bowen and George Steiner, and although he had been outvoted by the other two, he had wanted to give the prize to Aidan Higgins's *The Balcony of Europe*. I don't know whether Rory knew of this, but either way he was a keen admirer of Connolly, and wrote to me to say how much he had enjoyed my biography. I was flattered and gratified, and wrote to tell him so, but when this was followed by letters asking me if I'd review some new book of his, each sealed with a carefully drawn glass of red wine, I found that the iron had entered my soul. I haven't read any of his more recent books, but I still think of him as a far better writer than most of those who hog the review pages and are adored by the literary world. Derek Mahon always speaks warmly of him as a man as well as a writer, and he's someone I would trust.

I discovered early on that displays of brilliance are less highly valued by literary editors than a humdrum readiness to say what the book is about before venturing one's own opinions, and that reliability – delivering copy on time, and to length – is, for literary editors at least, the supreme virtue in a reviewer. My brilliant cousin Roger Lewis, a man of strong opinions, flamboyantly expressed, makes a habit of writing twice as many words as asked for: when he complains that his editors have cut all his best jokes – which are often very good indeed – I tell him that if he wrote to length it would make it far harder for them to do so. (Much the same could be said of his over-long demolition job on Anthony Burgess: since I once hurled an Enderby novel into the Irish Sea, unable to stand another word, I was gripped by his account of how he changed from being a keen admirer of Burgess's work to finding him unbearably flatulent and pretentious.) I must have reviewed at least a thousand books over the last forty years, and so far I've had an easy ride. 'Darling, I must have been very kind to you all those years ago in St James's Place,' Jilly Cooper wrote after I'd given her first novel top billing in *The Times*, ahead of duller and long-forgotten 'literary' novels – St James's Place being the elegant, bow-fronted London office of Collins, now the headquarters of a merchant bank, where we had worked together in the publicity department.

Since I am a coward and easily outgunned in argument, I move sharply sideways when I see writers whose work I've maligned heading in my direction at a party. Only once was I brought face-to-face with the victim of an unkind review. The roof garden at Barker's in Kensington High Street was, briefly, a favoured venue for publishers' parties, and at this particular party we had been equipped with name badges, clipped to our lapels with safety pins. I was standing in a little group, half-listening, half-gazing about me, and wondering how I could sneak a look at my watch without seeming impolite, when a middle-aged man in heavy specs came up to me and, bending forward, closely scrutinised my lapel.

'Ah,' he said, 'so you're Jeremy Lewis.' I agreed that I was. 'Well,' he went on, 'I have to tell you this: you ruined my life with your review of my book in the *Sunday Times*.'

'How awful! I'm so sorry,' I replied, adding – as one always does – that these things are always a matter of opinion, one man's meat, etc.

'Saying you're sorry isn't any good,' he insisted, utterly unmollified and not prepared to give an inch. 'I didn't get a single review after that. You killed my book stone dead, and I haven't written a word since.' I didn't remember his name, but I had a very dim memory of his book, a rather feeble memoir which I had reviewed at least ten years earlier. After delivering a few more broadsides he moved off, and I tried to resume the conversation with the other members of my group, hoping they hadn't noticed.

Reviewers, like publishers' readers, have to harden their hearts, to try to block out the fact that every book, however bad, is a labour of love, and a public exposing of the self. After that encounter I felt like giving up reviewing for a time, but the feeling didn't last. More recently, I was one of the few people to give an unkind review to Diana Melly's autobiography, in the *TLS*. Her friends and her publishers made plain their disapproval, but a week or two later Diana – whom I had never met – came up to me at a party, introduced herself and, far from launching a full-frontal assault, told me that I mustn't feel bad about it, that everyone is entitled to his own opinion and that of course she didn't bear a grudge. I like and admire her generosity of spirit, and since then we have become, at parties at least, the best of friends.

Waiting for the reviews of one's own books is, inevitably, a nerve-racking business. Kindly reviews by friends are welcome, but have to be heavily discounted: I much prefer to read those by people I've never heard of, and usually find myself agreeing with their less flattering remarks. Best of all are enthusiastic letters from members of the public, forwarded by one's publishers and usually arriving six months after they were written. Unlike so many reviews, they aren't compromised by acquaintance, sour grapes, vindictiveness or a desire to keep on the right side of the author. The one I enjoyed most referred to my claim, in *Kindred Spirits*, that our tabby cat Raymond had studied for his A-levels at Wolsey Hall, Oxford, before going on to take a degree at the Rapid Results College. Its writer was generally well-disposed, but puzzled by this particular incident: he had spent forty years as an extra-mural tutor with Rapid Results, but although he had dealt with students from every corner of the globe, he couldn't remember teaching a cat.

Reviewers themselves tend to be soft touches. Every now and then a long-awaited book would be delivered to Chatto which wasn't bad enough to be rejected outright, but was feebler and dimmer than expected. After weeks of tinkering and rewriting, we sent it out for review with a sinking of the spirits and a horrible suspicion that it would be torn apart with such savagery or derision that our reputation in the literary world, and my job in particular, would never survive the shame of it all; and yet, time and again, the reviews were far kinder than expected, apparently oblivious to defects that had seemed so glaring in the office. Various factors contribute to this. Even in this electronic age, the finished copy of a book has a gravitas, an apparent seriousness or value acquired, rightly or wrongly, in its translation from typescript or email attachment. As both George Orwell and Cyril Connolly ruefully remarked, professional reviewers willingly suspend their disbelief, separating – in their heads at least – books read for review from those read for pleasure, and applying a lower standard in the process: superlatives abound, and fiction reviewers in particular, faced with a batch of new titles, scatter 'brilliant', 'dazzling' and 'masterpiece' with wild abandon rather than admit that the sensible reader would do far better to reread Evelyn Waugh or Patrick Hamilton than waste a moment on this lot. In this they are very much like most literary publishers: without this element of double thinking, the whole business would grind to a halt, and we would all – writers, publishers, agents, booksellers, literary agents – find ourselves out of a job.

Finding oneself out of a job is a permanent hazard of the freelance life. What we all dread, far more than meeting one of our victims at a publishing party, is learning that a particular literary editor, who likes our work and keeps us in mind, is about to retire or move on to another job. However hard we try to ingratiate ourselves, the new incumbent will have his or her own favourites to advance, and all but a tiny, lucky elite will have to look for work elsewhere. The more elderly among us feel particularly vulnerable, as editors – and publishers – of our own age vanish from the scene, and those who take their places are hard pressed to remember who we are and what we have written. We try to tell ourselves, rightly, that the young need to be taught and encouraged, and that those in early middle age have mortgages to pay and small children to worry about; after which we set about finding another haven, however temporary or ill-paying it may be. It makes for an insecure, impecunious existence, working for innumerable masters over a lifetime, and never settling anywhere for long. Yet I far prefer it to institutional life of any kind, and enjoy not knowing what the future will bring. I hope to go on working for as long as my health holds out, and people are prepared to employ me. With luck it will see me out.

## TWELVE

# Oldies and Others

One day, towards the end of 1996, Richard Ingrams asked me if I'd be interested in a very part-time job at the *Oldie*. I had known him, though not at all well, for a good many years, and had contributed articles and reviews to the *Oldie* since he had founded it five years earlier. I liked the idea very much: helping Alan Ross with the *London Magazine* had given me a taste for that kind of work, and the freelancer's ideal is a part-time job which brings in some income, gets one out of the house, and provides all the benefits of office life – gossip, lunches and companionship – without the regular slog of nine to five and the horrors of office politics. I told Richard that I'd love to learn more. We met in a down-at-heel coffee bar next to the magazine's offices in Poland Street in Soho, and he suggested we should give it a whirl.

Christmas intervened, and I started work at the *Oldie* at the beginning of the New Year. It had been agreed that I would go in on Tuesdays, and that we would review the situation after a month. The *Oldie* staff was far larger then than now: David Ford, the genial business manager and Richard's son-in-law, worked on the ground floor, as did some other characters busying themselves on I never learned what; the first floor was occupied by Richard, his secretary-cum-assistant, two advertising men, and James 'Poshie' Pembroke, a red-faced, hyperactive Old Harrovian with a loud voice and blazing blue eyes who has ended up owning the magazine, following in the footsteps of Naim Attallah and the cricket-loving John Paul Getty. The accounts department was on the top floor, glass-roofed and home to a bad-tempered Czechoslovakian and a moon-faced middle-aged lady known as the Soup Dragon. The rest of the building was occupied by other members of Naim Attallah's benign and easy-going empire, the ingredients of which included, at various times, the *Literary Review*, Asprey's the jewellers, the long-dormant publishing firm of Quartet, a magazine devoted to jazz, and short-lived ventures into fancy chocolates and erotic key-rings. The first-floor office was an L-shaped room, with a long row of metal-framed windows looking over Poland Street, and I was to share a desk with Richard. Since he lived in the Chilterns and came up every day on the train, he got to the office at about 11.30, leaving at 4.30 and strolling round the corner to *Private Eye* when not engaged on *Oldie* business.

Two things impressed me at once about life on the first floor: the noise, and the apparent chaos. The desks nearest to the door were occupied by two ebullient advertising men, Tony West and Dave Sturge. Tony was a large and heavily moustached ex-policeman, with a paunch straining the buttons of his immaculate white shirt; Dave was a dapper, more reflective figure, keen on American blue-and-white-striped poplin shirts and black slip-on shoes referred to as 'idlers' back in the 1950s; both were extremely noisy, as was James Pembroke, who lived in a state of permanent overdrive. When not ringing up regular or potential advertisers – these included stairlift manufacturers, zimmer-frame merchants, massage parlours, retirement homes and makers of alternative footwear – Tony and Dave indulged in ferocious bouts of tribal chanting, repeating the same name or word over and over again in mock-African voices, and banging their desks in time with their fists. Early on in the proceedings they nicknamed me 'Jezza', and as soon as I put my head round the door on Tuesday mornings, a hooligan-like cry of 'Jez-za, Jez-za!'

would go up, with much pounding of the desks. Silence would then fall, while we got on with our various tasks; but then, for no apparent reason, the chanting would resume, with some other word or name repeated like a mantra. After David Ford left, he was replaced by an earnest-looking man with a beard and wire-rimmed spectacles: whenever he left the room the chant of 'Beard-ie, Beard-ie' burst forth, trailing off, *diminuendo*, when he stuck his head round the door, thinking (rightly) that someone had called his name.

The chaos was almost overwhelming, so much so that when Jenny Naipaul came from the *Spectator* to work at the *Oldie* she went rigid with shock and had to prop herself up against a desk: she had replaced Caroline Law ('Cazza'), who could take the tribal chanting no longer and had been lured away to *The Week* by my daughter Jemima, whom she eventually succeeded as editor. The epicentre of the chaos was Richard's desk. I had seen some heavily laden desks in my time – André Deutsch's and Alan Ross's were particularly fine examples – but this was in a different league. The disorder was deceptive, however: the papers at the bottom of the mound may have been years old, and composted down to a kind of mulch, but – like André and Alan – Richard knew exactly how and where to find the items he needed, and the system only broke down if, to his intense annoyance, some busybody or reforming spirit tried to tidy him up. His desk was larger than most, in that it consisted of two old-fashioned knee-holers pushed end to end, and I was allocated a space at the far end. I was in the short arm of the L-shaped room, which meant that although I could hear the tribal chanting, I couldn't see Tony and Dave drumming their desks with their heads tossed back, like wolves serenading the moon. To get to my seat I had to pick my way past piles of back-issues of the magazine, cardboard boxes brimming with submissions, and clip-files crammed with yellowing invoices. Once I had reached my chair, I had to step over an obsolescent vacuum cleaner, the nozzle of which trailed away under the desk; and before I could get down to work I had to clear a space for myself, pushing back the mountains of bumph which rolled towards me from Richard's two-thirds of our communal desks. My weekly clearances were ephemeral affairs: by the time I returned the following Tuesday my end of the desk had been entirely covered over, as if by a fast-moving glacier or an ever-encroaching Amazonian jungle.

My one-day-a-week job consisted – still consists – of correcting proofs, editing copy and, most important of all, looking through the slush pile. The *Oldie* is one of the few general-interest magazines that welcomes, and often publishes, contributions from the general public, and every week I find a couple of possible pieces: memoirs by retired actors, soldiers or schoolmasters, odd encounters of the 'I Once Met' variety, travel pieces featuring blocked lavatories and suchlike horrors, diatribes against this or that current absurdity. I always pass them on to Richard for his approval, and am happy to abide by his opinion on the grounds that he thought up and founded the *Oldie*, which – like the *London Magazine* under Alan Ross – draws its strength and its flavour from the fact that it reflects his taste and prejudices, and would not exist without them.

Richard and Alan are the most impressive editors I have worked with, and had much in common. Both are – or were, in Alan's case – extraordinarily sure in their judgements and quick to make a decision, for or against, while the rest of us dither over the borderline cases; both have low boredom thresholds, so that one tends to prepare what one wants to say in advance, and make it snappy, before their eyes glaze over and begin to look elsewhere; both delight in gossip, luridly delivered, and are happy to hear and retell the same stories over and over again; both are exceptionally easy to work with, being approachable, encouraging and devoid of pomposity or self-importance; and both are extremely funny, in print and in person. Although, as I soon discovered, we never commissioned articles (as opposed to book reviews), I was called the Commissioning Editor. I was pleased to be known as such, though it sometimes led to confusion when aspirant *Oldie* contributors asked if we would be interested in commissioning a piece, and I had to explain our policy.

Despite the years I had spent as a publishing editor, I much preferred the short sprint of magazine editing to the marathon of the full-length book. Early on in my freelance career I had done editorial work for Christopher Sinclair-Stevenson and other publishers, but now that I was writing books of my own, I felt exhausted at the thought of ploughing through other people's typescripts, trying to make sense of ugly or jargon-laden prose and to keep an eye out for factual errors, inaccurate or inconsistent spelling of names, and (in the case of novels) hair or eyes that changed colour in midstream. Reading, choosing, editing and commissioning articles and reviews seemed, by comparison, a wonderfully fast-moving business: a thousand-word article could be knocked into shape in half an hour at most, whereas editing a book could take weeks or even months; and since there was no question of taking work home after hours, it fitted in far better with my way of life. Although I haven't thought of a single new idea in my ten years with the *Oldie*, I have introduced some valued contributors: Alan Ross, D.J. Enright, E.S. Turner, Mordecai Richler, Denis Hills, Stephen Gardiner and David Hughes are no longer around to provide reviews or articles, but Isabel Quigly, Stanley Price, Virginia Ironside, John Moynihan, Lucy Lethbridge, Ian Whitcomb and my cousin Roger Lewis are – in the words of a regular *Oldie* column – Still with Us.

A veteran of *Punch*, the *TLS* and (even more improbably) the *London Review of Books*, E.S. Turner was our oldest and most prolific contributor, producing articles on swordsticks, hatpins, bird lime, shop-walkers and the like for our 'Olden Life' column. Best remembered for his books on butlers, boys' magazines, watering places and other aspects of English social life, he had started work on a Glasgow paper in the 1920s, and had been writing ever since. He continued to deliver copy until days before he died in his late nineties, typed up on an old manual, written exactly to length, delivered on time, and needing not a comma changed. So dependable was he, and so fertile in ideas, that two of his pieces had to be printed after his death. He lived near me in Richmond, so I suggested that it might be a good idea if we met for lunch. He warmed to the idea at once, and suggested a pizza and pasta joint near the bus station. I got there before him, and wondered whether the old boy, then well into his nineties, had chosen wisely, or had known what he was up to: the air pulsated to the sound of pounding rock music, and the only empty seats consisted of two high stools in the window. I perched myself on one of these, and awaited his arrival. A moment or two later I saw an upright figure heading down the hill towards me at speed, one hand waving a walking stick and the other held out to push open the door of the pizza and pasta joint, and a few seconds later he was shaking me briskly by the hand. The soul of affability, he looked like a less effete version of John Gielgud, with a blue Dutch-boy cap on his head and a gingery-white goatee glued to the end of his chin. He insisted on paying for lunch, and opened the proceedings by ordering a bottle of red, which we drained in a matter of minutes. 'We could do with another of those,' he said, looking eagerly round for the waitress. Under normal conditions I would have been more than happy, but I had a review to write that afternoon so, feeling a terrible killjoy, I said I'd better restrict myself to another glass. A look of disappointment flashed briefly across his face, but then we turned to other matters. I only met him once again after that, but dealing with him was always a pleasure; he invariably signed his letters with his Christian name, but calling him 'Ernest' never came easily.

Whereas Alan Ross was keen on *maître d*'s bowing low in smart restaurants in South Ken, Richard is far happier in a greasy spoon or, if eating lunch in the office, drawing from his briefcase a giant-sized packet of crisps, washed down with a large plastic keg of orange juice. Every fourth Tuesday I am paid to eat lunch, and Richard can dispense with the crisps. The monthly Oldie Literary Lunch in Simpson's-in-the-Strand attracts a loyal following of *Oldie* readers, some of whom come to every one. Many of them are retired folk, living in the country, and they combine it with shopping and, perhaps, the theatre in the evening. Three writers are invited to speak about their new books after lunch, and told to confine themselves to no more than ten minutes each; if one of them drops out at the last minute, Barry Cryer steps briskly forward, cracking the same jokes every time, and all the more enjoyable for it. High points have included a waiter pouring gravy into Peter O'Toole's lap, and Larry Adler being carried out, presumed dead, during the main course, his face the colour of a pale pea soup – only to reappear, looking more ashen than ever, just as the speeches were about to begin.

The *Oldie* is now in Newman Street: the editorial staff has been reduced to five, of whom two – Richard and I – are genuine oldies, while the long-serving Nick Parker, the deputy editor, must be half our age. I love every minute of it: working on the *Oldie* has been one of the great pleasures of my forty years in Grub Street.

My immediate predecessor in the job had been James Michie, the only poet allowed to practise his art in the pages of the *Oldie*, and the inventor of the 'I Once Met' column, in which members of the public describe their unexpected and comical encounters with famous names. I had got to know James during my publishing career, and liked and admired him a great deal. With his owlish horn-rimmed specs, he looked like a more substantial version of Woody Allen; like Woody Allen he was a keen ladies' man, and his funeral was remarkable both for its jollity and for the large contingent of faded beauties in attendance. As well as being an elegant, witty and consistently underrated poet and a distinguished translator of Horace and Catullus, James was a publisher for many years, and a very distinguished one in his day. He had been associated with the *London Magazine* in the days when John Lehmann was its editor; in the 1950s, when he was at Heinemann, he had been something of a whiz-kid, responsible for adding Michael Holroyd, Anthony Burgess and Sylvia Plath to the list, but after he moved to The Bodley Head, at the same time as Graham Greene, Eric Ambler and Georgette Heyer, he seemed to lose his appetite for the business. By the time I got to know him, in the early Seventies, he was known as the most literate, likeable and indolent of London publishers. He was responsible for editing William Trevor, Muriel Spark and Sebastian Faulks, but more diligent members of the firm complained that he came into the office some time after eleven, did the crossword while smoking a large cigar, headed off for a long lunch, put in some work around tea time, and ambled off home on the dot of half past five.

I was working as an agent with A.P. Watt when we met, and had just taken on as a client the youthful Paul Theroux, whose first book had been published by Alan Ross as a London Magazine Edition; he had then moved on to The Bodley Head, where James was his editor. I was thrilled to have Paul as an author, chiefly because I so admired his books, and also because I had never sold anything to The Bodley Head, a list I hugely admired for its air of elegant distinction, and because the books themselves were so beautifully designed, inside and out, by the incomparable John Ryder.

Although he was then far from being a bestseller, Paul's standing in the literary stock exchange was obviously rising: his books had been enthusiastically reviewed, Graham Greene had voiced his admiration in print, and his hardback sales had risen from the literary novelist's usual 1,500 to something closer to 5,000; he was clearly someone to watch, and to keep. His new novel, *The Black House*, may not have been as exotic or interesting as its precursors, but it was perfectly publishable; and if an author's standing is high, and rising, most publishers are more than happy to put up with a less good book in the hope that the next will see him back on form. I posted off the typescript, and sat back to wait for James's offer. Weeks went by, and not a word from The Bodley Head. Eventually James rang me, sounding particularly world-weary, to say that he and a colleague had read *The Black House*: it really wasn't very good, and his advice was that Paul should put it in a drawer and start work on his next. Paul was outraged when I reported this back to him, and told me to send it at once to another publisher. I posted it off to James's good friend Gillon Aitken, then the managing director of Hamish Hamilton, who took it on immediately, and Paul has been with the firm ever since. A few days later Petra and I were staying in Sussex, and were invited to drinks by Max Reinhardt, the managing director of The Bodley Head, who rented a cottage from old friends of Petra's parents. After the preliminary pleas-antries were over, Max drew me aside. Rejecting Paul Theroux had obviously been a great mistake, he said: would it be possible to resubmit the book to him instead? I explained that it was too late – and I never did sell a book to The Bodley Head.

Turning Paul down was seen as a bad mistake on James's part, still more so since he was one of the few good young writers on The Bodley Head's adult list, but although I had to feign a degree of indignation, I secretly admired his insouciance, his insistence on taking on only what seemed to him to be the very best, and his refusal to be cowed by publishing practice or the opinions of the literary world. Many years later I was able to do James a good turn. Dennis Enright's last act as Chatto's poetry editor had been to take on James's *Collected Poems*. Andrew Motion, Dennis's successor, hadn't shared his enthusiasm; the book had been poorly sold and promoted, and had rapidly gone out of print. One day, coming out of the *London Magazine*, I bumped into a lugubrious-looking James in Thurloe Place. He bemoaned the fact that his poems were no longer available, while agreeing that I had done him a bad turn by encouraging Chatto to honour its agreement to publish. Back in the office, I suddenly thought of how I could make amends. Christopher Sinclair-Stevenson, then publishing on his own account round the corner in Kenrick Mews, had just started a poetry list, so I dropped him a line extolling James's virtues. Christopher printed a handsome paperback edition: it went on to win the Hawthornden Prize, and quite right too.

Auberon Waugh had been a regular contributor to the *Oldie* from the start, writing a 'Rage' column in which he blasted off about current horrors and imbecilities, and serving for a time as the Wine Correspondent. I was one of his reviewers on the *Literary Review*, which he edited, but although I instinctively liked and admired him, I never knew him at all well or found him easy to talk to – unlike his sister Hattie, after whom daughter number two is named. Every now and then I'd find myself sitting next to him at lunch, and was instantly tongue-tied. Beaming and sporting a pair of round, wire-rimmed spectacles, he looked like a slimmed-down Mr Pickwick; but whereas Mr Pickwick hurried to set his interlocutors at ease, I quickly realised that, where Bron was concerned, it was up to me to make the running, and that if I failed to do so we might spend the rest of the meal in silence. Whether this reluctance to initiate a conversation stemmed from shyness, boredom or a kind of arrogance, I never discovered; whatever its causes, I would, after some panic-stricken scrabbling about in search of a subject, introduce a topic and hope for the best. 'I'm glad you asked me that,' Bron would reply in his precise, rather clipped way after I had asked his opinion on the novels of R.S. Surtees or some other subject dear to my heart.

He would discuss the matter with a great deal of animation and apparent enjoyment until the awful moment came when we both ran out of steam. A terrible silence would fall, broken only when I raised another subject, and the cycle was repeated once again.

Years earlier, Bron had been commissioned by Weidenfeld to write a biography of Cyril Connolly, and although nothing came of it, he very kindly lent me his notes when I took on the job. Like his father, he had long been fascinated and entertained by Connolly, and when my biography appeared, he put a drawing of a slothful, bed-ridden Connolly on the cover of the *Literary Review*. One day, some time after his review of my book had been published – he thought it, to my delight, the funniest biography he had ever read – Bron wrote me a letter. 'Dear Jeremy,' it read, 'You are a wonderful man. I hope nothing dreadful ever happens to you. Yours ever, Bron' – or words to that effect. I was flattered by his high opinion, but worried by his second sentence. Was I suffering from some incurable and painful disease, about which only I had been kept in the dark? Had I drunk so much at a publishing party, and behaved so atrociously, that I was in danger of imminent blackmail?

I was still puzzling it over when Bron rang me at the *Oldie*. 'I think we ought to get to know each other better,' he said. 'How about a drink in the Academy Club this evening?' The Academy Club was five minutes' walk from the *Oldie*; I went along as suggested and, after buying a bottle, we took it with us to a corner table. Despite Bron's warm words, neither of us could think of anything to say. Bron, once again, was leaving it up to me. I felt utterly exhausted, so much so that I couldn't go through the familiar hoops of raising a subject, and raising another when that petered out. We sat in companionable silence, one elbow apiece on the black tablecloth, and when the bottle was drained we made our separate ways home. I never saw him again, and he died not long after.

Nancy Sladek, Bron's longtime assistant, took over as editor of the *Literary Review* after his death. Despite the inevitable prophecies of doom and gloom, she has fully maintained the magazine's combination of levity and erudition, scholarship and readability. I was having a drink with her one day when she told me that she was pregnant, and when I asked her what she was going to do about the magazine, she asked me if I'd hold the fort in her absence. I'd never done more than stick my head round the door of the *Literary Review*, but happily took up her offer. The editorial assistants – Alan Rafferty, Tom Fleming and, in due course, Philip Womack – knew far more about the workings of the magazine than I ever did, but we struggled along somehow till Nancy returned, and I still help out two mornings a month, and call by whenever I'm passing.

The *Literary Review* and the Academy Club occupy adjacent buildings in Lexington Street in Soho; both are small early-eighteenth-century houses, with heavy black front doors, bare floorboards and grubby cream-painted panelling in the hall and on the landings, wobbly banisters alongside worn and carpet-free stairs, and decrepit and overgrown back gardens; the overall effect is very much like living in a cigar box. Situated on the first floor of no. 44, the *Literary Review* is, after the *London Magazine*'s garden shed in Thurloe Place, the most unusual and un-office-like office I have ever worked in, and all the better for it. A small, cube-shaped room with a fine marble fireplace and a carpet-covered hole in the floor in which unwary visitors may stumble or twist their ankles, it sometimes houses as many as five full- or part-time workers, myself among them. The walls are papered with covers of the magazine, and since space is rapidly running out they may colonise the ceiling before too long. Two tall and dusty windows, adorned with ruched and rotting brown silk curtains, look out across the street to other tiny cigar boxes, and the desks, floor and unoccupied chairs are covered by teetering mounds of books. Every now and then one of the mounds collapses, scattering proofs and finished copies in all directions

118

and, as often as not, colliding with another mound, so provoking an avalanche of paper.

A feeling of mild hysteria runs through the room at such moments, but despite such perils, and the difficulties of picking one's way through the mounds en route to a desk and a computer – more books have to be elbowed aside in order to reach the keyboard or write a label or a card to a contributor – the magazine is edited and put together with exemplary efficiency. The rates of pay are almost as modest as those that prevailed in Alan Ross's *London Magazine*, but although the *Literary Review* is not as highly esteemed as it should be in academia, it still attracts and retains some of the best writers and reviewers around; and long may it continue to do so.

For many years both the *Oldie* and the *Literary Review* were owned by Naim Attallah. Palestinian by origin but long settled in London, he had made his fortune in business before deciding to buy Quartet Books, an ailing, upmarket imprint founded in the Seventies by, among others, my old friend William Miller, who had employed me as a freelance reader when he ran Panther paperbacks, so enabling me to keep bankruptcy at bay while I struggled up the publishing tree. Before long Naim had made a name as the most exotic bird in the publishing aviary: clad in red lizardskin shoes and different-coloured socks, one red, the other green, his jacket linings an iridescent flash, he ran Quartet Books like a sultan, buying books on a whim while a bevy of aristocratic beauties manicured his nails, poured drops in his ears and did their best to avert his attention from the unwelcome discharge of bodily functions (according to *Ghosting*, Jennie Erdal's memoir of her time at Quartet, a major row broke out after he discovered that 'One of my girls has done a poo in the loo'). As a book publisher, Naim was better remembered for his parties than for his books, admirable and worthwhile as these often were; as a magazine proprietor, he was generous, benign and easy-going, an exemplary figure in that he was happy to support writers in the best possible way by providing outlets for their work, and keeping his publications going unless and until the money ran out.

'Tiger' – as he liked to be known in his Quartet days – was also a writer, lending his name to innumerable interviews with famous figures in the *Oldie*, a 1200-page tome on women ('I am *famous* for love,' we learn from *Ghosting*, and 'I *glow* in their company') and an article on women's knickers for the *Erotic Review*. It was his passion to write works that were both 'distin-guished' and 'poetic' that led Jennie Erdal to make the transition from being an editor specialising in Russian translations for Quartet to becoming a full-time amanuensis.

Dividing her time between her family in Scotland and London, she began by researching and writing up Naim's inter-views. This seemed harmless enough, but then she made the fatal mistake of agreeing to write a novel for him – something she had never contemplated on her own account. 'We are thinking about a beautiful novel, very beautiful,' Tiger insisted, and – unlike his reluctant scribe – he longed to reach the sex scenes ('Beloved, we *need* the jig-jig'). They spent weeks together in his house in the Dordogne, where he did the cooking while she typed in another room; and no sooner had the first novel been published than he demanded another, involving two girls who enjoyed simultan-eous orgasms even while they were on different continents. Jennie Erdal's life as ghost lasted fifteen years: she finally decided to break free when Tiger insisted on installing a 'hotline' at her home in St Andrews and took to ringing her up to forty times a day, driving her husband to despair.

*Ghosting* is sad, funny, affectionate and beautifully written, but although Jennie Erdal writes about other aspects of her life, Tiger dominates the proceedings to such an extent that whenever he vanishes from view one longs for him to bustle back onstage, batting his forehead with the palm of his hand, consulting one of the two watches he wears, splashing like an excited baby at the shallow end of his swimming pool in France, worrying that there may not be enough bread rolls on board a flight to Frankfurt and telling an air hostess that he needs to drink a great deal of water since 'My wee-wee is yellow' (a detail which Naim has hotly contested). Jennie Erdal's portrayal of Naim is both fond and admiring, and – for good or for bad – she has established him as one of the great characters of London literary life in the closing years of the twentieth century, akin in his colour and flamboyance to one of Dickens's more benign eccentrics. But, not surprisingly, Naim regarded *Ghosting* as an act of treachery on the part of someone to whom he had felt very close, and so resented her claim that she had not only written his books but even his most intimate letters that within three years of its publication he had written (and published) a Palestinian fable and two volumes of autobiography, the second of which covered a mere twenty years, and was as long as *David Copperfield*.

I reviewed *Ghosting*, very favourably, in the *Sunday Times*, but found myself torn between admiration for the book itself, liking for its author, and sympathy for its embattled subject, whose cries of woe and outrage served only to draw attention to Jennie Erdal's book, whetting the appetites of those who knew little or nothing about the London literary scene but were intrigued by so public a row and by the comic glimpses of the book's contents afforded by Naim's endless interviews with the press. In the aftermath of publication, I spent some time talking and writing to Naim in an attempt to make him feel better about it all, and not to waste so much time and energy fulminating and threatening litigation.

Most of what I said was cold comfort, I'm afraid. I pointed out that, however controversial they may be at the time, most books are soon forgotten, but taking the long-term view is of little use in the painful present; that although it might not seem that way, *Ghosting* was a very fond portrait, and that few of us were lucky enough to be portrayed in such flamboyant colours; that he would be best remembered as a literary philanthropist, a rare spirit who had used his money to good effect. In the end I reminded him that, for all its geniality and outward bonhomie and displays of other-worldliness, the literary world is as ruthless as any other, and that, as Graham Greene famously put it, all writers have a sliver of ice in their hearts: they are, by their very nature, indiscreet, selfish and self-absorbed, happily plundering the lives and secrets of those they know and love in search of their material. Journalists, editors and publishers – the people among whom Naim had chosen to spend his time when he acquired Quartet, the *Oldie* and the *Literary Review* – would often sacrifice loyalty and friendship in pursuit of a book or a story, and to agonise too much about their infidelities was a terrible waste of time and energy.

# THIRTEEN

# Odds and Sods

Literary festivals are a boom industry, and every town in Britain, it seems, yearns to host a gathering at which writers can promote their wares and pontificate at length. Cheltenham paved the way in the 1950s, and is still going strong; there are now more literary festivals in this country than I could bear to count, stretching from Aldeburgh to Kirkwall, and Hay-on-Wye, the most modish of them all, has opened branches in Brazil and Colombia. Up and down the country earnest book-lovers – mostly middle-aged, the men in socks and sandals, the women with hair scrubbed back in a bun or flowing free about their shoulders – squeeze into draughty church halls or bookshops to perch on plastic institutional chairs and listen in reverential silence while a poet reads from his work in a low, inaudible drone, or a novelist, with many 'Umms' and 'Aahs', struggles to explain the plot, or a biographer provides a brisk résumé of his subject's life. Supermarket red is on offer, and an opportunity to buy a signed copy and have a quick word with the guest of the evening before venturing out into the darkness.

I find it all quite baffling. I can see the point of music or theatre festivals, since both are performing arts, which depend on an audience: but books are meant to be read in privacy, in bed or the bath, and most authors are better encountered in print than in person. As Smollett observed in *Humphry Clinker*, the best speakers are usually indifferent writers, and vice versa. As a writer, I dutifully do my stuff if summoned, and usually greatly enjoy it; but I wouldn't dream of attending as a member of the public, far preferring to watch telly or go to the pub. Nor does one often meet the 'punters': at large festivals like Cheltenham they hurry off with a 'Can't stop, the next talk is about to begin,' rushing without apparent discrimination from novelist to politician to poet to cookery book writer. I hasten to say that literary lunches of the kind held every month by the *Oldie* at Simpson's-in-the-Strand are a very different matter: by the time the three speakers have risen to their feet the audience have consumed an enormous quantity of wine and are in an enthusiastic or riotous mood, and Richard Ingrams makes sure that none of the perorations exceeds its allotted span of ten minutes.

Although I was a distressingly ineffectual literary agent, I had some good authors on my list at A.P. Watt, all of whom loyally stuck by me despite my failure to get them deals of the kind they would have obtained from my bolder and more money-minded rivals: no doubt even the kindest of them would have left me in the end, but my getting the sack saved them from having to give me a well-deserved heave-ho. They included Jonathan Raban and Paul Theroux, and between them they urged me to take on a young short-story writer who has since become the most widely admired novelist of his generation: he has won the Booker Prize at least once, his novels are made into glossy-sounding films, and he has become as familiar a name to modern novel-readers as Angus Wilson was in the 1960s. He had, I was told, recently completed a writing course at the University of East Anglia under the aegis of Malcolm Bradbury, who thought very well of him and would happily provide a glowing testimonial.

I met my clients' protégé in a pub; he was young, slightly built and earnest, with a brush of hair standing on end and round wire-rimmed specs of the John Lennon variety. I liked him very much, but I wasn't so sure of his stories. Though carefully and competently written, they read like pieces by a rather conventional student who was determined to outrage middle-class opinion and stuffy good taste by writing about pickled portions of anatomy, incest, etc. Left to my own devices, I would almost certainly have turned them down, but I was very much in awe of Raban and Theroux, and proud to be associated with them, so I dutifully agreed to have a go. I tried them out on the *London Magazine* and *Encounter* and the few other places which published short stories, and back they all came with a polite note attached: these were essentially undergraduate stories designed to shock, moderately talented but no more, and not for them, alas.

And then, quite suddenly, everything changed. After reading one of my client's stories in Ted Solotaroff's *New American Review* – none of my work, I'm afraid – Philip Roth had decided that he was a writer of rare brilliance, and nothing was the same thereafter. From being a recipient of rejection slips, my client had become what publishing folk like to think of as a 'hot property'. All at once both Tom Maschler at Jonathan Cape and Tom Rosenthal at Secker were determined to publish a collection of stories by this young genius, and to my horror I found myself torn between the two Toms, both of whom were alarming and overbearing, albeit in very different ways. In the end I let Tom Maschler have his way – partly because I wanted to boast that I had placed a book with the presiding genius of London publishing, partly because Cape books were always much better designed than Secker's, and chiefly because he was even more intimidating than his rival.

When the collection eventually came out, the reviewers were equally besotted, including several of those who had, a year or two earlier, rejected one or more of the stories as adolescent shockers. V.S. Pritchett wrote a long, rhapsodic review; C.J. Driver, the South African novelist and future headmaster of Wellington, provided a sole dissenting voice; since then my erstwhile client has gone from one triumph to another, and – like Graham Greene – he has managed the rare feat of combining literary acclaim with bestsellerdom. Whenever I bump into him at a party, I like him as much as ever, but on the rare occasions when, curious to know what all the fuss is about, I dip into one of his novels, I feel much as I did thirty years ago: the pickled parts are no longer in evidence, but although the prose is as careful as I remember, it somehow lacks the vital spark, the animation that turns a literary exercise into an animate entity. But publishers, critics and readers are as prone to the Gadarene rush as Oxford Street shoppers in the New Year sales, and because of that the whole story had a curious fascination.

# BIOGRAPHICAL BUSINESS

FOURTEEN

# The Reluctant Biographer

In December 1989 I was finally hoofed out of Chatto & Windus, where I had led an inglorious existence for the past ten years as a so-called editorial director. Working there had proved a precarious and nerve-racking business. Norah Smallwood, my first boss, had long been notorious in the book trade for her terrifying ways, reducing distinguished men of the world to gibbering wrecks and provoking attacks of nervous diarrhoea in at least one of her fellow directors. Carmen Callil, her successor, was equally alarming, and many working hours were spent debating which of the two ladies was the more ferocious, and whether it was worse to be exposed to Norah's ice-blue gaze and withering sarcasms or Carmen's blistering heat. Raised voices, angry tirades, office vendettas and the cries of wounded underlings were not conducive to hard or pleasant work, but it would be wrong to blame my failures as a publisher on the termagants in charge. I loved the social side of publishing – the long lunches, the parties, the incestuous book-trade gossip – but I was never prepared to commit myself to it as fully as I should. I remained, in spirit, a part-time publisher, a spectator rather than an active participant, and as such I had to pay the price.

Part of this I saw as an extension of my childhood loathing for organised games, itself inspired by a combination of cowardice, physical ineptitude, a total lack of team spirit and the competitive urge, and a failure or refusal to take the whole business seriously or to make the necessary suspensions of disbelief. Pointless and absurd as they seemed to me at the time, team games are, it seems, a useful preparation for office life, part of the softening-up process that readies one for adulthood. I brought to publishing the same combination of fearfulness and scepticism I had earlier displayed on the games field, and it did me no good in terms of my career. Most of the books I really cared about were already on my shelves, and although Chatto published a better class of book than most, I found it hard to mind that much whether or not we bought the rights in most of those which were offered to us, let alone work myself into the paroxysms of short-lived excitement or despair that are so essential a part of the effective publisher's armoury.

Unlike my more driven or ambitious colleagues, I edited my books in the afternoon rather than at weekends, and was so allergic to correcting proofs or reading typescripts in the evenings at home that I eventually abandoned the charade of carrying papers home in my briefcase, which was reserved thereafter for sandwiches, a plastic mac and a novel by, ideally, Smollett, Surtees, Edith Wharton, Sinclair Lewis, Evelyn Waugh or Patrick Hamilton. I regarded meetings and paperwork as the most fearful waste of time, barely constraining my boredom as we inched our way down the agenda. But I was, for all my lack of commitment, a fairly competent editor, never afraid of suggesting structural changes and, if necessary, rewriting an author's work, albeit too much at the expense of his or her tone of voice. I was particularly pleased to have taken on Howard Jacobson's first novel, *Coming from Behind*, the wartime *Berlin Diaries* of Marie Vassiltchikov and David Smiley's *Albanian Assignment*, and although our children's book list was discontinued shortly after its publication, I had – to my amazement – so enjoyed a school play written by our daughter Jemima's English teacher in Oxford that I persuaded its author,

Philip Pullman, to submit *Count Karlstein* to Chatto; but since I never discovered a bestseller, and the books I took on looked increasingly ill at ease and out of place on the Chatto list, I was neither surprised nor particularly upset when Carmen gave me my marching orders. Despite a mutual love of cats, our relationship had been, for the most part, embattled, but she could not have been less alarming when the critical moment came. 'Darling, you must realise that I'm doing this for your own good,' she assured me. 'You'll be much better off on your own, and you'll thank me in the end.'

That was true enough, as it turned out, but in the meantime school fees and the mortgage were mounting up, and I had to bend my mind to other ways of earning a living. Among those offering advice was a fellow-publisher, a former Olympic fencer who was famously fertile in ideas. For no apparent reason, he had got it into his head that I ought to write biographies. I tried to explain that although I was a passionate devotee of memoirs and autobiographies, I hated reading biographies, thought them inherently second-rate and second-hand, and had no desire to write the wretched things. Carried forward on a tidal wave of eloquence, I went on to say that I regarded biography as the most ephemeral of literary forms, with Boswell and Lytton Strachey the exceptions that proved the rule, and resented the ludicrous claims made on its behalf by eminent modern practitioners; but he would not take 'no' for an answer.

He rang me up one day, sounding more steamed up than ever. He had, he revealed, the perfect subject for me, and would like to unveil it over lunch in a restaurant in St Martin's Lane. After the drinks had been ordered, he put his elbows on the pink table-cloth, gazed deeply into my eyes, and told me what he had in mind. 'Jeremy,' he said, in a tone of grave sincerity, 'you are tailor-made to write a biography of the Duke of Edinburgh, and I could pay you a very large sum indeed to do so.' Rather ungraciously, I greeted his suggestion with derision. I had, I told him, nothing whatsoever against the Duke – in fact I rather admired him for his tactless remarks – but I had no interest at all in the Royal Family, and could think of nothing I would like to do less. He was quite unfazed by this brutal rejection, but at the pudding stage he suggested, quite out of the blue, that I should write instead a biography of Cyril Connolly, a literary man remembered, above all, for his greed, his sloth and his complicated love life, and for two marvellous books, *Enemies of Promise* and *The Unquiet Grave*.

It seemed ungrateful to say 'no' twice in the course of a single lunch – and, despite my dislike of biographies, Connolly was an appealing subject. Although I'm not sure how much I would have liked him, I found his merciless self-knowledge and his romantic yearnings immensely sympathetic, as well as his refusal to commit himself to any one point of view ('I believe in God the Either, God the Or and God the Holy Both,' he once announced) and his cheerful admission that no sooner had he tried to take a stand on a particular subject than he immediately became convinced that the opposite was true: a cast of mind I found both congenial and familiar. We agreed that I would do a little background reading, and I headed off to the London Library to see what they had on the shelves. A few weeks later I had a call from Deborah Rogers, Connolly's literary agent. She told me, in the kindest possible way, that it would be a waste of my time to take things any further, since Connolly's widow, Deirdre Levi, was opposed to the whole idea of a biography, and could stymie any attempt by refusing the biographer permission to quote from her late husband's work. I capitulated at once – I couldn't bear the idea of doing battle with an enraged literary widow, a notoriously ferocious breed, and since the only point of a writer is his writing, it seemed idiotic to write a life without being able to quote from the work – and turned my mind to other things.

A couple of years later my phone rang at home, and I found myself talking to Michael Shelden, an American academic who had written an excellent book about Cyril Connolly's editorship of *Horizon*. We had never met, but I had been briefly in touch during my abortive explorations into Connolly matters. 'I've just done you a good turn,' he said. An unauthorised biographer had decided to go ahead with a life of Connolly in the face of Mrs Levi's objections, and various friends, including Stephen Spender, had urged her to retaliate by commissioning an authorised biography. She had asked my new friend from Indiana, and he – to my amazement – had recommended me. It seemed too absurd: I wasn't an academic or a professional writer, I had never written a biography before, I knew next to nothing about my subject-to-be, and my literary output consisted of reviews written to pay the bills, introductions to reissues of works by Surtees, Sapper and E.W. Hornung, and the waggish volume of autobiography devoted to my time as an undergraduate at Trinity College, Dublin. Why on earth had he chosen me? 'Well,' Shelden said, 'I liked the sound of your voice on the phone.' That seemed as good – or bad – a reason as any, and I gratefully accepted. He urged me to visit Deirdre Levi as soon as possible, and rang off.

By now I was thoroughly in favour of the whole idea, but my heart sank when Mrs Levi, who seemed very friendly, invited me to lunch near her home in Gloucestershire, and asked if I would bring with me a copy of *Playing for Time*, my facetious autobiography. As soon as she said this, I knew my number was up. To my horror, my publishers had given the paperback edition the worst kind of 'comic' cartoon cover of the kind then associated with novels by Tom Sharpe, heavily populated by men with bulging eyes and electrocuted hair and foam-flecked lips and bottles of stout jammed in their pockets. I had no copies left of the more decorous hardback; Mrs Levi would take one look at the cover, realise that I was not a serious candidate for the job, and turn instead to a Fellow of All Souls.

I was working at the time with Alan Ross, an old friend of both Connolly and his wife, so I took with me some recent issues of the *London Magazine* and dropped my paperback in the middle, hoping it would acquire some gravitas thereby. The lunch could not have been more genial or bibulous, and I took to the Levis at once: Deirdre has a marvellous drawling voice and a contagious laugh; her husband Peter – whom I had not expected to like – turned out to be one of the funniest men I had met, with the sleek, dark face of a benign and well-read badger. They took me to a quiet country hotel populated by elderly couples: the room was silent save for the click of knives and forks and whispered conversations, but all heads swivelled in our direction as Peter told us, in ringing tones, how Penelope Betjeman had set out for the Himalayas 'with a team of hand-picked lesbians'. Nothing was said about my book until the train for Paddington was about to pull out. I knew that the game was lost as I handed it out of the carriage window with its praetorian guard of *London Magazine*s; and as I trundled back to London I wondered what I could write about instead.

Next day the phone rang, with Deirdre on the other end. 'Peter and I simply *loved* your book, and we couldn't stop *roaring* with laughter,' she said. 'Cyril would have loved it too, still more so since some of it is set in just our part of Sussex, and you mention the Cuckmere Valley and Mr Rolfe the fishmonger in Seaford and Mary Ranger's bookshop, both of whom he always visited. Of course you must write his life.' And with that I embarked on my new career. Later I discovered that Deirdre had rung Alan Ross to ask if I'd be the right man for the job: I was a 'good fellow', he said, and that was as far as my scholarly references went.

I had no idea what to do next until Selina Hastings, an experienced biographer, showed me how to operate a card-index system (something I never mastered) and pointed out that since many of Connolly's surviving friends and contemporaries were, by then, in extreme old age, I should make haste and interview them before it was too late. I dutifully plodded off to see assorted octogenarians, including Peter Quennell, Steven Runciman and the formidable Gladwyn Jebb, a great iceberg of a man who received me, grudgingly, in his equally bleak and unwelcoming flat in Whitehall Court, where the very walls are lined with brown and white lavatory tiles. I soon realised that I knew far too little about Connolly to ask the right questions, while they – very understandably – recycled the same old stories from memoirs of their own.

Peter Quennell was a particularly nimble recycler. A lean, languid, dapper figure with a greying widow's peak, sharp, satanic features and the pink-and-white salami complexion of the heavy drinker, he had recently been ejected from the marital home by Marilyn, the last of his many wives, and was living in digs on the opposite side of the road. I rang the doorbell of a terraced house in Primrose Hill – an area regarded by Quennell as the London equivalent of exile in Siberia, far removed from his beloved Chelsea – and was ushered into a bleak, white-painted hall, with a bicycle propped along one wall and a strong whiff of boiled cabbage pervading the air. Elegant as expected, Quennell was wearing a charcoal-grey worsted suit, maroon waistcoat, white shirt, dark tie and black slip-on shoes. He waved me into a bare, featureless room on the ground floor, with stippled walls painted white, a single overhead light, a cheap-looking sofa on which he reclined at length, and one upright chair. After a few moments' desultory conversation he suggested, in hopeful tones, that we should move round the corner to a pub in Regent's Park Road where, I later learned, he held court with Kingsley Amis, Richard Hough and other convivial spirits. Once installed, he repeated, almost verbatim, what he had said about Connolly in various volumes of autobiography; that done, he made his excuses and left. Petra and Jemima had said they'd pick me up from the pub, so I stayed on, but I'd also given them Quennell's address. For some reason they called there first, and while Petra sat in the car outside, Jemima, who was then in her early twenties, banged on his door to flush me out. Famous as a ladies' man, Quennell was delighted to see her standing on his doorstep, beaming and bright-eyed, so he offered her a drink and ushered her into his lair. After a while he suggested that she might like to see the rest of the house, but she quickly made her escape.

I soon realised that even the most erudite and well-disposed were prone to amnesia and flights of fancy. Early on in the proceedings Isaiah Berlin told me a story which I knew, even then, should have featured Connolly's friend Dick Wyndham chasing Sonia Brownell into a duck pond, but came with the wrong *dramatis personae*. The film critic Dilys Powell, who had been a colleague of Connolly's on the *Sunday Times*, must have been well into her nineties when I called to see her in her house near Marble Arch. She was very deaf, so I made a funnel of my hands and, leaning forward in my chair, bawled my enquiries into one ear, while below us a yapping Yorkshire terrier fought to untie my shoelaces. She told me what I already knew from Connolly's great admirer, Godfrey Smith, and other veterans of the *Sunday Times*: of how he would come into the office every Wednesday after lunch to read through his proofs and choose another book to review, after which he might conduct a kind of informal seminar, reminiscing about the writers he had known and the perils of literary life before making his way home. And then, at some stage in the conversation, I mentioned his having been married. '*Married?*' she cried, jolting back in her seat, her bright blue eyes widening with disbelief. 'I never thought of him as a *marrying* sort of man!' Indeed he was, I explained, wondering how she had forgotten: not only had Connolly been married three times, with innumerable girlfriends in between, but his love life had long been the subject of lurid and often unkind gossip in the upper reaches of bohemia. 'But whom are we talking about?' she eventually asked, and when I explained she gave a great hoot of laughter and said, 'Oh dear, I thought it was Raymond Mortimer,' who had shared the prime position on the *Sunday Times* book pages with Connolly, and was certainly *not* a marrying sort of man. With that we agreed to abandon ship, and turn to other things.

After a month or so, I decided to call a halt *pro tem*. I would go away and do my homework before undertaking any more interviews. I wouldn't speak to another soul until I had immersed myself in as many published diaries, letters, biographies and memoirs as I could lay my hands on, and once I had familiarised myself with the cast of characters I would trawl through Connolly's voluminous papers in the universities of Tulsa, Oklahoma, and Austin, Texas. If some of the survivors had popped off by the time I got back from the States, that was a risk worth taking; still more so since I soon realised that although I was perfectly happy to be a voyeur at one remove, riffling greedily through the most intimate letters and diaries, I was far more craven and constrained when faced with flesh and blood, feeling myself to be an uneasy cross between a Peeping Tom and a double-glazing salesman. And the fact that Connolly had enjoyed such a complicated love life made the embarrassment factor greater than it might otherwise have been.

I soon discovered that sitting in libraries is one of the more soothing aspects of the biographer's life. It's very like being back at university, except that one reads to more purpose, and with a greater sense of luxury; riffling through books and papers, the silence broken only by the dainty coughs of one's fellow-researchers, the turning of pages and the soothing clack of other people's laptops, one inhabits a limbo in which the cares of everyday life have somehow dropped away. But spending long weeks in university libraries in the Mid-West has its drawbacks: at Tulsa the campus was deserted in the evening – the students had all commuted home by car – and once the Special Collections library had closed there was little to do except swim endless lengths of the pool and spin out a lonely meal in the student canteen.

One of the ways in which otherwise obscure American universities have put themselves on the scholarly map is by buying up the papers of eminent writers, and Tulsa had done better than most thanks to the volcanic energy of Tom Staley, a cowboy-booted academic turned impresario who, by the time I got there, had left to do even greater things for the Harry Ransom Humanities Research Center in Austin, Texas. Connolly's papers had joined those of Rebecca West, Edmund Wilson, Rupert Hart-Davis and Paul Scott; while I was there a large wooden crate crammed with V.S. Naipaul's paperwork arrived, and I joined the librarians in toasting its safe arrival while a graduate student wielded the crowbar. Immersing myself in the world of Eton and Balliol and then emerging into a prairie twilight was a curious sensation, as was coming across letters to Connolly from mutual friends: the Alan Ross file was crammed with his familiar postcards – the message scrawled on a *London Magazine* label pasted over the back of a card from someone else – and when I tipped it onto my desk they clattered out like so many roofing tiles. Every now and then I contemplated summoning up files from the André Deutsch archive, and rereading memos I had written a quarter of a century before when employed there as a junior editor, but there was never enough time.

I became so addicted to primary sources that I came to believe that one could only trust – or partly trust – letters and diaries written at the time: yet I found that they could be as unreliable as memory itself. Before I imposed my self-denying ordinance, I visited Anthony Powell, who had been at Eton and Balliol with Connolly, and had provided a shrewd if unflattering account of his old acquaintance in his memoirs. I remember the thickly striped mauve and white wallpaper in the hall of his rather gaunt country house, but I don't think he told me anything I hadn't read in his autobiography, nor – to my disappointment – did he serve up that disgusting-sounding combination of home-made curry washed down with claret and followed by Black Forest gâteau with which, according to proud entries in his *Journals*, he regaled gourmet friends like Roy Jenkins and V.S. Naipaul. Years later, in the last volume of the *Journals*, I found a reference to my visit. After comparing me to a friendly labrador, he got all the details of my visit wrong. None of it mattered in the least, apart from the labrador; but so much, I thought, for the reliability of the contemporaneous account. I wish, though, I'd visited Powell after I'd returned home from my long and lonely weeks in American universities, by which time I was far better equipped to interview survivors: names which meant nothing to me when I started out had become as familiar as those of my own acquaintances, and I knew enough of the small details of Connolly's life to ask the right questions, and to know when I was being fobbed off with an evasive half-truth.

I've written elsewhere in this book about some of those I went to see in the course of my researches – among them Barbara Skelton, Connolly's second wife and a celebrated *femme fatale*. One day, when we were eating lunch in her flat in Chelsea, an envelope was pushed under the door. We both assumed it was a circular, but it turned out to be a note from my unauthorised rival biographer, whose book had now been completed, and which was eventually published a year or so ahead of mine. Shortly afterwards, Barbara got hold of a proof. 'It's awfully good,' she told me; but then she turned against it so violently that she tore the proof in half after scrawling unkind remarks all over it, and hurled it into the dustbin. I rescued it when she wasn't looking, took it home with me, and started reading with a pounding heart.

It was well-written and full of things I'd missed or failed to notice, but the overall tone was hushed and awestruck. In his last year at Oxford, for example, Connolly spent part of his Christmas vacation in Minehead, where 'Sligger' Urquhart, the Dean of Balliol and a kindly bachelor don of the mother-hen variety, had organised a reading party consisting of himself,

Maurice Bowra, the waggish and overbearing Dean of Wadham, and a team of hand-picked undergraduates. Bowra had fallen hopelessly in love with one of the group, Piers Synott, a good-looking Anglo-Irishman whom Connolly described as the 'Narcissus of the Balliol baths', and he sought to woo the object of his passion with a medley of music-hall songs; but, after picking his nose throughout the rendition, the ungrateful youth told his admirer that his feet smelt, and the Dean – by now a 'broken man' – had to be taken by Sligger on a restorative walk through the surrounding countryside.

The music-hall songs and the nose-picking were details of the kind that spelt magic to me, and I fell upon them eagerly when trawling through Connolly's papers in the library at Tulsa, but my rival biographer, who had riffled through the identical papers a year or so earlier, seemed utterly unmoved by their revelations. Connolly, he tells us, 'seems to have been engrossed in Milton, Plato, Yeats and Proust' while in Minehead – and with that the reading party, freighted as it was with comicality and high emotion, was consigned to oblivion. The relish with which I hovered over the ignoble details of Bowra's courtship probably indicates an incurable frivolity of mind, evidence indeed of Connolly's claim that 'No two biographies are alike, for in every one enters an element of autobiography which must always be different'; but my rival's high-minded refusal to concern himself with nose-picking and the rest also suggests why so many modern biographies seem so dull. Quite apart from his other qualities, good and bad, Connolly was exceptionally funny, both in print and in person, but my rival's biography seemed a joke-free zone. His tone was unvaryingly reverential: so much so that after a while he wearied of referring to his subject by his surname, and called him 'the critic' instead ('That summer, the critic took his holiday in France . . .').

What so many biographers fail to remember is that psycho-logical insights and the accumulation of details must be accompanied by a modicum of artistry; that the biographer, like the novelist, needs to shape his material, to interlace (if possible) the funny and the poignant, the fast-moving and the slow, the quiet and the noisy. All too often biographers are so intent on hurrying their protagonist through his paces that, like a bad host, they quite forget to introduce us to the subsidiary characters, who are bustled on and off stage without a word about their backgrounds, education, looks, proclivities or mode of dress (than which nothing is more touching and revelatory). A sure and familiar sign that the biographer has failed to make the necessary introductions comes towards the end of his labours: eager to strike a valedictory, autumnal note, he tells us that old friends of his subject have died ('That July, Jim learned that his close friend Colin had died of a heart attack') – but since no mention has been made of Colin until now, the emotional impact is not all that it might be. Equally irritating is a failure or refusal to be specific: to say – *à propos* some minor character – that he went to Uppingham rather than 'public school' and Magdalen rather than Oxford, or joined the 14th Lancers rather than 'a cavalry regiment', brings everything into sharper focus, and may trigger further associations, if only among a handful of readers.

Writing a biography of someone who died well within living memory, with friends and relations still thick on the ground, is inevitably a tricky business. Deirdre Levi had proved the most exemplary literary widow, cooking delicious lunches whenever I loomed up and answering even the most impertinent questions with frankness and great good humour while Peter took Petra off to the local pub to drink enormous quantities of perry (these would be supplemented with champagne on their return, and wine with the lunch). I had become extremely fond of both her and Peter – he was one of the funniest talkers I have ever known – but even so I dreaded the moment when she reported back to me about my version of events, the brick-sized typescript of which I had posted off to her in a fever of anticipation, and was afraid that this could well mean the end of our friendship. I needn't have worried. Far from taking umbrage, she could not have been more complimentary, but suggested that I might have been pulling my punches towards the end. Connolly's relations with women were entertaining but deplorable – he liked to have several on the boil at once, and would bad-mouth them to each other, while declaring undying passion to them all – and late in life, when he was living in Eastbourne, he had started his last extra-marital affair. I had tiptoed daintily round it for fear of upsetting Deirdre, but she would have none of it. 'I do think you ought to say more about Shelagh,' she said, so in she went.

Not everyone shared her enthusiasm. Like many other writers – Auden most famously so – Dennis Enright abominated literary biographies: what mattered about a writer was his work, not his life, and lives of writers, unless written by the subjects themselves, were intrusive, trivial, irrelevant and somehow immoral. He enjoyed reading my memoirs (or 'me-moirs' as he called them), but although he always asked politely enough how I was getting on with Connolly, he did so between gritted teeth, and I would hurriedly change the subject in favour of cats, a shared enthusiasm, or the bad old days at Chatto & Windus. Since Dennis died at the end of 2002, I have published my biographies of Smollett and Allen Lane, and am now at work on the Greene family. I have loved every minute, and although half of me still shares Dennis's disapproval, the other half has been utterly corrupted. I combine an uneasy sense that we biographers are, by definition, denizens of the literary second division with the hope that the detailed and sympathetic recreation of someone else's life could be worthy to stand alongside the labours of the great novelists: it attempts, after all, the resurrection of the dead, and what could be more miraculous than that?

FIFTEEN

# Footnotes

Among the people I was told I must talk to about Cyril Connolly was the Anglo-American gossip Alastair Forbes; partly because he had known Connolly extremely well, and partly because he was an influential figure in the world of upper-class bohemia, who would expect to be asked and could prove troublesome if not consulted. Ali was a familiar figure both by reputation and on account of the seemingly interminable reviews he wrote for the *Spectator* and the *TLS*, in which the names of famous people he had known were linked together by long, Jamesian sentences crammed with parentheses and short on full stops. An American educated at Winchester, he had got to know Winston Churchill during the war, almost certainly through his son Randolph, and had worked as a journalist after the war; he knew Peter Quennell and Duff and Diana Cooper, and was the sort of person who popped up in the diaries and letters of Evelyn Waugh, more often than not in the footnotes. He had gone to live in Switzerland, occasionally resurfacing in London in the bar of White's, and might have been entirely forgotten if John Gross, when editor of the *TLS*, had not decided to use him as a reviewer, specialising in gossipy upper-class memoirs and allowed a good deal more space than most in which to ventilate his views. As such, he was loved by some, and mocked by others: his admirers relished his indiscretion and the sense he gave of providing an insider's view;

his detractors thought him a snob and a windbag, and a waste of much-coveted editorial space.

I knew what he looked like – or had looked like, back in the 1950s – since in volume two of her memoirs Barbara Skelton had included a photograph of him, standing in the garden of her cottage in Kent: a blond, good-looking, well-built young man of medium height, standing very upright, with a thick head of fair hair brushed back in a widow's peak and (or so I assumed) a pinkish face and bright blue eyes. Shortly after Connolly's death in 1974 he had written a very long and affecting piece in the *TLS* about his friend's last weeks on earth, from which one might have assumed that he was one of Connolly's closest and dearest friends, and the one person he would have hoped to have to hand during his dying days. He was very much the sort of person Connolly would have known; and yet, during all my long months of research in libraries in America and Britain, I had not come across a single reference to, or a letter from, Ali Forbes. It was very odd, but I felt sure that when and if we met, all would be made plain.

Although I was interested to meet Ali Forbes, I rather dreaded it as well: he would, I was sure, be dauntingly sophisticated and *blasé*, greeting my humdrum queries with condescension and weary disdain. We met eventually at Barbara Skelton's funeral in Worcestershire. A rather dashing figure wearing a sky-blue shirt that matched his eyes, a bow tie and an expensive-looking tweed suit, he looked exactly as expected. He couldn't have been more pleasant or more friendly: he was, he explained, heading back to Switzerland the next day, but he would love to talk to me about Connolly, and would call me next time he was in London.

As good as his word, he rang me from White's on his next visit. I offered to jump on the train and hurry in to the West End, but he would have none of it: he had hired a car for the duration of his stay, and wanted to get his money's worth. Did he really want to trail out to East Sheen, I asked, remembering the chimes

on the doorbell and the clip-on Tudor beams, and catching sight
of the balls of cat-hair rolling over the kitchen floor, the torn and
fading covers on the armchairs, the water stains on the ceiling
and the unswept leaves piling up in the garden beyond. He could
think of nothing nicer, provided I could tell him how to get there.
Petra, I explained, was out at work, so lunch might not be quite
as delicious as it should be, but that was no problem: bread,
cheese and pickle, washed down with beer, would suit him
perfectly. After I had put the phone down I sped off to Waitrose
to stock up with beer and a better class of Cheddar, hoovered
the ground floor, plumped the cushions, and got out my notepad
and pencil.

Shortly after one, a large white convertible drew up outside
the house, and Ali Forbes stepped out. Luckily I spotted his
arrival through the dining-room window – I was busy laying the
table – so I was able to pre-empt the chimes by flinging open the
front door before he had a chance to press the buzzer. As we sat
down to lunch, he was affability incarnate. We made general
conversation at first, and then turned to his friendship with Cyril
Connolly; and it was now that things began to go wrong. We got
on very well, but I could not get a straight reply to anything
I asked. I would ask him a specific question, and he would reply
by talking about something completely different. I would try to
haul him in, and he would slither out of the net. I was deluged
by names and anecdotes, none of which had anything to do with
the subject supposedly under discussion. It was, perhaps, like
reading one of his articles before it had been subjected to an
editorial blue pencil: a rambling, inconsequential monologue,
amiable enough but of no real interest or relevance. Worried that
he might think I was paying insufficient attention, I took to
doodling and scribbling in my notebook, pretending to take
down what he was saying. After a couple of hours he looked at
his watch and said he must be hurrying back. Baffled and worn
out, I saw him to the door, and watched him speed off down the

street in a cloud of autumn leaves. I had done my duty by seeing Ali Forbes, but I had learned nothing whatsoever from him.

Equally unforthcoming was the painter Derek Hill, another avid gossip who prided himself on knowing all the right people in society and the arts. Although he was not greatly admired by art critics, I rather liked his accurate and proficient portraits, many of which still line the stairs in the old John Murray offices in Albemarle Street and the walls of Oxbridge common rooms, and his less conventional landscapes, often painted at his home in Donegal. Not long before I was commissioned to write the Connolly biography, Christopher Sinclair-Stevenson, then running his own firm, rang me to say that he thought Derek Hill should write his autobiography, and asked me if I'd like to visit him and find out whether he warmed to the idea. When not in Ireland or his house in Hampstead, or on his travels abroad, Hill could often be found in Long Crichel, an elegant but homely red-brick eighteenth-century house in Wiltshire which had been shared over the years by a shifting cast of homosexuals, including the music critic Desmond Shawe-Taylor, Raymond Mortimer, Patrick Trevor-Roper, the eye surgeon and brother of the historian, James Lees-Milne's close friend Eardley Knollys, and Derek Hill. Hill was alone in the house that day, apart from a housekeeper of the homely, roly-poly variety, who cooked us lunch and fussed about the place, tut-tutting and clucking under her breath.

Hill was a well-preserved, nut-brown, roundish-looking man with bright blue eyes, a petulant mouth and an even more petulant tone of voice, suggestive of someone always on the verge of taking umbrage. He was, as I later discovered, affable enough once one had weathered the initial storm, but the opening deluge, with its accusations of neglect, tardiness and general lack of consideration, was sometimes hard to endure. Over lunch he told me that he was keen to write his memoirs, and I could quite see why: he had led a far more interesting life than most, spending long periods in Russia and Germany in the Thirties when not consorting with the Mitford sisters, making himself into an expert on Islamic and Byzantine art, and rubbing shoulders with every grand or glamorous name one could think of, from Patrick Leigh Fermor and Ivor Novello to Bruce Chatwin. Afterwards he suggested, to my alarm, that we should head upstairs to his bedroom to look at his photograph albums.

His bedroom was surprisingly austere, with bare boards on the floor, few pictures or decorations, and a minimum of furniture. We perched side by side on a black metal-framed prep-school bed, and he handed me the first of several enormous leather-bound scrapbooks, each of which was at least a foot thick and eighteen inches high. He had, I soon discovered, kept and pasted in every invitation, photograph and postcard that had come his way since he left Marlborough, plus the odd menu, train ticket, dance card and the like; all had been arranged in chronological order, carefully dated and annotated in ink underneath. It was a riveting treasure trove, and I could happily have sat there for a week slowly turning the pages. Quite how these marvellous scrapbooks could be converted into an autobiography was beyond us both: Derek (as he had now become) seemed to assume that they could be somehow transmuted into print by some form of osmosis.

I soon realised, from some notes he had pencilled in an exercise book, that he was no writer, and that the only possible solution might be to photograph a selection from the scrap-books, converting them into a coffee-table book with an appropriate introduction. Back in London, I reported my findings to Christopher. Understandably enough, he was overcome by exhaustion at the prospect: such a book might sell rather well in the 'carriage trade' bookshops like Heywood Hill or John Sandoe, but it would involve a vast amount of work, and the thought of having to deal with Derek at his most petulant was too much to be borne. The idea was quietly dropped; but I've often wondered what happened to the scrapbooks, those meticulous and touching records of a busy social life, and a fascinating social document as well.

Towards the end of my Connolly researches I went to see Derek in his magical house in Hampstead, crammed with canvases propped against walls, *catalogues raisonnées* and pieces of Oriental art. He had intimated that he would like to talk to me about Cyril, as he called him, and that he had known him pretty well. I was ten minutes late in arriving, which excited a flurry of remonstrations and some angry pursing of the lips, but once I had gone through the rituals of apology he was all benevolence and good will. I got out my notebook, only to find that I was dealing with Ali Forbes all over again. He seemed incapable of giving a straight answer. I was subjected to a frenzy of name-dropping and *non sequiturs*, none of them adding anything to my knowledge of Cyril Connolly or his world; after a while I gave up, and once again pretended to be scribbling in my notebook.

When the book was finally published, Derek was one of the first to arrive at my launch party. He hurried to the table on which finished copies had been laid out, and turned at once to the index. 'But I'm not here,' he said, looking wretched and petulant. I wished, at that moment, I'd found some way of smuggling him into the story, but – as with Ali Forbes – I'd come across no references to Derek in any of the Connolly papers, nor had he told me anything of interest. 'But Derek, you're in the Acknowledgements,' I replied, and I may have added some lie to the effect that the publishers had insisted on cuts, to which he had fallen victim; but I knew he didn't believe me.

Despite this terrible blow to his *amour propre*, Derek remained in touch. By now I was working with Richard Ingrams on the *Oldie*, and we persuaded him to become an occasional contributor, writing short pieces on bootmakers and varieties of mustard. Richard and I visited him in July 2000 as he lay dying in the

Edward VII Hospital in Wimpole Street: he looked a sad and shrunken figure, festooned with drips and tubes, but his face lit up when we handed over a copy of the *Oldie* containing his latest contribution. Ali Forbes, on the other hand, was less forgiving. He was given the lead review in the *Spectator* in which to pronounce on my Connolly book. He dismissed it in a few lines as badly written and ill-informed, after which he proceeded to tell us once again how well he knew Cyril, and what good friends they had been. None of it quite rang true.

# SIXTEEN

# The Sage of Trenarren

In the days when we still had family holidays, we spent a couple of weeks every summer in Polruan, a vertiginous Cornish village overlooking a busy estuary crammed with amateur yachtsmen flying the Red Ensign and enormous East European cargo ships, which arrived looking clean and well-scrubbed, picked up a load of china clay from further down the river, and left coated with the fine white dust which lay all over the leaves at the working end of the town, like a permanent sprinkling of snow. On the other side of the estuary, ten minutes away on a tiny ferry boat, was the little town of Fowey, dimly remembered from my prep-school days as the original of Sir Arthur Quiller-Couch's fictional Troytown: Sir Arthur's house – yellow, with a white painted verandah on the first floor – was at the top of the ferry steps, and a granite obelisk commemorating the great man stood on a headland overlooking the estuary.

An elegant little town of winding lanes and brightly painted Regency houses, Fowey boasted a nineteenth-century Gothick castle, antique dealers, delicatessens, restaurants with Michelin stars and second-hand bookshops specialising in the works of Daphne du Maurier, Fowey's most famous former resident, as well as those of Quiller-Couch, A.L. Rowse, Geoffrey Grigson and other Cornish authors, many of them reprinted in the red-covered paperbacks of Tony Mott's admirable if short-lived

Cornish Library. Weekend sailors togged out in luminescent yellow stormproof jackets, faded pink trousers and blue-and-white Ted Heath boating shoes and guernseys moved importantly about the quaysides and talked in loud voices in the ships' chandlers; and there was a swelling population of theatrical and literary types, including the crime novelist and cricketing biographer Tim Heald, recently relocated from East Sheen.

Whereas Fowey had long been a middle-class town, Polruan was – superficially at least – rather more plebeian. Fanlights, french windows, gleaming stucco and white-painted columns were in short supply; the stone-built houses looked like dumpy cottage loaves, with small, deep-set windows glowering out against the prevailing south-westerly winds and low doors of the kind I banged my head upon; the main street was more perpendicular than anything on offer on the other side, and – in those days at least – the village shop was better equipped with white sliced bread, tinned carrots and fizzy drinks than with ciabatta or sun-dried tomatoes. But all was not as it seemed. Polruan was far too attractive to be restricted to gnarled old fishermen and their wives, or the humble folk who worked in the shops, restaurants and hotels of Fowey. It was known, within Oxford at least, as North Oxford- or Summertown-*sur-mer*, and many of the houses were owned by benign-looking dons who decamped to Cornwall for the long summer vac and stood halfway up the steep main street or on the quayside, clad in knee-length khaki shorts and gazing absent-mindedly into space while their apple-cheeked wives struggled with the shopping and fought to control hordes of noisy, ill-kempt children.

We went there first towards the end of our spell in Oxford, renting a cottage then, and for many summers to come, from an affable American academic. The cottage didn't have a telephone, and one summer I wasted a good deal of time feeding money into the village phone box in order to ring Mervyn Horder, a retired publisher who had got it into his head that I ought to become the Editorial Director of Duckworth, and sent me urgent postcards instructing me to ring him at once. His father, Lord Horder, had been the Royal Physician, but Mervyn had opted for publishing rather than medicine. At some stage he had owned Duckworth, but although he could still be spotted in the Old Piano Factory, the firm's unusual headquarters in Camden Town – they had moved there from Henrietta Street after being bought by Colin Haycraft – he was no longer a director, and was in no position to offer me a job of any kind, let alone that of Editorial Director: but that was no bar to his making long, conspiratorial phone calls, his voice modulating from a shriek to a whisper.

Mervyn was a regular contributor to the *London Magazine*, specialising in literary and publishing anecdotes, and, as a highly competent pianist, wrote both the music and the libretti for songs which he happily performed at publishers' pantomimes and the like. A spindly, grey-haired, rumpled-looking character, sporting a pair of wire-rimmed specs, he used to call in at the *London Magazine* to deliver his copy and be entertained to lunch in the Italian on the other side of Thurloe Place. Eventually he felt he must reciprocate, and persuaded Alan to join him for lunch in Camden Town. Alan loathed North London, but he eventually agreed to go, put on his smartest tweed suit and boarded a taxi to bear him north of the Park. Two hours later he returned looking ashen-faced and shaky: Mervyn had not only taken him to a pub – despite the long hours he had spent as a young man in the Wheatsheaf and the Marquis of Granby, Alan loathed pubs as much as he loathed North London – but had bought him, for lunch, a sausage on a stick. A few months later Mervyn invited me to lunch, and took me to the same pub in Parkway. It was a blazing hot day, and the place was filled to overflowing with builders with a thick patina of white dust on their boots, downing pints and wiping the sweat from their brows. Seated in a far corner was my host. Mervyn must have been in his early eighties by then: he was wearing a skimpy bathing costume, rubber flip-flops and a vest, and had shaved and waxed his legs for the occasion. Mervyn was very good company, combining a certain hesitancy of speech with torrential flows of anecdote; unlike Alan, I enjoyed my lunch, though it was too hot to eat a sausage on a stick. When I got back Alan told me, *à propos* the bathing costume, that Mervyn had once been surprised in a public lavatory wearing a full frogman's uniform, including flippers and goggles. He spluttered with laughter as he told me: I suspect the flippers and the goggles were his own embellishments, and in due course I added a trident to complete the ensemble.

Whatever the truth of Alan's allegation, nothing came of my Editorial Directorship, and I don't imagine Colin Haycraft had the faintest idea of what Mervyn had been up to. I always enjoyed Colin's company: he had an Oxford blue in squash – 'I would have *thrashed* him,' he said when I asked him whether he would have beaten Alan Ross, who had also played for Oxford – and with his round face, round specs, round body, beaming smile, black mop of hair and overall exuberance and bounce, he resembled nothing so much as an animated squash ball. He was, I suspect, a good deal brighter, in academic terms at least, than most of his publishing colleagues and rivals, almost all of whom he loved to ridicule, accompanying his diatribes with great shouts of laughter; but the relish with which he played the part of the publishing maverick had a self-destructive element. During the Seventies he made Duckworth into one of the most interesting literary imprints in London, and gave the most drunken parties I've ever attended in the Old Piano Factory, serving cocktails in triangular glasses with the colour, consistency and flavour of lighter fuel: but he was notorious for paying his authors next to nothing, and for being tricky and devious in negotiation. He detested literary agents – he often told me, quite erroneously, that those who can't write become publishers, and those who can't publish end up as literary agents – and would, out of sheer perversity, refuse to deal with them or even answer their letters. A particular *bête noire* was Michael Sissons of A.D. Peters, widely admired as one of the most effective, literate, businesslike and straightforward of current practitioners. Duckworth had long controlled the rights in Evelyn Waugh's early travel books and Hilaire Belloc's *Cautionary Verses*, but although they were supposed to account for royalties every six months, neither a statement nor a cheque came through. More than once Michael wrote to say that, if Duckworth failed to account, they would be in breach of contract, and that the rights would revert to the authors' estates, both of which were administered by A.D. Peters: Colin paid no attention; the rights were reclaimed and resold to another publisher, Duckworth had to pay the very considerable legal costs of both sides, and were left with a warehouse full of unsaleable stock of steady-selling backlist titles of the kind they could ill afford to do without – and all because, like a naughty schoolboy, Colin liked to thumb his nose at what he regarded as the publishing establishment.

Quite early on in our Polruan visits I got in touch with an old publishing acquaintance, Raleigh Trevelyan, who had a house not far from Fowey, and had urged me to pay a visit. As a very young man Raleigh had taken part in the Anzio landings, his account of which, *The Fortress*, is one of the finest books to have come out of World War II. After being demobbed he had gone into publishing, initially at Longmans and then at Michael Joseph, and combined a career as a well-regarded editor with writing books of his own. I had got to know him in the early Seventies, when I was working at A.P. Watt. We had one or two lunches, most of them spent in companionable but gloomy silence. Raleigh is a shy, reticent man under normal circumstances, but his dislike of Edmund Fisher, the current Managing Director of Michael Joseph, had rendered him totally speechless. Eventually he could take Michael Joseph no longer, and after a brief spell at Hamish Hamilton he became a part-time editor-cum-literary adviser at Jonathan Cape; and it was while I was at Chatto, part of the same publishing group as Cape, that I got to know him again, finding him a likeable and civilised companion on summer outings and at communal Christmas parties.

I did Raleigh a good turn one year, when the Chatto, Cape and Bodley Head Christmas party was held in the Arts Club in Dover Street. The club has two large reception rooms in which parties are held, and ours was on the first floor; the ground-floor suite had been booked by an oil company, and the familiar din of braying voices, raucous laughter and the pulling of corks was blasting up the stairs, like so much hot air rising. On one of several trips to the lavatory in the basement I noticed, on my way down, that the lights had been dimmed and the music turned up, and that several dishevelled couples had taken to the dance floor, the men clutching secretarial buttocks in one hand and a glass of red in the other, the women with both arms draped round their partners' necks. On my way back, I noticed a solitary, upright figure standing by himself, clutching a wine glass and speaking to no one. It was Raleigh: he had been there, he said, for the last hour, wondering why he recognised no one, but too polite to ask. Urging him to take his glass with him, I escorted him up the wrought-iron staircase, where he rejoined his colleagues from Jonathan Cape.

When not travelling down the Orinoco or amassing information for the *Companion Guide to Sicily*, Raleigh and his friend Raul Balin divided their time between a flat in Shepherd's Market and the house in Cornwall. I had never met Raul, but when I rang from Polruan to arrange a meeting, a guttural foreign voice answered the phone, and immediately invited us to lunch at St Cadix the following day. To get there we had to drive along narrow winding lines, following the river Fowey north. After several false stops and much cursing and consulting of maps, we eventually arrived a mere half an hour late. Nothing could matter less, we were told as we were ushered indoors, apologising profusely as we went. Built around the remains of a medieval monastery, the house is a wide, white-painted, two-storey Regency farmhouse of the kind one associates with a Jane Austen heroine; trees and a farmyard surround it on three sides, and on the fourth a water meadow leads to an inlet of the river, where a rowing boat was tied to a post. Inside were books, rugs and paintings by their great friend Mary Fedden. Raul was an exuberant, jovial figure, whose ebullience perfectly counter-pointed Raleigh's shyness and reserve, and we both took to him at once. He stood very close when speaking to one, chest to chest, and prefaced most statements with a cry of 'No, but . . . '; although he had lived in this country for at least thirty years, he retained a strong Spanish accent, and his speech was punctuated with the Welsh-sounding guttural rasps I had noticed over the phone.

There were two other lunch guests, old friends who had arrived before us, and while Raleigh emanated quiet bonhomie, Raul bustled about, pouring out drinks and seizing one or both of us by the upper arm to show us a particular painting or a view from a window. Before long it was time to move into the dining room. Raleigh took his place at the head of the table; Raul was in charge of the placements, ushering us all to our chairs and then, once we had been installed, leaning over our shoulders to fill our glasses, and hurrying in and out of the kitchen with dish after dish before eventually taking his place at the far end of the table. It was the first of many such encounters with Raleigh and Raul, whose delight in each other's company was ended only by Raul's death fifteen years later.

Among the Cornish neighbours whose names cropped up on that first lunch was A.L. Rowse, best known for his histories of Tudor England, his controversial views on Shakespeare, and the relish with which he dismissed rival scholars as incompetent second-raters. As a published poet and the author of at least two volumes of autobiography, he regarded himself as a literary man and not just a dry-as-dust academic, and claimed an acquaintance with Cyril Connolly. Born in 1903, he was three months younger than my subject, but whereas Connolly was a product of Eton at its most rarefied and self-regarding, Rowse was the son of an almost illiterate china-clay worker, and had grown up in poverty near St Austell, a mile or two round the coast from Fowey: looking across the estuary from the top of the hill at Polruan one could see the white, pointed peaks of discarded china clay gleaming on the skyline above Fowey, like miniature snow-covered Alps. Both men had won scholarships to Oxford, but Rowse was a good deal more diligent as an undergraduate, noting with pleasure in his memoirs that whereas he had got a first, 'the Brackenbury Scholar at Balliol, C.V. Connolly' only scraped a third. And although Rowse was at Christ Church, the grandest and most aristocratic of Oxford colleges, he had neither the means nor the inclination to socialise with its *jeunesse dorée*, whereas Connolly mixed exclusively with other Old Etonians: but Rowse did contribute to an anthology of Oxford poets edited by Graham Greene – as did Harold Acton, who was, with Brian Howard, the most celebrated, or notorious, of Christ Church's rich young aesthetes and *poseurs*.

Although Rowse referred to various meetings with Connolly in his memoirs, and had contributed to *Horizon*, references to him in Connolly's papers were extremely thin on the ground, and I had a strong suspicion that, whatever Rowse might have to say on the subject, they hardly knew one another: but – quite apart from vulgar curiosity about so celebrated a literary and academic pugilist – I felt I should go through the hoops, so I wrote to Rowse to ask if I could visit him next time we were in Polruan. Back came a postcard by return of post, the writing elegant and clear, with not a quaver in sight: he would be delighted to see me at Trenarren House, but not between two and four in the afternoon; as for Connolly, 'I regard CC as having a streak of genius. The clue to him is that he was *Irish* – which he hated. Irish gift of the gab, playing up to the English like Shaw and Wilde (as at Eton); the self-indulgence; spells of indolence; self-pity; play-acting, playing up to his persona; originality; gifts. He loved literature; was a poet *manqué* in my view. And he was a gent. Best of luck, ALR.' It seemed a pretty accurate summing-up, though I wasn't sure about the Irishness argument; nor, as it turned out, did ALR have anything more to say on the subject.

I have always hated mixing business with pleasure, and after days spent walking round the headlands, bathing off Pridmouth Bay and carousing with friends, the last thing I felt like was interviewing a waspish nonagenarian: Rowse's postcard couldn't have been friendlier or less alarming, but I remembered seeing him on television denouncing politicians, writers and fellow historians as second- or even third-raters in an angry, high-pitched squawk, and my heart sank at the prospect. Over lunch at St Cadix, however, Raleigh and Raul assured me that 'Leslie' Rowse was really a dear old thing, not at all alarming and very keen to see me, so – feeling like a criminal *en route* for the stocks – I made my way to the nearest phone box and rang Trenarren House. The phone was instantly snatched from its cradle, and a shrill, rather matronly voice – Rowse's own, I quickly gathered, though it could well have belonged to Mervyn Horder – demanded to know who I was and what I wanted. I burbled out my lines, and it was agreed that I would report for duty at eleven o'clock the following morning.

Petra and our friend Alastair Langlands agreed that they would drive me over, drop me off, go for a walk, pick me up a couple of hours later, and whisk me home for a restorative drink and lunch; so, deposited at the side gate bang on time, I made my way across crunching gravel to the porch. Not many miles from where the young Rowse had grown up in poverty, Trenarren House was a handsome, grey eighteenth-century manor house, set in a southwards-facing cleft in the hills; before it, a well-shaved lawn led down to rhododendron bushes, and beyond them shimmered the sea. Faintly dilapidated, crammed with books and paintings and engravings of Oxford colleges, the house inside was very much that of a gentleman-scholar. Rowse had, I gathered, written over a hundred books, most of them published by Macmillan or Jonathan Cape: they ranged from *Richard Grenville of the Revenge* and *Tudor England* to a biography of his cat. On his frequent trips to the Huntingdon Library and American universities, Rowse had made a point of ringing home to talk to his cat: I knew how he felt, and although I had never tried to conduct a telephone conversation with any of our cats, I often tried – without much success – to persuade them to purr down the phone to Petra when she was away from home. *Peter, the White Cat of Trenarren* had been published by Raleigh's old boss Michael Joseph, a passionate cat-owner and himself the author of at least one feline biography.

Of its prolific author there was as yet no sign. I had been let in by his housekeeper, Phyllis, a homely, talkative Cornishwoman in her early eighties, limping along on a stick; and as she showed me round, pointing out objects of particular interest with a wave of her stick, she explained that nowadays Dr Rowse spent most of his time in bed, seldom venturing downstairs even for meals. The tour completed, she escorted me up a broad flight of stairs, across a landing, and into the great historian's bedroom.

It was a large, light room with tall mullioned windows looking out across the lawn to the sea, and it smelt, faintly but disconcertingly, of urine. Rowse lay propped up in bed against a barricade of pillows, and he ordered me to draw up a chair and sit alongside but facing him. His face was the colour of ivory, bisected by a pair of old-fashioned horn-rimmed specs, and topped by a gleaming quiff of silver hair. He was wearing pyjamas, striped in mauve and black and white, with a loosely knitted shawl round his shoulders. He started talking as soon as I entered the room; every now and then he laid his hand on my knee, and he made, from time to time, a camp gesture with his wrist, like a railway signal returning to the horizontal. This was often accompanied by laughter, and a curious high-pitched hoot.

'I know all about you, dear,' he said after a while. 'You're a second-rater who read English at Oxford and thinks he knows all the answers.' 'No, I'm not,' I replied. 'I'm a second-rater who read history at Trinity, Dublin, and I know next to nothing.' This seemed to please him a good deal: he let out a shriek, murmured, 'Ah, fabled Trinity,' and something about the superiority of all historians to Eng. Lit. academics, closed his eyes, and seemed to fall fast asleep. While he dozed, I got up very quietly and paced about the room, examining his books and pictures and gazing out to sea, half-wishing I was in it.

Awake again, Rowse resumed his favourite topic – the prevalence of second-raters. Could I think of *any* first-raters, in or out of Oxford? he wondered. As always on such occasions, my mind went completely blank. Most of the first-raters I particularly admired were of a pensionable age, but I dreaded exposing them to possible ridicule, or failing lamentably to justify my choices and caving in under a barrage of derision; and if I were to come up with any candidates, I would have to put them forward with the right mixture of diffidence and defiance. Would he think James Lees-Milne and Patrick Leigh Fermor too lacking in academic ballast? What did he make of Richard Cobb? Would he have heard of Dennis Enright, or Alan Ross, or my Trinity friend Derek Mahon, the finest poet of our generation? Hugh Trevor-Roper seemed incontrovertibly first-rate, but it was very likely that they had fallen out over high table politics or the Tudor Poor Law, so I couldn't risk him (since then I have read Trevor-Roper's contemptuous views of Rowse in his letters to Bernard Berenson, and no doubt his disdain was returned with interest). Eventually I came up with Isaiah Berlin and Nirad C. Chaudhuri, the Indian sage who was even older than Rowse. Both, he conceded, were indeed first-raters; and, with that agreed between us, we turned to Connolly himself. 'Who is more

overlooked by the third-rate Eng. Lit. academics – Cyril or me?'
he wondered afterwards in a letter. 'I never disliked him,' he went
on *à propos* that antithesis of the academic man. 'I merely disapproved of his silly way of life, his wasting his gifts, weakness of
character. He thought me "censorious" – well, that was right.'

The interview over, Rowse settled back on his pillows and
closed his eyes, and I tiptoed dutifully out of the room. Petra and
Alastair were waiting downstairs, and Phyllis asked them if they
too would like a guided tour. She was obviously extremely fond
of her temperamental master, and proud of him as well. 'He's a
terrible old devil,' she told us as we poked about the kitchen and
the scullery, neither of which, from the look of them, had been
touched since the 1920s. 'You should hear him when he's angry!'
On the way out we came across Rowse clinging to the banisters,
halfway down the stairs; he was still in his pyjamas, his silver hair
shooting from his head like a parakeet's crest, his spectacles
flashing fire. 'Who *are* these people?' he demanded. 'Have they
come to see you or *me*?' Quite unawed by his wrath, Phyllis
ordered him sharply back to bed, making shooing motions at
him with the backs of her hands.

I never saw Rowse again, but until he suffered a stroke from
which he never really recovered, we engaged in an affectionate
correspondence. For some reason he had decided that I was, if not
a first-rater, at least a kindred spirit, and he was complimentary
about a pamphlet I wrote about Connolly for the University of
Texas: 'I think you've got him absolutely right, if too sympathetic.'
He addressed me as 'Jeremiah', suggested ideas for future books –
these included a book about his publishers, the Macmillan
family – and urged me, without success, 'not to go in for
Cyril's habit of self-deprecation – very middle-class – which La
Rochefoucauld knew was only a way of recommending oneself'.
Already rather fond of my formidable correspondent, I was
extremely flattered by his attentions, and when he suggested
that I might like to take up the mantle of his Shakespearian

researches, I could hardly bear to tell him that no one could be worse qualified for the job: I have always had a blank spot about Shakespeare, hate seeing his plays on stage, and haven't read a word of him since I left university over forty years ago. 'Dear Jeremiah,' Rowse wrote by return, 'I am *shocked* to think that you are not up in the work of the leading authority on the Elizabethan i.e. Shakespeare's Age. As bad as Cyril with his Third?' Nor, to my relief, was I alone in my ignorance, for 'Cyril was rather poor on Shakespeare,' it seemed.

As for the ostensible purpose of my visit, one matter remained unresolved. In one of his autobiographies, Rowse described how, shortly after the publication of *Enemies of Promise* in 1938, Connolly came rushing into his 'dark-panelled rooms in the front quad' at All Souls and, spotting an annotated copy of his book on a table, eagerly devoured his host's marginalia; after which, 'I sat him down to a tutorial on the German mind and philosophy; concluding by reading to him that marvellously penetrating passage in Santayana's *Egotism and German Philosophy*, in which he diagnosed and precisely pin-pointed the disease during the First War, before it became so brutally self-evident in Nazism.'

None of this quite rang true. Though reconciled to the place in old age, Connolly hated Oxford for much of his life, and never went there unless he had to; Stuart Hampshire, who saw a fair amount of Connolly in the Thirties, told me that he was quite sure that he never visited All Souls at that time; and Connolly's own papers suggested that the two men were unacquainted. In 1942 Connolly was appointed, for a brief, unhappy spell, literary editor of the *Observer*, and its proprietor, Lord Astor, dropped him a line to say that he hoped he wouldn't employ a 'militant atheist' like Rowse as a reviewer. Connolly wrote a pretty sharp reply, refusing to be dictated to and defending his right to employ the likes of Rowse; in his letter he said that he had never met his contentious reviewer, but shortly after, following one of his rare visits to Oxford, he told his hostess, Billa Harrod – whose husband, Roy, was an economist at Christ Church – that he had 'greatly enjoyed meeting Rowse'. This hardly suggested the degree of pre-war friendship Rowse had described in his book; I was keen to include the story of Rowse's seminar in my book, but not if it proved patently untrue. I had no desire to put the old boy on the spot, let alone accuse him of telling a whopper, so I wrote him a tactful letter pointing out the slight discrepancy between his version of events and Connolly's letters to Lord Astor and Billa Harrod. 'Fancy Waldorf [Astor] writing like that! it is quite unlike him,' Rowse replied, before going on to admit that 'You are quite right, Cyril had only met me once and could say tactfully that he didn't know me . . .' All in all, it seemed wiser and kinder to let sleeping dogs lie: in one of his letters, Rowse had enclosed a book of his poems, and from them I got a strong – and tragic – sense of how, behind the boasting and the bombast and the ridicule of second-raters, lay a rather shy, virginal creature, who felt himself to be not just unloved, but unlovable as well, and had craved, but never known, physical and emotional affection.

'I have been wondering how you were getting on – slow-coach, too meticulous,' Rowse wrote in one of his last letters to me. I wish he had lived long enough to read my biography, though the hardback is too heavy to read in bed, and he would certainly have thought it far too long. 'Vy pleased we rather agreed about poor dear Cyril,' he concluded. 'So – Good Luck with your Reading – and Catching Up! ALR.'

# SEVENTEEN

# Battling with Barbara

The one person I rather dreaded meeting was Connolly's second wife, Barbara Skelton, a notorious *femme fatale* to whom the adjective 'pantherine' was invariably attached. In addition to Cyril Connolly, she had been married to George Weidenfeld and Derek Jackson, the millionaire Oxford don and amateur jockey; her lovers had included King Farouk (who beat her with his dressing-gown cord on the steps of his palace), Feliks Topolski, Peter Quennell, Alan Ross, Kenneth Tynan and a plainclothes detective who came round to investigate a burglary. Her alarming reputation seemed to be borne out by her memoirs, comical and bitchy in equal measure, and by her tawny-haired, high-cheeked, almond-eyed good looks, like a ferocious ice maiden painted by Cranach. She was living in France, and with Alan Ross's encouragement I dropped her a line and asked if we could meet. She wrote back to say that she would be in London shortly, and suggested a time and place for our rendezvous.

She was staying with her friend Jocelyn Rickards, who was married to the film director Clive Donner and lived in St John's Wood. I had never heard of Jocelyn Rickards, but was quickly enlightened by those in the know. She was, it seemed, another *femme fatale* of the 1950s, and had been the mistress of Freddie Ayer, Graham Greene and John Osborne: but whereas Barbara was hawkish in looks and temperament, Jocelyn was rounder, with a *retroussé* nose and pug-like features, and altogether less intimidating. Years later, Richard Ingrams and I employed her, by then nearly blind and very stout, as the *Oldie*'s audio-books critic, while Clive, whose only failing was a stumpy pigtail holding his snow-white hair in place, provided us with gossipy memoirs of a life in films, typed in capital letters with no punctuation. All this lay in the future: in the meantime, I found myself ringing a doorbell in a wall at the end of a *cul de sac* off Grove End Road, and rather dreading my first encounter with a *grande horizontale*. Eventually the door opened, and I was ushered into a lush, overgrown secret garden, far removed, in spirit at least, from the huge red Thirties mansion blocks that loomed all round it. Clive and Jocelyn had gone out, I was told, so Barbara and I had the place to ourselves – and we were to help ourselves to the champagne, put in the fridge specially for the occasion.

Barbara, my hostess for the afternoon, was of average height, with grey hair cut in a bob, smooth, almost golden skin, a small, straight nose, a long, humorous mouth, and green, lynx-like eyes peering keenly out from behind a pair of bat-winged, pink-framed specs of the kind I associated with Edna Everage rather than a *femme fatale*. She was wearing a white cotton shirt, tight black silk trousers, and black slip-on shoes, and although she must have been in her late seventies, she had the figure and the elasticity of a woman in her thirties. Only those terrible specs let her down; but she was too vain, in a man's company at least, to keep them on for long, and having once whipped them off she peered short-sightedly about her, bringing books and bottles ever closer till they swam into focus. She spoke in a low staccato, often ending a sentence, in the French manner, with an interrogative 'yes?' or 'no?', her voice rising to the concluding question-mark. She had problems pronouncing her 'r's, her vocabulary combined old-fashioned slang with flurries of

French, and both delivery and content combined derision and affection, menace and comicality.

'You'd like some champagne, yes?' she asked as I blundered from the bright light of the garden into a darkened hall; and as I struggled with the cork she made little purring noises of approval, adding, '*You're* not much good as an opener, I must say,' when it failed to twist in my hands. Our glasses filled at last, we trailed through to the sitting room, where Barbara lay back in a wicker chair, her eyes half-closed and her cat-like profile silhouetted against the late-afternoon sunlight slanting in through the french windows. I was very taken with her silvery laugh, her innate good sense on literary matters, her lack of pretension and the snorts of derision with which she dismissed so many of those she had known in that seductive, raffish world where bohemia and society intersect. We drained a second bottle of the Donners' champagne – I had no problems with the cork this time – and as I made my way unsteadily home, I felt that a good day's work had been done.

I didn't see Barbara again for several months, but I kept bumping into her, in print if not in person. As I ungallantly discovered after her death, when asked to write about her for the new *Oxford Dictionary of National Biography*, she was born in 1916, the daughter of an unsuccessful soldier and a former Gaiety Girl. (Not long before I delivered my piece to the *DNB*, OUP introduced a half-witted and short-lived editorial policy of banning capital letters except for real names, so peopling their books with lopsided characters like the duke of Windsor or cardinal Newman: I fought hard to convince them that an uncapitalised 'gaiety girl' made no sense at all.) By her own account Barbara was a temperamental child: 'bun-faced, with slanting sludge-coloured eyes', she once lunged at her mother with a carving knife, and was alerted to the perils of sex when a priapic uncle invited her to search for sweets in his trouser pockets. While in her teens she moved from Kent to London, where she lost her virginity to a middle-aged margarine millionaire, and worked as a model for Hartnell and Stiebel, and for Schiaparelli in Paris.

During the war, 'Skeltie' became the archetype of what Peter Quennell described as the 'Lost Girls' of the period, 'adventurous young women who flitted about London, alighting briefly here and there, and making the best of any random perch on which they happened to descend'. She lived for a while with one of General de Gaulle's entourage, 'a balding stocky man with a pale reptilian face', but before long she had become a denizen of bohemia, dividing her favours between Quennell and the painter Feliks Topolski: they came to blows over her one night in the Gargoyle Club, with Topolski ruffling his rival's impeccable widow's peak. 'There was something about her slightly slanted eyes, her prominent cheekbones, and smooth olive skin that suggested the youthful concubine of a legendary Mongol chieftain,' Quennell once wrote of her, adding that 'her narrow-waisted, rather wide-hipped body recalled the celestial dancing-girls I had once encountered at Angkor Wat'. He compared his infatuation with Hazlitt's for Sarah Walker, and recalled how Barbara 'had an air of secret self-possession and, illuminating her face in rare flashes, a half-provocative, half-malicious smile'. A later lover, the painter Michael Wishart, suggested that her eyes 'had the mysterious, drowsy look of a baby panther. To catch her eyes was more or less to enter into a conspiracy: she drove her admirers mad by her combination of elusiveness and volatility, sulking one moment and bubbling over with laughter the next, bestowing and then, quite suddenly, withdrawing her favour.'

All this sounded horribly familiar. I had worked, for ten years, for two publishers who had operated, very successfully, on similar lines, seeming to offer up friendship and even affection and then suddenly whipping them away, so that one never knew where one stood, and was permanently off balance; equally familiar was the way in which Barbara was, in Quennell's words, 'extraordinarily quick at detecting one's limitations and exposing one's pretensions, and always adroit at holding up a glass where one saw one's silliest face reflected'. Even as a comparative outsider and, as it would turn out, a late friend of Barbara's old age, I soon saw how 'she had acquired a knack, perhaps half-unconscious, of distinguishing her lovers' weakest points, just as certain wasps, accustomed to paralyse their prey, know exactly where to sink their stings'. Or, to quote Wishart again, 'as feline in appearance as she later proved to be in character, she had the tantalising quality of needing a tamer, while something indefinable about her indicated that she was untameable'.

For a time, Barbara and Peter Quennell shared an attic in Bedford Square over the offices of *Horizon*, rented from Cyril Connolly, but in 1942 she went out to Cairo, at Donald Maclean's suggestion, to work as a 'cipherine'. There she added to her list of lovers the conventionally good-looking, firm-featured actor Anthony Steel, best remembered by those of us who grew up in the 1950s for films in which he trudged across Africa in knee-length shorts and a khaki shirt with the sleeves rolled up, as often as not in the company of Stewart Granger, whose hair was so heavily brilliantined that it came out blue in Technicolor. But her most celebrated Egyptian liaison was with King Farouk. He had not yet become the bloated, mountainous figure of later years – according to Barbara, he came to resemble 'a huge sawdust teddy bear, badly sewn at the joints' – but her persistent fondness for him reflected, in part, her disdain for conventional good looks: she once cited Erich von Stroheim as her *beau idéal*, and Topolski, himself a slender, rather graceful figure, recalled her 'penchant for male beasts, hairy and excessive in bulk'. What she did value, on the other hand, were cleverness and humour: she had a nimble wit and a highly developed sense of the absurd, both in person and on paper, and although formally uneducated she was widely read, with an instinctive feeling for writing that put most literary types to shame. Though many found her silent, threatening and farouche, a glowering presence radiating waves of boredom and disdain, laughter always worked far better than conventional disapproval.

No one was funnier or cleverer or better read or less conventionally good-looking than Cyril Connolly, who was to become the one real love of her life, to be looked back on with affection and admiration – tinged, as ever, with the familiar dash of derision. They met again not long after her return from the Middle East, and before long he was in hot pursuit. His morale, never the sturdiest of growths, was at a low ebb in the late 1940s. He was rapidly losing interest in *Horizon*, which he had edited since the outbreak of war; his two best-known books, *Enemies of Promise* and *The Unquiet Grave*, were behind him, but although his ever-hopeful publishers, Hamish Hamilton and Cass Canfield of Harper & Row, commissioned a life of Flaubert and a book about south-west France, neither would ever be written, and his future books would consist of reprinted essays and reviews, artfully arranged. He dreamed of being a novelist, a calling for which he had no talent whatsoever, but although he lay in the bath laughing at his own inventions, nothing was forthcoming; he was about to embark on a form of servitude, as one of the *Sunday Times*'s two lead book reviewers, to which he would remain subjected until his death in 1974, and which provided him with yet another excuse for failing to write the full-length masterpieces he liked to believe were simmering inside him.

He was a forceful presence on the literary scene, known for his wit and his charm and his tendency to sulk, yet for all his eminence money was always in short supply, and the bank manager's letters a matter of dread. The slim youth of Eton and Balliol had long given way to the portly, pleasure-loving man of letters, famed for his greed and his sloth; he had become bored with the long-suffering Lys Lubbock, who had been with him ever since his first wife, Jeannie, went home to America at the outbreak of war, unable to cope any longer with his lifelong addiction to being in love with two or more people at once, and to pining for those he had lost. Perched behind the wheel of her scarlet Triumph roadster, the hood down and her fair hair flying in the wind, Barbara must have seemed the perfect antidote to the wastes of middle age. They were married in a Kent register office in 1950, with PC Wellington Boot doing duty as a witness. The ceremony over, Barbara hurried off to an appointment with the dentist, after which they settled down to married life in her tiny, inglenooked cottage in the village of Elmstead, a few miles north of her home town of Hythe.

Barbara's life with Connolly, and her farcical infatuation with his new publisher, George Weidenfeld, have been described at length in her two volumes of autobiography, and in the two biographies devoted to her husband. Locked away in Oak Cottage, a mist coming in off the sea and the gulls screaming overhead, they fought, as Connolly put it, like a couple of kangaroos. Barbara found herself saddled with 'a slothful whale of a husband' who lay in bed till midday sucking the sheets and repeating, 'Poor Cyril, poor Cyril,' like a mantra, or wallowed for hours on end in the bath muttering, 'I wish I were dead' or 'a million miles from here', and then pottered angrily about the house, rearranging his collection of china and silver and brooding over the exotic plants he had bought for the garden. Barbara longed to have children, but too many abortions had taken their toll; they made do instead with guinea fowl and geese and a hysterical coatimundi called Kupi which her friend John Sutro had brought back from Uruguay: according to Barbara, it was such a nuisance on the flight back to England that Sutro's fellow passengers begged him to hurl it out of the window, and once established in Oak Cottage it chased the geese, dug up the exotic shrubs and bit its master in sensitive parts of his anatomy. Running true to form, Connolly pined for Lys and bombarded her with pitiful letters bemoaning his plight and begging her to have him back. One morning, as I was working my way through a mound of photocopied letters from Connolly to Lys, Petra picked one up and started to read. 'How old is this man?' she asked when she got to the end: a reasonable enough question, since although from a literary point of view Connolly's letters to Lys, and the other women in his life, were extremely sophisticated, in emotional terms they were those of a lovesick, self-pitying teenager.

And then, quite suddenly, Barbara fell in love, and everything was changed. Some three years younger than Barbara, George Weidenfeld had arrived in England from Vienna in 1939. During the war he had worked for the BBC, monitoring broadcasts from Germany, and written a book about Goebbels's propaganda techniques. After the war he determined to become a publisher, and to get round the prevailing paper quotas he and André Deutsch founded a book-format magazine called *Contact*, which attracted first-rate contributors, and gave him an *entrée* to the literary world. In due course he set up as a book publisher with Nigel Nicolson: although he never showed any interest thereafter in books for young people, he got off to a flying start when Marks & Spencer commissioned him to produce a line of children's books, and moved on to become one of the most distinguished and enterprising publishers in London.

Despite the advances that had never been repaid and the books that had never been delivered, Connolly and the ever-patient Hamish Hamilton had come to a temporary parting of the ways. Weidenfeld, like Hamilton before him, employed Connolly as a literary adviser, and before long he had published *The Golden Horizon*, an anthology of the best pieces that had appeared in Connolly's magazine, which had finally folded in 1950, almost simultaneously with John Lehmann's *Penguin New Writing*. He also published Barbara's autobiographical first novel, *A Young Girl's Touch*. But his literary partnership with Barbara's husband was short-lived. Passing Weidenfeld's house in Chester Square, and finding the front door mysteriously open,

Connolly entered, as if in a dream, and discovered his wife and his publisher *in flagrante*.

Before long Barbara's affair, and Connolly's cries of anguish, were the talk of literary London. Though consumed by remorse, Barbara – like her new lover – was overwhelmed by an intense if transient physical passion, and found it impossible to stay away. Weidenfeld believed he was rescuing her from an unhappy marriage; though neither was in love with the other, their affair acquired a hideous and unstoppable momentum, as a result of which Barbara destroyed the one relationship in her life which she would look back on with genuine affection. She and Connolly were divorced, with Weidenfeld cited as the co-respondent. Protesting all the while that she loved Connolly more than ever, she found herself, like a reluctant sleepwalker, taking part in a dismal marriage ceremony in Caxton Hall before setting out for a honeymoon on Ischia. According to Barbara, she took radioactive mud-baths while her new husband lay on the sand in a pair of city trousers with the legs rolled up, his face buried under a pile of newspapers. Connolly was staying at the other end of the island with Auden and Maurice Bowra; Barbara soon got in touch, and, when Weidenfeld's back was turned, 'Hubby' took a partial revenge.

Life as a publisher's wife proved utterly uncongenial. Barbara refused to play the part of a charming and compliant consort, turning up at grand parties in a pair of gym shoes and openly deriding her husband's instructions to 'gush' over editors, authors and important guests; Weidenfeld loathed her cats, which scratched the furniture and peed in the grate. Embattled from the very beginning, they remained together for a matter of months, and when, in due course, they got divorced, Connolly was cited as the co-respondent.

Contrary to literary mythology, Barbara never remarried Connolly: nor was she in a position to do so, since he had fallen in love with a young woman called Deirdre Craven, a child was on its way, and in October 1959 he married for the third and last time. Barbara was distraught, and took herself off to New York, where she worked as a dentist's receptionist and in a bookshop, visited Cuba, and had affairs with Charles Addams, Kenneth Tynan and Bob Silvers, the founder of the *New York Review of Books*. Quite forgetting how they had bickered and fought, Connolly wrote her endless letters grumbling about the constraints of domesticity and looking back with longing to life in Oak Cottage. When, in due course, she moved to the South of France, he came to stay in her *mas* on his way to and from travel assignments for the *Sunday Times*, and it was while he was with her in the summer of 1974 that he suffered the heart attack that preceded his final collapse and death.

Like many other beautiful and stylish women, Barbara was briefly married to the unappealing but immensely rich Derek Jackson, an Oxford Professor of Spectroscopy, former fighter pilot and amateur jockey whose family fortune was founded on the *News of the World*: they stayed together for a matter of months, but he left her – as he left his other wives – a generous settlement, and for the rest of her life Barbara, hitherto impoverished, was never short of a penny. She lived for a time, tempestuously, with the French writer Bernard Frank, who had earlier been involved with Françoise Sagan; in due course she moved north, to a village sixty miles south of Paris, and a flat in an unfashionable outskirt of the city. Old friends lost touch, or died, or moved away; Barbara began to brood on the possibility of moving back to England, and it was then that I got to know her.

Some months after our first meeting, she asked me to stay: she was keen to help me with my book, and we could spend a few days together in her cottage near Nemours, raking over the past and trawling through her collection of photographs. The Channel Tunnel was still being dug, and I couldn't afford to fly, so I hopped on a bus at Victoria and took the Metro out to her flat in the far south-east of Paris, beyond the *Périphérique*. The flat was in an undistinguished modern block. It had a transient, unsettled air, as though she had alighted there briefly and reluctantly, and was about to decamp at any moment. This proved to be the case, for hardly had I stepped through the front door than she was shooing me out again with impatient flicks of her wrist: we had no time to dilly-dally, she told me, but must make our way to the country before the rush hour engulfed us.

Barbara was wearing a man's shirt, a pair of light tweed trousers and pink gym shoes, and as we moved into the hallway she strapped on a black leather money-belt and draped a tobacco-coloured tweed overcoat round her shoulders. One of her ankles was in plaster, and as she hobbled down the stone stairs into the courtyard she revealed that she had recently returned from the Jura, where two friends, both much younger than her and permanently high on pot, had abandoned her halfway down a mountain: she had twisted her ankle in the descent, and her friends were friends no longer. We loaded up her Renault Clio with things we might need at the other end, and set off, violently, in a southerly direction. Barbara was a dashing but erratic driver: in towns she drove, very slowly, in the middle of the road, a long snake of honking motorists unravelling behind her, but once in the open country she hurtled along, skimming the approaching traffic by inches and jamming on her brakes at the very last moment when she came up behind another car. She liked to drive with the windows open and the radio on full blast; she was forever fiddling with the tuner, darting from one station to another and cursing the crackles in between.

While Barbara's Paris flat was dispiritingly bleak, her country cottage could not have been more different. The country round was green and lush and rolling, with low blue hills in the distance and plane trees rustling in the wind; the village itself was drowsy and shuttered and grey, its quiet broken only by the sporadic snarl of a motorist pounding through at ninety miles per hour.

Hidden behind an eight-foot wall, the 'Cott' was a long, elegant, whitewashed affair, with overhanging eaves, an orchard rolling away at the back, and a walled garden in front. The hall was paved in black-and-white chequerboard marble, while the sitting-room floor consisted of thick black-stained boards, with Persian rugs thrown over them. There was a gigantic fireplace, large enough to stand up in; much of the furniture was of the homely, farmhouse variety, interspersed with heavy marble-topped tables and deep, luxurious armchairs it was hard to struggle out of. Upstairs, the bedrooms were painted in pale matt colours, apple-green and sky-blue, and visitors could see themselves reflected, dimly, in the blotched and mottled glass of eighteenth-century mirrors, the frames of which were decorated with urns and garlands picked out in gold on a background of pink or pistachio plasterwork. There were books everywhere, teetering in mounds on every available surface. The pictures were bright and mostly modern, and over everything hung the faint, rather musty smell that I came to associate with every place in which Barbara lived.

Under the window in the sitting room stood a large painted wooden chest. 'I bet you'd like to know what I keep in *there*,' Barbara said – whereupon she whipped it open to reveal a cornucopia of letters, discarded short stories and odd, inconsequential pages of diary, all thrust higgledy-piggledy into supermarket carrier bags. Many of these letters, she told me, were from Cyril Connolly, and I recognised his spidery scrawl on sheets of bright blue Basildon Bond peeping out from a Waitrose bag. A haul of this kind is what every biographer dreams of, but although I had my notebook at the ready, there was no suggestion that I might like to spread its contents out on the dining-room table and see what it contained, and I was far too diffident to ask. 'I *might*, just *might*, let you take a look at these one day,' Barbara said in her taunting, half-teasing way, and closed the lid of the chest. Nothing more was said about its contents for the rest of my stay, but a day or two later she burrowed deep inside and fished out a jiffy-bag crammed with photographs. Many of them, taken in the 1950s, showed her in the nude, lying in long grass, but the *pièce de résistance*, produced with a silvery laugh, showed a gigantic erect penis bursting from the trousers of a pinstriped suit, like a storm-lashed lighthouse on a rock: to one side lay an old-fashioned fly-button, and away in the distance, tastefully out of focus, was the beaming face of its proud proprietor, a well-known figure on the literary scene.

Much as I came to like her, Barbara was never easy to talk to, and conversation tended to come in spurts, with awkward silences between. Connolly himself lay like a barrier between us, a subject to be circumnavigated or postponed, but relief of a kind was provided by Barbara's two cats, referred to as the 'Pussers'. Barbara shared Connolly's love of animals, far preferring them, I suspect, to humankind: no doubt amateur psychologists would have diagnosed the Pussers as substitute children, and her passion for them as frustrated maternal urges. A mother and son, they were dark brown Burmese, and had travelled from Paris with us, mewing angrily in their baskets on the back seat and jolting suddenly forward whenever Barbara jammed on the brakes. Though a keen cat-lover, I found it hard to warm to the Pussers: they were a disconsolate, ill-tempered pair, and, like their mistress, they combined elegance with unpredictability, disdaining conventional offers of friendship and occasionally rounding on well-wishers with a snarl and a sideways swipe of the paw.

Like an over-anxious mother, Barbara never left them alone for a minute, but followed them anxiously about the house, commenting on their every deed and worrying about their health and safety. Very occasionally they would drive her mad with irritation, and with a cry of '*Ça suffit!*' – they were French-speaking cats – she would lock them in the sitting room, where they mewed piteously while she told them that they were bad

Pussers, that she had had quite enough of them for today, and that they must stay locked up until they could behave better. She refused to allow them out of the house in case they were run over or eaten by a fox. This seemed a miserable business, so I persuaded her to allow the Pussers into the front garden, hemmed in as it was by the eight-foot wall, which even the most determined fox would be hard-pressed to scale. She insisted that I should keep an eye on them, so I sat in a deckchair on the terrace reading a book, while they disappeared behind a bush.

Nor were Barbara's anxieties restricted to the Pussers. At the slightest provocation – a dead fly, or some gravel from the Pussers' tray which they had flicked onto the carpet – she would unravel the Hoover from under the stairs and set to with a concentrated frown; and as she prowled about the house, she wiped every available surface with a tightly screwed-up wad of kitchen paper, her hand moving over the surface in tight, fast-moving circles. In the intervals of scouring she complained about the 'fucking Frogs', and how unfriendly they were: she had no friends in the village – and precious few in Paris, come to that – and the neighbours were conspiring against her; she was bored and restless in both places, pacing furiously up and down like a lioness in a cage. She took her typewriter, an Olivetti portable, wherever she went, and it stood open on a round marble-topped table: from time to time she would interrupt her pacings to clatter out a paragraph or two, carefully concealing them from intruding eyes. The most worrying aspect of moving back to England, she declared, was deciding where to house the Pussers during their six-months' quarantine period; so instead of discussing Cyril Connolly during our evenings together, we pored over the brochures provided by catteries in Kent and Sussex, the most promising of which displayed, on its notepaper, a broadly beaming cat in tweed plus-fours and a pork-pie hat, striding out on its two back legs, a walking stick in its right paw and a pipe firmly clenched between its jaws.

Three months later, Barbara was in touch again. In my thank-you letter I had rashly volunteered to help with her move back to England, and she was keen to take me up on my offer. 'I have suddenly decided to write and say YES YES YES,' she wrote. 'I would like you to help me over with the transportation of the Pussers. I would pay all your expenses, natch, and I know you would jolly along the whole affair and make it less painful. The poor Pussers are booked into their prison near Lewes on 6 Oct and are being picked up by a gaoler at Dover. We would drive over in that rotten little car, get drunk on the boat, and on to London with me thoroughly doped and MAYBE relieved, as both are in disgrace at the moment. Am waiting on tender hooks for your reply.'

Once again, I reported for duty at Victoria Coach Station, but this time nothing ran smoothly. The boat was delayed at Dover, and the bus was hours late leaving Calais; I'd told Barbara to expect me in the late afternoon, but by the time we picked our way into Paris it was well past nine. When I rang her from a phonebox, she sounded like a child whose party had been ruined. 'Well, you're no use to me, are you?' she said. She had been packing up the flat all day without any help, and was quite exhausted and going to bed. It was far too late for me to come round, but if I was to be of any use at all I should turn up first thing the following morning; and with that she slammed down the receiver, and left me to my own devices. I crept away and restored my morale with my old university friend Suzanne Lowry, then the Paris correspondent of the *Daily Telegraph*, who gave me a bed in her attic.

It was raining next morning, and as I trailed out to Choissy on a suburban commuter train I dreaded what awaited me. But after a good night's sleep Barbara was on cracking form, and we set about packing her possessions into cardboard boxes. A newly opened bottle of Scotch was perched on the draining board in the kitchen: Barbara suggested that we should fuel ourselves with regular swigs, and by the time the removals men arrived at eleven we were well away. Every now and then Barbara asked me whether we should entrust a particular painting or precious object to the *déménageurs*, or take it with us in the back of the car: I invariably recommended the *déménageurs*, at which Barbara, standing very close, would wag her finger in my face and remind me that if anything was lost or broken in transit, she would know whom to blame.

By the time they left it was mid-afternoon. We were filthy and whisky-sodden and underfed, so Barbara suggested that, rather than make a spectacle of ourselves in her local restaurant, we should eat up the contents of the fridge. This was all very well, but we had packed the plates, the knives and forks, the glasses and the salt and pepper: we would have to throw ourselves on the mercy of her neighbours – all of whom, Barbara told me, were embittered and lonely old spinsters, who disapproved of her deeply, spent their days peeking out at her from behind their lace curtains and making tut-tutting noises, and had never addressed a single word to her in all the years she had lived there. Unalarmed by this, and emboldened by whisky, I banged on the door of the flat above, and asked its inhabitant – an old lady in a flowered and padded dressing gown, with dyed amber-coloured hair and steel-rimmed specs – whether we could possibly borrow the crockery and cutlery we needed. She bustled vigorously about, and when I told her that Madame Skelton was leaving that evening, she gave a little cry of dismay, threw her hands in the air, produced a bottle of *eau de vie* and some Duralex tooth mugs, rounded up a contingent of other old ladies, all of them wearing padded dressing gowns and tinted steel-rimmed specs, and hurried downstairs to Barbara's flat to say how much they would miss her, and how sad they were to see her go, to the accompaniment of endless drinking of toasts.

Once we'd eaten our frugal meal, and returned the plates, glasses and knives and forks, Barbara set about loading the

179

Renault with all those items that had not been entrusted to the removals men. Pride of place, in the back seat, was given to the Pussers, each occupying a basket of its own and angrily giving voice. Behind the driver's seat we wedged an enormous sack of cat litter, and behind the passenger seat a round wicker basket crammed with half-empty bottles of whisky, brandy and assorted liqueurs. Several large suitcases filled up most of the boot, and the gaps were plugged with shoes, a pair of cowboy boots and an assortment of dresses on wire hangers. An original drawing by Toulouse-Lautrec was pushed down one side, and on top of it all, straddling the boot and the back seat, and occasionally brushing the backs of our necks, balanced a large painting by Sidney Nolan, in which a despondent water fowl with scarlet legs could be seen picking its way through a swamp, with factory chimneys puffing in the background.

We locked the door of her flat for the last time, and set off in the direction of the *Périphérique* in a series of heavily-laden jerks. Exhausted by her day's labours, and the toasting in *eau de vie*, Barbara was, by now, in a filthy mood; every few minutes she removed both hands from the wheel in order to pull on, and then pull off, a pair of brown string and leather driving gloves, and the car lunged wildly to left or right before being brought under control at the very last moment.

Although she had lived in France for the last quarter of a century, Barbara seemed to have no idea of its geography; nor did her car come equipped with maps of Paris in particular, or France as a whole. She told me, crossly, to keep an eye open for signs reading 'Calais' or 'le Nord', but when, some twenty minutes round the *Périphérique*, heading at speed in an anti-clockwise direction, I pointed to a sign that read 'Calais A1', she flashed on past before eventually grinding to a halt in one of those motorway maintenance areas that are filled with sand used to grit icy roads or extinguish cars that have burst into flames.

Somehow we managed to back out of the sandpit in the face of the rush-hour traffic, and made our way to the nearest exit slipway. By now Barbara was tired and tearful, insisting it was all my fault and seemingly resigned to spending the rest of the day in some obscure corner of north-eastern Paris. Although I loathe driving under any circumstances, and had little experience of doing so on the wrong side of the road, I became unexpectedly masterful, ordered Barbara into the passenger seat, took the wheel and headed back in the direction of the A1. As Paris fell away behind us, Barbara's spirits revived, helped along by generous slugs of whisky from the wicker basket, drunk straight from the bottle. 'Why are you driving so *slowly*?' she asked, as the rain drummed against the windowpanes and I peered blindly through the spray from a thousand lorries. '*Faster, faster*. We'll never get there at this rate.' We found a hotel in Ardres, a pretty village to the south of Calais. Rather than spend the night in the car, the Pussers were smuggled into Barbara's room, from which they mounted desperate attempts at escape. Next morning one of them refused to get back in its basket, but darted frenziedly about the room. I was amazed how lithe and supple Barbara seemed as, half-laughing and half-cursing, she hurled herself between the beds in hot pursuit.

A thick black cloud was hanging over the English coastline as we boarded the ferry, and Barbara's spirits began to flag. I bought her a double vodka to fortify her against the imminent loss of the Pussers and the steady approach of England, borne on the breeze in a steadily intensifying whiff of fried onions and fish and chips. As the white cliffs loomed above us, and the ferry drew alongside the pier, Barbara ordered me to defy officialdom and hide the Pussers about my person, but before she could put her plan into effect two men in peaked caps had whipped them away and bundled them, mewing, into the back of a van. 'It's all your fault that the Pussers have been removed, and I hold you entirely to blame,' Barbara told me with her familiar mixture of levity and malice, pawing my wrist with a feline forefinger. 'If you'd done as I asked you, none of this would have happened.'

From Dover we headed a few miles down the coast to Hythe, where Barbara had spent her childhood. The pavements were crammed with senior citizens of Barbara's age, many of them propped up by sticks or pushing tartan shopping bags on wheels, all of them clad in anoraks and shapeless trousers in dispiriting shades of grey and beige, the women clutching enormous white handbags that banged about their ankles. As we picked our way westwards, Barbara revealed that I would shortly experience something not vouchsafed to any of her husbands, lovers or friends: I was about to meet her sister, who was still living in Hythe. They had never been close, even as children, and Brenda, now a widow, was extremely proper and conventional: she wouldn't offer us anything to drink, and for lunch she would serve up slices of supermarket ham, a bowl of lettuce, a tomato apiece and a potato salad, with Branston pickle and Heinz salad cream by way of condiments.

Why, I wondered, were we taking time off to have lunch with Brenda if they got on so badly and had nothing in common? Barbara gave one of her silvery laughs, and revealed her master-plan. Some years earlier she had given Brenda a painting by an eminent French artist of whom I had never heard – a confession that was greeted with French mutterings of the *zut alors* variety, and much raising of the eyes to heaven. She had given a very similar painting, by the same eminent artist, to her goddaughter, Cressida Connolly, of whom she was extremely fond. It seemed quite wrong that the two paintings should ever have been separated from one another, and since Brenda was incapable of appreciating the one Barbara had given her, and would never notice its absence, we should unhook it while her back was turned, load it into the back of the car, and drive off with it as soon as lunch was over. My job was to engage Brenda in conversation, or ask to be shown round the garden, while Barbara, feigning a visit to the lavatory, stole upstairs and did the dirty work. When I expressed reservations about the whole business, I was told not to be so feeble, and warned that I was in danger of being struck off her list of friends.

Brenda lived in a neat 1930s suburban house, high above the town, with a trim front garden, Crittall windows, wine-coloured fitted carpets and a few well-dusted ornaments laid out on shelves and low teak tables. She looked like a chunkier version of her sister, with the same bright eyes, high cheekbones and Scandinavian colouring, but whereas Barbara was clad in a cowboy shirt with the top three buttons undone, a pair of skin-tight jeans and the cowboy boots we had hurled into the back of the car, Brenda sported a maroon twin-set, a 'sensible' plum-coloured tweed skirt which looked like a bramble hedge, and fur-lined suede boots. She seemed, beside her sister, homely, familiar and reassuringly easy to talk to, very much in the mould of a retired schoolteacher or librarian. Defying Barbara's gloomy prediction of a glass of sweet sherry at most, she had invested in a half bottle of whisky, which stood open and primed for action on an immaculate formica-topped table in an equally pristine kitchen; I spotted on the sideboard the slices of supermarket ham on a plate under clingfilm, the lettuce, tomatoes and potato salad, and the jars of Branston pickle and Heinz salad cream.

Barbara toyed with a lettuce leaf, pushed her lunch aside, and paced angrily up and down, puffing on a cigarette, while Brenda and I made polite conversation. To my relief, Barbara's nerve seemed to have cracked as far as the visit's *raison d'être* was concerned, and Brenda's painting remained firmly *in situ*. Barbara vented her frustration by telling me that I was eating far too slowly, and that we must hurry on to London *tout de suite*; with that she stalked out of the house and, after making apologetic farewells to Brenda, I joined her in the car. Barbara took the wheel, skimming the oncoming traffic so closely that – since this was a left-hand drive car – I flinched towards her with every approaching car or lorry.

Shortly afterwards, Barbara moved into a fourth-floor flat in an expensive but unprepossessing sixties block on the corner of Sydney Street and the King's Road, where she paced up and down like a tigress, occasionally pecking at her typewriter, while the Pussers trailed in her wake. Back in England, she was as bored and lonely as ever. The English, she conceded, were a good deal nicer and friendlier than the French, and she much preferred their sense of humour; on the other hand – here I ran my finger uneasily round the collar of my shirt, and strove to change the subject – they were so dull and unintelligent and lacking in style and sparkle compared with their neighbours across the Channel. After Paris, London seemed hideous and depressing; the television was no good, the shops a disgrace, the food repulsive, the restaurants a parody of the real thing. Had I been braver I might have asked her why, if she so disliked and despised us, she had bothered to come back, and why she didn't pack up and go back to France; but I knew perfectly well – as she often admitted, with a silvery laugh – that she had groaned in exactly the same way about the 'fucking Frogs', and would go on groaning till the day she died.

For all her brittle bravado, Barbara was a vulnerable and isolated figure. She was prone to debilitating attacks of depression and would take to her bed for hours on end, a bottle of anti-depressants on the table beside her, rereading Flaubert and Chekhov or simply gazing into space, her fingers twitching on the counterpane. She longed to be diverted, but those prepared to indulge her seemed pitifully few. Most of the people she had known in her heyday were dead; she had precious little family, and few with whom she wanted to be in touch; she was viewed with hostility and resentment by many of her fellow-survivors of upper-class bohemia, either because she had mocked them in print, or because, in the case of the women, she had over-excited their husbands, or because they remembered her farouche behaviour and her sullen silences, and thought her too tricky and too tiresome to be borne. And, for all her devotion to Connolly, she had never really belonged to his world. She was a good deal cleverer than most of the upper-class groupies who hung on his every word, and unlike them she could put pen to paper, to lethal effect; but she was, in the last resort, considered to be both common and tarty, and as such she remained an outsider.

The number of people who came to see her, or invited her out, was pitifully small: Alan Ross, the Donners, Cressida Connolly and her husband, Ali Forbes, Carol Topolski, Marilyn Quennell, and Glur Dyson-Taylor, who had been the third Mrs Quennell, and had known Connolly and his first wife, Jeannie, in the 1930s, when they too were living in the King's Road. I was a far newer friend than any of these, but felt I formed part of a lifeline. I dreaded ringing her up, but soon realised that the important thing was to make her laugh: she was always keen to be amused and to see the comic side of things, and once one had provoked the silvery laugh, the smouldering and the sulking were temporarily set aside. Petra and I soon became extremely fond of her, in the nervous, uneasy way in which one might become fond of some beautiful undomesticated animal that was liable to whip out its claws at any moment. 'Well, *you're* not much of a friend, are you?' she'd say if I failed to ring every other day at least. She remained as flirtatious as ever, but if I gave her so much as a formal peck on the cheek she went rigid, as if she'd been plugged into the mains.

Barbara's closest friend, on a day-to-day basis, was the caretaker in her block of flats. Tim was a genial Irishman who, when not at home in Ealing with his dogs, lived in a glass box on the ground floor, crammed with buckets and mops, and spent much of his time moving slowly up and down in the lift, a fluorescent affair with pink pile carpeting on ceiling, walls and floor. When not travelling in the lift, Tim liked talking to Barbara, and *vice versa*: she quizzed him, without success, on his sex life, while he advised her on her plumbing, the importance of making a will, her health in general and her eyesight in particular, and the workings of her television set. Before long he had assumed heroic proportions, and Barbara would pass on his decrees in an awestruck whisper; they provided a perfect means of breaking the conversational ice or, if she was in one of her black moods, providing momentary cheer. Tim's hair was a constant subject of debate. He wore a tweed cap which he never removed, and his hair hung below it in rust- or carrot-coloured curls. Barbara was convinced that it was dyed, and varied in colour from day to day, and whenever we spoke I asked her what shade of red he was wearing that day: after giving the matter some thought, she would dissolve into peals of laughter and blurt out 'Pillarbox' or 'Aubergine.' What went on beneath the cap remained a mystery until one day Barbara rang in a state of high excitement to say that Tim had, quite suddenly and for no apparent reason, whipped off his cap and, bending low before her, revealed a cranium as bald as an egg. This remained a single sighting, and was never referred to again. Every now and then Tim would fall foul of Barbara's paranoia, and she would accuse him of riffling through her papers or, on one occasion, making inroads on her supplies of butter; but before long he would be restored to favour.

All this was entertaining enough, but it wasn't advancing my career as a biographer. One day, greatly daring, I raised the subject of my reading the letters in the plastic bags with which she had tantalised me on my first visit to France. She brooded for a while before coming up with a solution satisfactory to us both. She had never been able to read Connolly's handwriting: she would allow me to read his letters on condition that I typed them out at the same time; that way we could both enjoy them.

It seemed a dotty idea – there were hundreds of letters, jumbled together and hopelessly out of order, and matters were made worse by Connolly's refusal to date his correspondence – but there appeared to be no alternative. Barbara lent me her old portable, stretched herself out on the bed, and, using her dressing table as a desk, I began to work my way through the mound.

Barbara soon became bored by the proceedings. '*Now* what's Cyril saying?' she would ask; I would read out bits from the letter in question, Barbara would give a shriek of mirth ('So *that's* what he was up to!') and, with luck, place the letter in some kind of context. But it was, I knew, a doomed venture: after a week's typing, endlessly interrupted, I had barely made an impression on the great wodge of sky-blue airmail letters. At this rate I would spend the next ten years at least working on my biography; some other way round would have to be found. After Barbara's death I was presented with a complete tran-script of those troublesome letters by a mutual friend who knew how much I wanted to read them, could decipher Connolly's spidery scrawl, and – miraculously – had managed to put them in some kind of order after much quizzing of postmarks. They were not the most edifying documents, with Connolly revealing himself at his most treacherous and self-pitying, but without them my biography would have been much the poorer.

A few months after her return to England, Barbara, restless as ever, decided to divide her time between London and a country cottage. Kent was familiar, and on the way to France, but it was too built up and too close to Brenda; and since she had no ties elsewhere, she plumped for Worcestershire, which was at least near to her beloved Cressida. One day she rang to say that, on an impulse, she'd bought a cottage between Evesham and Pershore: it was ghastly, and she hated it already, but she'd love to know what I thought of it. Once again we set off in the Renault Clio, the familiar snake of angry motorists building up in the Cromwell Road as Barbara inched her way forward in second gear; once again we squabbled over the map-reading, with Barbara holding me to blame when we found ourselves immobilised behind a herd of cows.

Situated on the edge of a village, on the slope of a gently rolling hill, and looking onto an orchard, with cows grazing between the trees, the Worcestershire 'Cott' was far worse than I had expected. It occupied a narrow triangle of land between the orchard and a busy rat-run, down which the traffic snarled eighteen hours a day; the garden, also wedge-shaped, was dank, sunless and carpeted with moss, while the house itself was a monument to English bad taste. It was a low, whitewashed nineteenth-century building from which every good feature had been ripped by its previous owners and replaced with something so dreadful that the only solution lay in total demolition. The front door had been elbowed aside by a teak monstrosity with a built-in fanlight enlivened with panes of coloured glass; the wooden window frames and mullioned windows had given way to sheets of plate glass and plastic frames; the fireplace in the sitting room had been torn out in favour of a bogus rustic affair made up from slabs of pinky-grey composite stone, like a Battenberg cake with a 'distressed' oak beam laid on top; all the old doors had been replaced by flat plywood affairs with flimsy gold handles. Worst of all were the ubiquitous tiles: corset pink in the kitchen, with grey flowers embossed upon them, while those in the bathroom were embossed with Spanish gypsy girls clicking castanets and Rhenish castles perched over jade-green lakes. 'You don't like it, do you?' Barbara asked in her accusatory way. I urged her not to waste another penny trying to remedy the irremediable, but she wavered between cries of 'Of course you're right – it'll have to go' and half-hearted improvements. These included persuading a friend to construct an elaborate chicken-wire cage for the Pussers, which led out of one of the kitchen windows and allowed them to enjoy some country air without being free to roam in the orchard or be run over by a motorist.

After a neighbour had rung to say that the 'Cott' had been broken into and burgled, Barbara finally decided to get rid of it. Once again she wheeled me into accompanying her on a last visit to clear out her things; once again I succumbed, partly because I enjoyed her company, and partly because I was still hoping to read those elusive letters in the supermarket shopping bags, and didn't want to fall out of favour with their proprietor. As we drove down she revealed that she had no time for Mrs X, the widow of one of her former lovers, and was convinced that she was conspiring against her. I had never met Mrs X, but she seemed to be a good and dependable friend of the kind Barbara could ill afford to lose: a keen DIY practitioner, she had made more than one trip to the Cott with her Black & Decker, and it was she who had single-handedly designed and built the Pussers' chicken-wire cage. On her last visit, Barbara revealed, Mrs X's behaviour had been particularly atrocious. They had opened a bottle of wine before dinner, and the cork had fallen on the floor. Later in the evening the cork had mysteriously vanished: it was obvious that Mrs X had stolen the cork simply to annoy her. Why on earth, I asked, should Mrs X *want* to steal a discarded cork? It seemed much more likely that, during the course of the meal, one of them had got up from the table, and kicked the cork aside as she headed off for the sink or the stove. 'Do you *really* think so?' Barbara asked, after greeting my explanation with a sceptical hum. 'But that wasn't the end of it,' she continued. 'Do you know what happened when we got back to London the following day? I wanted to refer to my address book, but couldn't find it anywhere. I searched all over the car, and then I looked down and there it was at my feet. It was obvious what had happened: Mrs X had taken it from my bag and hidden it in order to get at me in some way, and then dropped it at my feet . . . ' It was useless to battle such paranoia: Mrs X had been expelled from Eden, and no doubt I would follow in due course.

We spent the day packing up, Barbara wiping the kitchen surfaces with screwed-up wodges of kitchen paper, using the same tight, circular movements I remembered from the cottage in France. At the end of each session of scrubbing she would mutter 'Pattati, pattata' – the inflexion rising on the final 'a' – before moving on to the next. The Hoover lay permanently poised for action, like some prehistoric creature of the swamp: every now and then Barbara would seize hold of it and set to with the same frowning intensity, paying particular attention to the armies of dead flies on the window sills.

That evening, worn out by our labours, we opened several bottles of wine; and although we staggered off to bed the best of friends, next morning Barbara radiated sullen disapproval, like a fractious and over-tired child. We packed the car with books and clothes and ornaments in a miasma of mutual hostility; and water turned to ice when – the car laden to the gunwales, the cottage locked up, and Barbara simmering in the seat beside me – I turned the ignition and nothing happened: the lights had been left on all night, and the battery was dead.

'It's all your fault,' Barbara repeated again and again as we trudged into the nearest village in search of a garage. I was ungallant enough to point out that she'd been the last person to drive the car, at which she altered her line of attack: the village policeman had a down on her because she'd refused to change her French numberplates for British ones, and he had come round in the middle of the night and switched on her lights as an act of revenge. She told me later that I was too angry with her to realise that this was meant to be a joke – 'You can't have thought me *that* dotty, can you?' – but when, three hours later, we finally set off, Barbara at the wheel, the mood was sulphurous.

We drove in silence as far as Woodstock, where Barbara asked me if I'd take over, since she was exhausted. The sun was beating down as we flashed along the M40, and Barbara began to complain of a splitting headache: would I *please* slow down, and would I *please* not drive in such a way that my right-hand wheel occasionally strayed onto the broken white lines that separated one lane from the next? Somehow we battled our way to East Sheen, where lunch was waiting. 'Well, *that's* the end of a beautiful friendship,' Barbara told Petra as we burst through the front door, but lunch soon brought her round. 'He was in a *filthy* mood,' she explained, over several glasses of wine. Afterwards we drove back to Sydney Street to help her unload; in a bravado display of motoring, Barbara did a U-turn in the middle of the King's Road, mounting the kerb opposite the Town Hall and ending with her front wheels jammed up behind a pedestrian barrier.

It turned out that there was rather more to Barbara's headache than a hangover or petulant exhaustion. Not long after our unhappy expedition, she began to complain of constant headaches and faltering sight. She shunted from one private doctor to another, each more expensive than the last; each assumed her to be rich, neurotic and hypochondriacal and prescribed yet another anti-depressant, all of which were declared useless after being washed down with a glass of vodka. Tim recommended an oculist in the King's Road, so I arranged for her to have her eyes tested and helped her to choose a more flattering pair of specs; but, unlike the expensive doctors, Petra was quite sure that there was something far more seriously wrong.

A day or two later, Barbara rang to say that she was feeling so terrible that she had decided to book herself into a 'loony bin' which catered for the very rich who were so depressed that they felt they were going mad, and could cope with life no longer: they were expecting her at 2.30 that afternoon. 'Couldn't you drive me in?' she asked, with that familiar mixture of menace and seduction. It was impossible, I said: I was expecting someone to arrive at any minute, and couldn't put them off, but I would ring Tim, and ask him to order a taxi and go with her to the loony bin. Tim, as always, was happy to cooperate; but I knew from Barbara's flat, dismissive reaction that I had failed her in her hour of need, and I never saw or spoke to her again.

Once admitted to the loony bin, Barbara – or so I later learned – cowered and shivered in a corner, or curled up on her bed in a foetal position. The following day Jocelyn Rickards went to see her, and was amazed when Barbara – normally so reserved and undemonstrative – flung herself into her arms and clung to her like a frightened monkey, begging her not to let her go. Soon afterwards she was diagnosed as having an inoperable brain tumour. The headaches and the fuzzy sight and the paranoia and the increasing ill temper were all explained; far from making a fuss about nothing, she had been dying all this time. She was moved to the Cromwell Hospital, with its emerald-green windows and the traffic roaring past. Torn between guilt and regret, I bought her an enormous pot plant, and lugged it up to the third floor; but Jocelyn came to the door, took the plant from me, and explained that Barbara was too ill to see anyone.

Shortly before Christmas 1995, the Donners drove her down to Cressida Connolly's house at Wick, near Pershore in Worcestershire. It was, I gathered, a hellish journey, with Barbara complaining about the pain in her head whenever the car went over a bump; but at least she was going to die surrounded by the people she loved, and with the Pussers standing by. In her marvellous funeral oration – both touching and funny, and made all the more effective by her exact imitation of Barbara's lilting intonation, each sentence seeming to end on an interrogative – Cressida described how, after she and her husband Charles had decided that Barbara should end her days with them, she had rushed into Blackwell's medical section and looked up the section on brain tumours in a medical encyclopaedia, only to discover that sufferers often became extremely irritable. 'My heart sank,' she told us. 'Knowing how cross Barbara could be without a large cancer in the brain, I dreaded to think what she might become with one.'

And yet, during the month Barbara spent at Wick, 'all her rancour, sadness and fury fell away, leaving only the best intact: her intelligence and curiosity, her elegance, her marvellously soft skin – and a loving side I had never seen before'. Barbara had been thrilled when she was brought a mango in hospital by Alan Ross, whose affair with her over forty years earlier had driven Connolly wild with proprietorial fury – quite unreasonably, since she was married to George Weidenfeld at the time – and, according to Cressida, her love of good food remained with her to the end, as did her liking for champagne. Her attitude to dying – 'this business' – was humorous and unafraid. ' "Now," she said briskly, "do we have the fire business or the worm business?" I told her I preferred the fire business, but that, as a nature-lover, she might prefer the worm option.' Shortly before she died, as Cressida sat beside her holding her hand, Barbara sighed and muttered, 'Yes, very nice. This is a very nice business, I must say.'

She died at the end of January 1996, two days short of her eightieth birthday. A day or two later Petra and I drove down to Worcestershire for the funeral, with Alan Ross and Petra's old school friend Jane Rye. Although she had once hoped to be buried near Connolly in Sussex, she had preferred to stay near Cressida and Charles and their children, and had opted for worms rather than fire. It was bitterly cold and dank in the village church, and after the service was over, and we had processed round the grave, we drank champagne and warmed ourselves before the fire in Cressida's enormous dining room, a great vaulted chamber with a flagstoned floor, a beamed roof and a minstrels' gallery. Jocelyn Rickards and Clive Donner were there, and Ali Forbes, who had flown over from Switzerland, and Brenda and her daughter, and an aged, whiskery cousin, who had last seen Barbara in the 1950s.

As we were leaving, Cressida thrust into my arms a striped raffia shopping basket. 'I think this is meant for you,' she said. Back home in the suburbs, I took a closer look at its contents: a bathing costume, some schoolboy stubs of pencil, heavily chewed, and a thick brown envelope crammed with papers, all pushed in anyhow: letters, odd scraps of typed-up diary, covered with scribbles and scrawls, abandoned stories and fragments of autobiography. Some, the paper yellowed to the colour of tobacco, dated back to the war years; others were whiter and less creased and torn, and on them I recognised the typeface of her tiny portable Olivetti. Barbara had gone on writing, or trying to write, to the end of her life, and she often talked of writing memoirs of friends who had recently died, like Peter Quennell or Patricia Highsmith. Trying to sort out this rubble of papers, I suddenly spotted my name, followed by the epithet 'silly arse'. I couldn't bear to read on, nor have I dared to take another look, but the world went very cold, and I felt, as biographers are prone to feel, like an imposter, an outsider who had presumed on a friendship that had never really existed, and who could never belong to the world he sought to evoke and understand.

Writing to thank Cressida for lunch, and to congratulate her on her oration, and on arranging the funeral so well, I mentioned Barbara's unflattering epithet. 'I found this in a carrier bag full of Waitrose receipts,' she wrote back, enclosing another page of heavily annotated typescript. 'I thought it might make amends for the silly arse remark: hope so.' 'It was one of those friendships, regardless of age, that can spring up overnight,' Barbara had written under my name:

> Friendship can be ignited by admiration, physical attraction, similar tastes or a mutual sense of humour. It can come about late in life, and peter out as soon as it has arisen. You can go on meeting, but the original affinity loses its intensity. There are many different kinds of friend: a selfish friend, an unselfish friend, one who gives good advice, another unsound. The worst kind, of course, is the fair-weather friend, and there are plenty of those about. Some people have the gift of friendship, others don't.

The piece petered out before I could discover what kind of friend I was, but I learned that I was 'a big, tweedy, smiling man wearing green corduroy trousers and highly polished shoes', that I shared her enthusiasm for wine, and that – at first meeting – I 'appeared to be extremely jovial and easy to talk to, with a likeable tail-wagging charm, not at all intimidating or highbrow'. I wasn't sure about the tail-wagging business – it was almost as bad as Anthony Powell comparing me to a 'floppy labrador' in his *Journals*, or James Lees-Milne likening me to a scoutmaster in the *Spectator* – but otherwise it seemed fair enough. I was sad that Barbara didn't live to read my biography: I hope she'd have liked the jokes, both Connolly's and mine, greeting each one with a silvery laugh.

But that was not the end of the affair. Barbara had also given me various diaries and papers of her own, and these included some unkind remarks about her second husband, George Weidenfeld. Alan Ross had told me how upset Weidenfeld had been by her bitchy if comical account of their relationship in her memoirs; and now I was not only reopening old wounds, but adding second-hand salt of my own. After I'd finished my book, I sent Lord Weidenfeld the relevant pages with a note saying how sorry I was to bring all this up once more, and asking if he could bear to check it for inaccuracies. The weeks went by, and I heard nothing; Cape wanted to get the book into production; I dreaded a writ for libel, or a terrible cry of rage.

I got home one evening, and my youngest daughter, Hattie, told me that a foreign-sounding man had rung a couple of times: could I ring him back? Heart pounding, I picked up the phone and rang Weidenfeld at his home on Chelsea Embankment. A purring, slightly inflected voice told me that the chapter I had sent him was most elegantly done, that he was full of admiration; when I apologised for raising old ghosts he assured me that I should not worry, that it was all ancient history, but would I mind terribly if he suggested some very small corrections? Of course not, I cried, bending low with gratitude and pleasure. He hoped I wouldn't mind, but a particular date was wrong: no problem. I had misquoted from the Latin: I was happy to stand corrected. Was there anything else in need of amendment? Well, he said, it was rather a pity that I'd made mention of – and here he referred to an unkind observation of Barbara's, culled from the papers she'd left me rather than the published memoirs. It wasn't libellous, and I was loath to lose it, so I said nothing, and the conversation moved elsewhere.

'Now,' he suddenly said, 'I'm going to tell you something in the strictest confidence, and you're not to use it in your book. Do you know who told me, when I was in New York, that Barbara had left me and returned to Cyril?' I didn't, and begged him to reveal all about this key moment in Connolly's career. It was, he said, Caroline Blackwood: but that was for my ears only. This was, from my point of view, a fact well worth the knowing: while married to Barbara, Connolly was always hoping to seduce Caroline Blackwood, earning himself a sharp kick from her then husband, the painter Lucian Freud. Since

Caroline Blackwood had recently died, it seemed innocuous enough: but although, unlike the waspish aside to which Lord Weidenfeld had objected, it was a small but valuable part of the jigsaw, I'd promised not to use it, and that, it seemed, was that.

After I put the phone down, I wrote George Weidenfeld a brief note of thanks; and I begged him to reconsider about Caroline Blackwood, while assuring him that my lips were sealed unless he changed his mind. A day or two later the phone rang, and the great publisher was on the line. He had a proposal to make, and I craned eagerly forward in my chair: if I would remove that waspish observation of Barbara's, he would allow me to include the Blackwood revelation. I was more than happy to accept his terms; yet although I was immensely relieved to be able to go ahead, my overriding feeling was one of liking and admiration for my partner in the deal. Despite the carpings of envious competitors, I had always thought him the most glamorous and intelligent of publishers, a worldly, empurpled Renaissance pontiff adrift at a Methodist meeting, and now he had joined my pantheon of heroes.

While I was researching the biography, I wrote, as one always does, to old friends of his to ask if they would be prepared to talk to me. These included Lucian Freud, several of whose drawings had been published by Connolly in *Horizon*. He wrote me such a disobliging letter in reply that I have never dared to look at it since, but some time after my book had been published he rang me up out of the blue. He had, he said, greatly enjoyed my biography, and wanted to know if I could do him a favour: a painting by him of Barbara Skelton was being sold at Christie's in King Street, and since I had seen a fair amount of her while researching my book, he wondered whether I could write a short piece about her for the accompanying catalogue. Had I been an austere and honourable figure, I would have replied 'I don't know how you have the effrontery to ask! Certainly not, after the letter you wrote me'; as it was, I bowed low over the phone, muttered something about how thrilled and flattered I felt, and – at his suggestion – hurried off to King Street to examine the great work. Such are the rewards of the literary life – and besides, I needed the money.

# FOREIGN CORRESPONDENT

# EIGHTEEN

# Conversing in Como

A year or two after my biography of Cyril Connolly had been published, I was sitting in my study one afternoon, fighting off sleep, when the phone rang and a voice announced itself as belonging to Grey Gowrie. I knew who Grey Gowrie was – as well as writing poetry and making occasional appearances in *Private Eye*, he had been a minister in Mrs Thatcher's government, and during my time at Chatto I had edited books by his younger brother, Malise Ruthven – but although we had never met I felt I had gone up in the world when he addressed me in the friendliest possible terms, as if he were speaking to an old and valued friend. 'Drue Heinz and I have been reading your biography of Cyril Connolly, and we think it's extremely good,' he said, after a brief exchange of pleasantries. 'She wonders whether you would like to join us for one of her *conversazioni* at her *castello* on Lake Como in six weeks' time. It would be marvellous if you could.'

I had never met Mrs Heinz either, but I knew her to be fabulously rich, and an unusually generous sponsor of the arts, and of writers in particular, offering impoverished authors with writer's block accommodation at her castle in Scotland, helping to fund the London Library, and financing one of the most distinguished and sought-after literary prizes. Cyril Connolly – perpetually broke, keen on the high life, and one of nature's freeloaders – had enjoyed her hospitality in the West Indies and at her house near Ascot, and I had spoken to her about him on one of her visits to London, where she had a mews house in Mayfair. Once a year, Lord Gowrie told me, Mrs Heinz invited a selected group of writers to her castle on Lake Como, there to spend four or five days discussing their particular areas of literary expertise: crime writers, art historians, novelists had all enjoyed her hospitality, and now it was the turn of literary biographers. There was nothing to be done; one had merely to accept, and turn up at the airport on the right day. It sounded perfection, and still more so on a rainy March day in the suburbs. I said 'yes' right away, and hurried downstairs to break the news; and I spent the next six weeks feeling very grand and pleased with myself, like an important writer at last.

I wanted to look my best when the day of departure dawned, so I got up early to wash my hair, shaved with more care than usual, polished my shoes till they shone like aubergines, and made sure, when packing, that I took clothes that somehow combined elegance with informality, as well as some copies of the most recent *Oldie*. By the time I got to Heathrow, most of the other guests had assembled. There were twelve of us in all, many of whom I knew already: they included Selina Hastings, Victoria Glendinning, Hilary Spurling and my publisher at Cape, Dan Franklin, and his wife Lucy Hughes-Hallett, whom I had first met twenty years earlier on a freebie to Israel. All this was very encouraging, and as we strolled on board the aeroplane and ordered our free drinks, trading vigorous literary gossip as we went, life seemed very good indeed.

It was blazingly hot in Milan – much to the discomfort of our leader, Grey Gowrie, who was still wearing his winter garb of an elegant but heavy lovat tweed suit, with a tan-coloured Ulster flung over his shoulders in the manner of Sherlock Holmes. His luggage, containing suitable summer wear, had for some reason been misdirected to Glasgow, and would be unable to rejoin its master for some time; and for the first two days of our long weekend he puffed about in his tweeds, looking so uncomfortable that I broke into a light sweat when he headed in my direction. After commiserating over his loss, we clambered into a bus and set off for the foothills of the Alps.

The rim of Lake Como is as heavily lined with houses as the Downs at Peacehaven or Rottingdean, albeit of a grander and more elegant variety. As we rounded a bend in the lake I noticed, to our right, the bright yellow hotel from the terrace of which, fifteen years before, Charles Sprawson had dived into the lake to swim to the other side and back: three hours later he had hauled himself up by a stepladder onto the terrace, mauve and juddering with cold, spraying water in all directions, and looking like a beached whale among the smartly clad locals strolling up and down after church or enjoying a pre-lunch Cinzano or Martini. Some twenty minutes further on, we drew up outside a set of elaborate wrought-iron gates, which opened slowly inwards at the press of a button. Before us a curvaceous drive wound uphill through English-looking lawns and bushes, punctuated every now and then by a palm tree; mountains loomed up in the background, as stony and perpendicular as those once imagined by Flemish painters who had spent their lives at sea level; a church was perched on top of a particularly vertiginous and inaccessible outcrop, and, had one looked hard enough, some naked hermits with knee-length beards should have been spotted scurrying among the rocks. We passed through a gate in a castellated curtain wall, and the *castello* stood before us. Pink, square and upright, with crenellations on the roof and gothic doors and windows, the main house reminded me of the kind of building that might have featured in an Osbert Lancaster backcloth for a Glyndebourne production in the 1950s. Behind it, on the far side of a gravelled courtyard, stood a handsome ochre-coloured building containing guest rooms and the room in which our *conversazioni* would take place;

white outhouses and cottages spread up the hills behind it, one of them housing the set of rooms I was to share with James Atlas, a New York editor and the author of a forthcoming biography of Saul Bellow; in front of the pink *castello*, over-looking the lake, was a gravel terrace on which we ate our breakfast, and beyond that an oblong formal garden was laid out, with a fountain playing in the middle, a turret at each corner, and a wall which, on its far side, dropped sheerly down to the English-looking gardens below, where the odd peacock could be seen jerking its head to and fro. Grey Gowrie, looking hotter than ever, introduced us to our hostess; we were shown to our quarters, and told where and when to gather for our pre-dinner drinks.

Next morning we assembled in the ochre-coloured building for the first of our *conversazioni*. We sat round a long table, like directors attending a board meeting; at the top end sat Grey Gowrie, playing the part of chairman, and the Irish historian Roy Foster, in the role of managing director. Mrs Heinz sat to one side with the late George Plimpton, the elegant, affable editor of the *Paris Review*, whose funny, graceful accounts of his attempts to compete with the leading sportsmen of the day I had so enjoyed when working for André Deutsch nearly thirty years before; his job was to man a gigantic, old-fashioned tape recorder, the spools of which spun slowly round as the morning wore on, recording our every word for posterity and, in suitably edited form, for the pages of the *Paris Review*, which was owned by our hostess.

Each of us, in turn, was asked to make a short impromptu speech, introducing ourselves and explaining how and why we had written our most recent biography. Since I had only written one, I felt worse qualified than most of those present; I am very easily afflicted by feelings of intellectual inadequacy, and am no good at thinking on my feet, and as my fellow-guests articulated their theories of biography and the role of the biographer with enviable fluency and awe-inspiring displays of supercharged brainpower, I cringed back in my seat, hoping that a coffee break would intervene before I had to give voice. When eventually my turn came round, I tried to tell some funny stories about my dealings with Barbara Skelton and the other *grand guignol* characters who had loomed so large in Connolly's life. No one laughed and, utterly unnerved, I began to gabble, dropping names to left and right in my attempt to entertain and illuminate. 'I think, Jeremy, that we've had enough of this anecdotage,' Roy Foster declared from the far end of the table, at which I dutifully ground to a halt. Had I been quicker-witted I would have replied, 'But surely, Roy, even the most highly regarded biographies are, in essence, a string of anecdotes glued together': but I felt so overawed and dispirited that I lapsed into a sullen silence, contributing nothing to the social or intellectual life of the proceedings thereafter. As I gazed unhappily out of the window, the bright Italian sunlight seemed to shine with diminished voltage, and Eden seemed Eden no longer; I wished I was back in East Sheen, getting ready to go down to Waitrose or even mow the lawn, far removed from the literary world and the problems of biography.

From now on, to my discredit, I behaved like a bolshie school-boy, glowering at the back of the class and sighing ostentatiously: in my fevered imagination, Grey Gowrie and Roy Foster assumed the role of school prefects, while my fellow-seminarians were transmogrified into exemplary pupils of the most irritating variety, mustard keen, good at games and, unlike me, sure to win scholarships to Oxford or Cambridge. Our hostess had arranged outings to restaurants and boat trips on the lake to provide some light relief from intellectual debate, but I trailed along at the back, speaking to no one and scuffing my shoes in the dust. I admired the way in which she combined diffidence and resolution, controlling the proceedings while saying little and happily taking a back seat during our discussions; my graceless behaviour was a poor return for disinterested hospitality in an Arcadian setting, and although at the time I felt, in a half-guilty, half-defiant way, that it was entirely justified, I look back on it now with shame and regret.

Despite my ignoble and self-pitying behaviour at the *castello*, I continued to see Drue Heinz from time to time, most regularly at the party held to celebrate that year's winner of the Hawthornden Prize. And then, one March day a few years later, she rang us up out of the blue. 'What are you and Petra doing this Easter?' she wanted to know. 'I wondered whether you might like to come out to Lake Como. It won't be a *conversazione* – just a gathering of friends.' Feeling both gratified and a fearful hypocrite, I put my hand over the receiver, wheeled round to ask Petra her views, and eagerly accepted.

Once again I set out for Heathrow, only this time with Petra alongside to keep me company and boost the morale. After we'd booked in we headed off to buy ourselves a late breakfast of coffee and a *pain au chocolat* apiece. Richard Dorment and Hattie Waugh were sitting at the bar, eating oysters and draining the last of a bottle of white wine. It turned out that they too were heading for the *castello*, and that in itself seemed a very good omen. Although he spends much of his life flying round the world to cover new exhibitions and galleries for the *Telegraph*, Richard, like Petra, is terrified of flying, and can only summon up the courage to step on board a plane by filling himself to the brim with alcohol; another bottle of white wine was ordered, and once we had taken our seats on the plane he summoned up what looked like a triple vodka.

Again we took a minibus from the flat, dusty plains round Milan to the foothills of the Alps, passing again the yellow hotel where Sprawson had plunged into the icy waters of the lake; again we halted briefly outside the ornate metal gates of the *castello* before winding our way uphill to where Mrs Heinz was waiting to greet us. Thereafter all was sweetness and light. Hilary Spurling was already in residence, toiling over Volume II of her *magnum opus* on Matisse; so too was a jolly party consisting of David Hockney and his friend John Fitzherbert; his immensely tall and gangling manager David Graves and his wife Ann, who looked like Jean-Louis Barrault playing the clown in *Les Enfants du Paradis*, had appeared in innumerable Hockney paintings over the years, and, it turned out, had been born within hours of Petra in exactly the same nursing home; and Lord Northbourne, the inventor of the iceberg lettuce, and his wife.

Snow was still to be seen on the Alps at the far end of the lake, and it was cold and wet. Despite the rain, David Hockney painted every day on the terrace, perched under an umbrella, the occasional raindrop adding verisimilitude to his watercolours. He smoked incessantly, was deaf as a post, talked wonderfully well about every subject known to man, and wore flamboyant check suits with huge pockets in the lining from which he withdrew brushes, paints, a sketchbook and a collapsible canvas bucket; to his credit, he was a stickler for protocol, and made a point of wearing a tie every evening at dinner. One afternoon he said he would like to paint me in ink and watercolours, so I hurried off to my room to wash my hair, which develops an irritating curl over the forehead when greasy. We had two long sessions in his cottage down by the gates: he sat very close, leaning forward on a stool, staring intently and breathing heavily, his pens in his mouth when not in use, a cigarette in his free hand; I wasn't sure what I was supposed to do, apart from sitting still, so I stared back with equal intensity. Every now and then he would lean back and light a fresh cigarette, and we would talk about this or that till it was time to resume. I was immensely chuffed at his wanting to paint me, though he gave me unduly narrow shoulders and, seeing through all artifice, included the greasy curl.

On my first visit to the *castello* I had longed for it all to end, but now we dreaded having to say goodbye. At Milan airport Richard headed for the bar and returned carrying a tray laden with four glasses of white wine, which he drank like medicine, one after the other. On the plane home we agreed that it had been the best possible Easter, spent in perfect company – and it made me regret all the more my churlish behaviour on my first visit.

## NINETEEN

# On Safari

Every now and then we're offered a 'freebie' at the *Oldie*, and when a travel company suggested a week in Kenya, I hurried to accept. I had no particular desire to go there: what I really looked forward to was the sense of living in limbo, momentarily freed from the worries and responsibilities of everyday life, and the intense, short-lived friendships that the freeloader makes with his fellow travellers, very few of whom he ever sees again. I remembered how, on a freebie to Gibraltar, the military historian Robin Neillands and I had become instant best friends, spending long hours in bars together and persuading our driver to take us for lunch in Ronda while the rest of the party went shopping; or how, as the only members of the expedition, a girl from a magazine group in Peterborough and I spent several days together in Malta, and how – although I no longer have any idea of her name, and have never seen or heard from her since – I became an avuncular confidant, doling out advice and lending a friendly ear at dinner every evening. This time, it seemed, we would be spending the first part of the trip on safari, in the Masai Mara, and the second on an island in the Indian Ocean. I had fond visions of sitting round a campfire with hacks of both sexes – the men rather red in the nose, and watery about the eyes, the women equally convivial but less obviously battered by life – while the whisky bottle circulated, of long alfresco lunches on a palm-lined beach, followed by a short snooze and, in the cool of the evening, a little light sightseeing. It sounded like perfection, peopled by kindred spirits.

On this occasion, I didn't meet any of my fellow-hacks until we arrived at Nairobi airport, where we were bustled into a Land Rover and driven to the air terminal in the middle of the city. There were four of us, it seemed: a couple in their late twenties, both of whom worked for a lifestyle magazine; and John Kampfner, the future editor of the *New Statesman*. The young couple seemed interested only in each other, and far from paying any attention to the suburbs of Nairobi, they spent the entire half-hour journey holding hands and gazing into one another's eyes: he was skinny, with long black hair, sloping shoulders and a shortage of chin; she was draped in diaphanous white robes, and had tattoos tastefully placed about her body; both were pale, slow-moving and self-absorbed. Kampfner seemed an altogether better proposition: he was nearer my age, I instinctively liked the look of him, and he seemed to be both knowledgeable about, and interested in, the country we were visiting. We talked between ourselves all the way into Nairobi, and I looked forward to getting to know him better over the next few days: but no sooner had we arrived at our destination than he announced, to my disappointment, that he was heading off on a mission of his own, and that we would see him no more.

Within minutes of his departure we were being driven out to another airport to catch a plane to the Masai Mara. This involved a good deal of waiting around in the departure lounge, so I made strenuous efforts to get to know my new companions. It proved an uphill business. I asked all the questions, and received none in return; both spoke in a lifeless monotone, their voices as limp as their gait and their gestures. They worried about the availability of Diet Coke on their travels, but little else seemed to excite them in any way. After a while I gave up all attempts at conversation: I had two books to review, and when not reading I watched an airport worker standing on a stool and sporadically flicking the wings of a plane with a blue and yellow feather duster.

Late that afternoon we took off for the Masai Mara. Since the plane stopped every ten or fifteen minutes, rather like a commuter train, we flew close to the ground: the vegetation was spinach green, the earth the colour of goulash, and whenever we landed we did so in a cloud of maroon dust. We arrived at our destination, and were driven in another Land Rover to our camp on the edge of a river. Each guest, or pair of guests, was provided with a tent: dotted among the trees, and linked to the dining and reception areas by boardwalks, each had its own shower and lavatory, a carpet on the floor and another pinned to the wall behind the double bed, a cupboard and dressing table, a cloud of mosquito netting and the usual baffling array of dimmer switches. Our cases were carried for us by barefooted, scarlet-jacketed Masai: when not seeing to our every need, they spent a good deal of time sweeping the duckboards, and two of them patrolled the campsite at night to keep lions, jackals and other predators at bay.

As soon as I had unpacked I hurried to join my hosts for a drink. Middle-aged, English and wearing the inevitable khaki shorts and knee-length socks, they were a pleasant married couple of the Home Counties variety, and we got on extremely well. Just as we were settling into our second Scotch we were joined by my travelling companions. They were, they explained, rather exhausted by their travels; no, they didn't touch alcohol, but a Diet Coke would be very welcome. After which they relapsed into silence; nor did they open their mouths during dinner, except to point out that they were both vegetarians, and would not be partaking of the braised gazelle or whatever the dish of the day happened to be.

Just before we turned in, our host told us that he planned an early start next morning: shortly after dawn was far and away the best time to see wild animals on safari, and we would be leaving in the Land Rover at six. Anxious to seem a good sort, I was up on time, and made my way to the reception area where my host and a Masai driver were waiting, both clad in khaki bush shirts and freshly ironed knee-length shorts. There was no sign of my travelling companions. 'What's happened to your friends?' said my host at ten past, taking an angry glance at his watch. Five minutes later, he stalked round to their tent and rattled on the guy ropes. He didn't look best pleased when he reappeared. 'They say they're too tired, and that they're going to have a lie-in instead,' he reported, in disgusted tones. 'Well, we'd better go without them. We've missed the best of the day as it is.' Eager to disassociate myself from such poor behaviour, I unleashed an appreciative torrent of 'Ooohs' and 'Aaahs' and worked hard to ask intelligent questions as we bumped our way across the safari. Tawny-coloured, and with a range of blue hills in the distance, the Masai Mara looked a large-scale version of Richmond Park in autumn: elephants, giraffe, lions, hippos and the rest stood in for the deer, and I tried to look concerned when told that only a week or two earlier a Japanese tourist had been eaten by a lion after he had unwisely climbed out of the Land Rover to take a photograph.

The Drips – as I now called them, to myself at least – were still asleep when we returned to the camp some three hours later. 'What a shower,' said my host as he ushered me towards the breakfast table, where sausages and bacon were sizzling in a pan. Shortly before lunch the Drips sidled out of their tent; in the afternoon they came with us to visit a circular Masai village, but added little to the proceedings. 'Since you missed this morning's expedition, I've arranged for our driver to take you out tomorrow instead – so make sure you're ready at six,' our host told them before we turned in that night, fixing them both with a beady eye. I woke early next morning, and since I had nothing better to do I thought I might as well go along for the ride. Once again, I joined the driver alongside the Land Rover, which was throbbing and ready for action; once again, there was no sign of the Drips. We both went round to their tent and rattled the guy ropes, and after a minute or two a feeble voice said, 'I think we'll stay in bed, if you don't mind – we both need to sleep.' The driver and I set off to inspect a different (if very similar) stretch of safari: we made another trip after breakfast, and my host and his wife provided us with a packed lunch and a bottle of wine, which we enjoyed off the bonnet of the Land Rover.

The Drips, or so I gathered, spent the day drooping in deckchairs: he read a paperback fantasy novel while she filed her nails and gazed thoughtfully into the void. That evening, over drinks, my hosts waxed furious about the Drips, who had wisely retreated to their tent with a supply of Diet Coke: they had put themselves out to arrange an interesting visit, they were going to take up the matter with the tour operators, what could the Drips write about the Masai Mara when they had made no effort to see it, etc., etc. Few things are more enjoyable than working oneself up into a frenzy of righteous indignation, and by the end of the evening we had consumed several large whiskies and a couple of bottles of wine, and were in a thoroughly good humour.

Next morning we said our farewells, and took the flight back to Nairobi, where we changed planes for the flight to Lamu, on the Indian Ocean. The plane was a tiny ten-seater, and we were the only passengers. About half an hour out of Nairobi, huge gobbets of rain began to drum on the window panes. The sky turned black and then purple, lightning flashed about us like ack-ack fire, and the booming of thunder obliterated the drone of our engine. We were flying through a tropical storm of Wagnerian proportions, and the plane bucketed about like a cork in a high sea, lunging from side to side and suddenly dropping hundreds of feet before regaining its momentum. I was terrified, gripping my armrests and closing my eyes whenever we went into a free-fall, but took comfort from two quarters: the Indian co-pilot, who turned round in his seat and made thumbs-up signs every time we plummeted earthwards, his laughter growing louder with every fresh roll of thunder; and the effect of it all on the Drips. Mr Drip appeared to be in a coma, juddering with fear, his mouth hanging open and his skin more waxen than ever; Miss Drip became hysterical, screaming and tearing her hair with operatic frenzy. I took an unworthy pleasure in their distress, and although I had never been so frightened before, it encouraged me to play the part of the stoical Englishman, gazing unconcernedly out of the window and pretending to read my book. We arrived in bright sunshine at Lamu airport, where Miss Drip had to be carried out of the plane, foaming lightly at the mouth.

Lamu is a small island near the Somali border, settled originally by Arab slavers and frequented nowadays by jetsetters: according to the brochures, the warm winds wafting off the Indian Ocean are lightly scented with the fragrance of cloves, but as we approached the little town of Lamu by boat we were greeted by an overpowering stench of raw sewage. With its white-washed houses and minarets and narrow lanes, it looked attractive from a distance, but the poverty and the dirt and the smell were too oppressive to be borne. We wandered round for a time, and Miss Drip – rather rashly, I thought – added to her collection of tattoos, but it was a relief to be whisked off to the other end of the island in a high-powered motorboat.

Separated from the malodorous township by mangrove swamps, our destination was a sandy bay which had been converted into a luxury holiday resort. All the buildings were made of wood, with wide verandahs, huge latticed windows flung permanently open, and heavy roofs made from palm fronds; there was a swimming pool, an open-sided bar built from palm-tree trunks, and tables and chairs shielded from the sun by trelliswork interlaced with brightly-coloured flowers. Guests were housed in wooden huts on the edge of the beach, with dry sand underfoot and palm trees swaying overhead. The huts were mounted on stilts, and because the climate was so balmy, there was no glass in the windows, and our bedrooms were open to the elements: despite such apparent simplicity, each hut was provided with its own shower and lavatory, an enormous double bed and thick carpets underfoot. Everything was in perfect taste, and the camp was run by a friendly and convivial Englishwoman, who urged us to join her in the bar as soon as we had unpacked. It seemed the perfect place in which to spend a few days.

But not even this demi-paradise could rouse the Drips from their torpor. Far from joining our hostess and the other guests in the bar – let alone sampling the local brews – they preferred to sit by the pool, drinking Diet Coke and reading their books. Next morning, on my way to a swim, I asked them if they were going to test the water: but no, they didn't like swimming in the sea, and would rather stick to the pool. Over lunch, our hostess told us that she had arranged for us to be taken out in a replica dhow to visit a coral reef. At this the Drips turned ashen, and gazed unhappily into their wooden platters. They would rather not go, they said: they might be seasick, and they would prefer to spend the afternoon by the pool. Our hostess didn't seem too pleased about this, but luckily some of the other guests were happy to make up the numbers. I was horribly seasick once the dhow reached the open sea, and – unlike my companions, most of whom were tough, sunburnt farmers in their thirties – I made heavy weather of jumping overboard in flippers and goggles in order to swim out to the coral reef, and then somehow dragging myself back up the side of the boat while it tossed about in high seas. Without my specs, I saw nothing of the coral reef, let alone the dolphins and multi-coloured fish; but I was glad to have made the trip, both for its own sake, and because it further inflamed my indignation *vis-à-vis* the Drips.

Nor was I alone in this. On our last morning on the island, our hostess and I walked a couple of miles along the beach into the nearest village, since she wanted to show me where and how the locals lived. We looked round a school, where I handed out the ballpoint pens and T-shirts we'd been asked to bring with us, and I was bowled over by the brilliance of the women's clothes, so welcome after the dispiriting blacks and beiges that prevailed at home. 'Who are those *awful* friends of yours?' our hostess asked as we trudged home across the sand, and before I could issue my standard disclaimer she had launched into a tirade almost identical to that unleashed by the couple in shorts in the Masai Mara. That afternoon we took the ten-seater back to Nairobi: to my disappointment, the sky was as blue as the sea we were leaving behind, with not a thunderstorm in sight. I was glad to find the Drips were several tiers behind me in the plane back to London, and we parted at Heathrow without saying goodbye. I have never seen or heard of them since, but I wasn't surprised to learn that the magazine for which they both worked had gone out of business.

# TWENTY

# Auschwitz Visit

We visited Auschwitz in 1998, four years after my father died, and I thought about him as we poked about the huts in Birkenau, the doors banging in the wind behind us, and tried to read the labels on the great piles of luggage, now preserved behind glass, which the inmates had brought with them, and surrendered on arrival. He had visited a similar place over forty years before, and I wished I'd asked him more about it.

For the last thirty years of his life I hardly spoke to my father at all. This was not because we had had a row, or had come to dislike one another. We had been very close when I was small, and we both, I suspect, longed to be able to talk, to make our fondness plain: but he had retreated from life while still in his forties, and could only be himself when fooling about with my daughters, who teased him and ruffled his hair, and regarded him as a fount of jollity and affection. When left alone together we made stiff, formal conversation before relapsing into an awkward silence, broken only when someone else came into the room.

As a young man he had everything to hope for. Tall and well-built, he was good-looking, clever and athletic. He had a big-featured face, with large, round eyes, a granite jaw and thick, wavy hair brushed back from his forehead; he had the most beautiful hands I have ever seen, with long, spatulate fingers that seemed to tilt upwards at the end. He was Welsh on both sides, but after an expensive English education he had put all that behind him. He had spent his childhood in Bedwas, a grim little mining town in Monmouthshire, and grew up in a large, dark red Edwardian villa with stained glass in the front door. It was crammed with ornate and hideous furniture, much of it made from an unappealing gingery-yellow wood, Turkish memorabilia picked up on visits to Constantinople, and innumerable volumes of fairy stories by Andrew Lang, the illustrations to which, by H.J. Ford, depicted dwarves, goblins, witches and damsels swathed in sinuous Pre-Raphaelite vegetation, and were so terrifying that I could only bear to look at them through the partially opened fingers of one hand. My grandfather was a small, dark Welshman with a black moustache and black eyebrows who had done well as a businessman, and had eventually been pricked to be the High Sheriff of Monmouthshire. Years later, when we were living in Prince of Wales Drive, on the south side of Battersea Park, my father was pricked for the same post, even though he hadn't lived in Monmouthshire since he was at Cambridge: but he was far too large to fit into my grandfather's black knee-breeches and cutaway jacket and white frilled shirt and triangular Wellingtonian hat – all of which, plus a ceremonial sword, had been carefully wrapped in tissue paper and stored away in a black tin trunk – and had to decline. According to my literary cousin Roger Lewis, one branch of the Lewis family had done very well as pork butchers, but I imagine my father was embarrassed by this, and I only learned about it very recently.

My grandmother was thought to be classier than her bustling, faintly pompous husband, who had a coat of arms designed for himself when he became High Sheriff, and amassed a collection of trowels, the blades of which were engraved with details of foundation stones he had laid. A tall, gentle, dreamy woman who liked to read and play the piano, and walked about the house humming to herself, much to my mother's irritation, she was descended from a long line of Church of Wales clergymen, and claimed to be somehow related to John Morley, the late-Victorian statesman, publisher and biographer of Gladstone, and to Sir Oliver Lodge, a long-forgotten scientist famed for his interest in ectoplasm and other manifestations of the paranormal. Their three children were more similar to their mother than their father, being unworldly, timid, well-built, fair-complexioned and artistically inclined. The eldest, a girl, died from a brain tumour when she was still in her teens, and the youngest, my Aunt Rosemary, was fearful, kind and unalarming; all the family's hopes and expectations were vested in my father.

My grandparents' house was full of my father's work, reverentially preserved. Although he read omnivorously and, unlike me, remembered what he read, he never had literary ambitions, and his attempts at song were invariably discordant; but his long, prehensile fingers were more than just an enviable physical attribute. He drew and painted landscapes, portraits and detailed botanical specimens, carefully annotated and with Latin names attached; he loved working in wood, carving busts of himself and his siblings, floral devices of the kind one finds on the rood screens in remote Welsh churches, and modernistic cigarette boxes with the same precision and delicacy that he would later bring to his work as a surgeon, and to carving the family joint. The apple of his parents' eyes, he was sent to prep school in Hereford, and then on to Malvern, where he did well academically and on the games field, and won a scholarship to Pembroke, Cambridge, to read medicine. He rowed in the victorious Cambridge boat in 1936, the only product of his riverless school ever to do so, and because in those days Boat Race oarsmen became short-lived national heroes, his photograph was plastered all over the papers. An American film studio offered him a screen test, but he decided not to take things any further when they told him that he would have to have his teeth out if he was to make it in Hollywood: which was just as well, since he was far too shy and self-conscious to have been an actor. He was chosen to row for Britain in the 1936 Berlin Olympics, but he turned this down as well since he was starting his medical studies at St Thomas's, and they wouldn't allow him to take the time off.

He met my mother sometime in the late Thirties. They made a fine-looking couple, and her ebullience and force of character compensated for, and complemented, his reticence and shyness. She had left her home in Gloucestershire at the age of fifteen, vowing never to return, and, after training as a nurse and then a secretary, had done a variety of jobs. She spent summers working in a holiday camp on Jersey, had briefly managed a troupe of midgets, and worked for a time as a secretary-cum-receptionist for Boriswood, a short-lived firm of literary publishers best remembered for publishing the works of Georges Bernanos, the Catholic novelist, and James Hanley's novel *Boy*, which had been rejected by innumerable other publishers on the grounds of obscenity: every now and then my father and a Cambridge friend would stick their heads round the front door of the offices in Greek Street, wearing false beards, and ask if they had any dirty books for sale. In the early years of their marriage my parents lived in a series of mews houses and flats in South Kensington, and spent a good deal of their spare time in pubs, punting on the river at Marlow or Maidenhead, and dancing in nightclubs: years later, when my sister and I were in our teens, and far shyer and less adventurous than most, we would listen for hours on end while they told us endless tales of this pre-war paradise lost, and be overcome by feelings of inadequacy and failure.

During the war my father served as a medic attached to the Guards Armoured Division. He landed in Normandy, where, when not directing traffic or seeing to the wounded, he lay in a slit trench reading his way through a pile of red-covered Everymans, each marked as his own by the elegant pencilled signature on the top right-hand corner of the endpapers designed by Eric Ravilious, who had been reported missing a couple of years earlier. At some stage on the advance across northern France he skinned a dead sheep, salted the fleece, pinned it out on the bonnet of his jeep to dry, and sewed it onto the collar of a khaki American jacket: I wore it for many years at university, and have it still. He noted his progress across France and Belgium and into Germany in a tiny pocket diary, the entries restricted to little more than a word or two ('Arrived Brussels' or 'Very hot'). Years later, when I was in my teens, and had just read *The Scourge of the Swastika*, he told me how, as a medic, he had had to go into a concentration camp, and had seen the most dreadful things, and how his commanding officer was so outraged that he had thwacked the German Commandant across the face with his swagger-stick. He told me that story more than once, though never in later years: his diary, cryptic as ever, restricted itself to the word 'terrible'. Which camp it was I never found out, but he detested Germans for the rest of his life.

Like many of those who had been through the war, he had a soft spot for the Poles – a liking shared by our youngest daughter, Hattie. After she left university she spent several months in Cracow, teaching English in a language school and in a cigarette factory in the suburbs. Back in London, I wrote an account of our visit to see her, part of which reads as follows.

We have decided to screw up our courage and go to Auschwitz. We need to make an early start as, maddeningly, the last bus back to Cracow leaves at 3.15, leaving us only four hours in which to look around. We take a taxi from Hattie's flat to the bus station, where antiquated silver monsters growl and judder over the pot-holes, belching black smoke, and our fellow-travellers breakfast on dry-looking bagels. Trundling west from Cracow through green, rolling country, I brood on our motives for visiting Auschwitz, an experience I half long for and half dread: voyeurism and vulgar curiosity justified by a feeling that one owes it to those who died there to see where and how they suffered, and that it would be mad *not* to visit a place that is so infamous, and looms so large in one's consciousness.

About ten miles from our destination an old man in a pale grey, double-breasted worsted suit, orange shoes and a tweed cap flags down the bus, clambers on board and asks for a ticket to Oświęcim. To him it is, I suppose, the local market town and a modest industrial centre, as it was some sixty years ago, but it seems odd to think of Auschwitz as a commonplace destination, like Chichester or Milton Keynes. With his flat, round face, sturdy build, high cheekbones and pale blue eyes, he looks like everyone's idea of a Pole, and I find myself wondering what he has seen and known and experienced. Has he lived all his life in Oświęcim? Did he take just such a bus into market all those years ago? He's a good twenty years older than me, so he must have been of an age to be involved in the war, but in what capacity?

I was born in the year of the Wansee Conference, when the Final Solution was set in motion by Himmler and Heydrich. Two years later – by which time Auschwitz-Birkenau was fully operational – I was photographed, in woollen knitted shorts and aertex shirt, perched on a gatepost in a sun-washed Sussex garden: with my straight, flaxen hair and regular features, I look exactly like the sort of child SS geneticists strove to breed in Aryan stud-farms, where blonde, blue-eyed girls were impregnated by members of the master race. Brooding on this, I'm struck once again by the comparative mildness of English life and history, embodied in the tiny, benign-looking dolls' houses, each with its garden, car and drying clothes flapping in the wind, that line the road as one drives into London: a world in which Lewis Carroll rather than Hieronymus Bosch is the presiding genius, and Sherlock Holmes's comfortable drawing room in Baker Street prevails over the Cabinet of Dr Caligari. No doubt the relative geniality of our history goes some way to explain the

English virtues of modesty, tolerance, eccentricity and civilised debate; no doubt, too, it explains a certain whimsicality and feyness, and an uncomfortable suspicion, voiced by Virginia Woolf and Cyril Connolly, that compared with the great French or Russians, English novels often read as if written for children. But that seems a small price to pay to be spared the full horrors of the twentieth century.

As we near our destination, the country becomes flatter and sandier, less green and more forested. After driving through a suitably sinister pine forest, we arrive in Oświęcim, a scruffy little town bisected by railway lines, with an Opel dealer in the outskirts and a hideous concrete hotel in the middle. The bus drops us off in a side street, and we walk up what could well be the approach to a school, with a church at one end and institutional-looking buildings to either side. Eventually we reach a large car park, crammed with luridly painted tourist buses debouching OAPs, men and women in shell suits and hordes of schoolchildren, giggling and shoving in time-honoured fashion. We decide to visit Birkenau first, and then come back to Auschwitz proper: it's a mile or two further on and much less visited, and since it covers a far bigger area, we can get our walking done before it gets too hot. We climb into an empty transit bus, and set off in the direction of Birkenau.

Whereas Auschwitz was originally a Polish army barracks, Birkenau was set up as an extermination camp in which those who were not consigned to the gas ovens on arrival were worked to death before being gassed. As our bus mounts a bridge over a railway line, we catch our first glimpse of what must be the world's most notorious building, long and low and plain-featured, with a gabled gatehouse in the middle through which the cattle trucks transported their wagonloads of misery: it's smaller than expected, and its pink brick warmer and brighter. It's a bright, breezy day, the clouds scudding fast across a brilliant blue sky and tall, pale green poplars sighing and rustling in the wind: it takes time to adjust to the notion of Auschwitz in colour, with larks trilling overhead, farmers going about their business in the fields beyond the rusting barbed-wire fences, the blue line of the Carpathians shimmering in the distance, and a great bank of trees beyond the crematoria going sha-sha-sha in the breeze like those recalled by Cyril Connolly, heading south through France in an open car at a time when Oświęcim was still a small and unremarkable Silesian country town.

We pass through the gatehouse and follow the railway line, past the sidings where those selected to become slave labourers were separated from those condemned to die at once, and on towards the crematoria. The railway line bisects the camp: to the left are the brick huts once occupied by women prisoners, all of which are still standing; to the right are the men's huts, most of which were knocked down just before the Russians arrived, leaving only the blackened chimneys standing. The place is deserted, apart from a party of shell suits in the distance. Eventually we reach the far end. A hideous monument, vaguely reminiscent of Easter Island, commemorates the millions who were murdered here. The gas chambers and the crematoria at Birkenau were blown up by the Germans shortly before the Russians arrived, and little remains other than piles of red-brick rubble: explanatory notices do their best, but it's hard to make sense of it all. An all-male party of Orthodox Jews are photographing each other among the ruins: with their Homburg hats, white shirts buttoned at the neck, three-quarter-length black breeches and black frock coats, they look like so many magpies. Later, in the lavatory at Auschwitz, I bump into one of the elders of the group, a dignified old gentleman with a long white beard, clutching a cane; once again, I wonder what he remembered or had experienced.

Leaving the trees behind us, we head towards the women's huts. Built of the same pink brick as the gatehouse, they are more widely spaced than I'd imagined, adrift in seas of waving grass and dandelions. All identical, they are long, single-storeyed buildings, with windows to either side of a door in the middle – some of which have been embellished with strips of wood to give the impression of panelling and even pediments. To one side of the front door is a small room like a porter's lodge, the plaster on the walls of which, though faded and broken, seems to have been covered in a dark blue wash; straight ahead is a vestibule or open space, from which aisles run either way the length of the hut. In one of these lobbies I notice the remnants of wallpaper, a red and black pattern like the marks of a bird's claws, on a background of dirty cream; in another is a child's painting of children setting out to school. On the wall above the door are stencilled instructions in black Gothic script: 'Sauber Sein ist Deine Pflicht!' ('It is your duty to be clean!') and 'Verhalte Dich Ruhig!' ('Keep Calm!'), plus warnings about the danger of drinking the water. At the far end of each hut is a small, square room in which the brick floor seems to slope down, from all sides, to a drain in the middle: I assume these to have been washrooms of a kind, though since the camp was built on marshland, and the huts lack proper foundations, the water must have drained straight into the ground, making the whole place even soggier and more pestilential than before.

The main body of the hut reminds me of the sheds in which my Gloucestershire grandfather kept his cattle: the same dark wood, the same uneven brick floors with runnels to allow liquids to drain away, the same spiders' webs beneath the rafters and draped against the clouded windowpanes, the same smell of creosote, the same coo and flurry of pigeons strutting and beating their wings in the eaves overhead; but the cattle stalls and the warm straw and the gentle sound of munching have been replaced by wooden bunks, three-tiered, eight people to a bunk, with a wooden ladder up the side. It is very dark, despite the brightness of the day outside, and the doors keep banging shut in the wind, then blowing open again, then banging shut once more.

I dig my nails into the timber upright of a tier of bunks, as if by doing so I could somehow squeeze from it its secrets, and make contact with those who had lived and died here. These are terrifying and dreadful places, peopled by ghosts. I dread being locked inside by a door slamming shut, of having to spend a night on a bunk, too frightened to cry out: by some cruel irony, the ghosts I fear are those of the victims rather than their persecutors, of tiny, emaciated figures in soiled and filthy blue-and-white pyjamas hemming me in and clutching at my clothes rather than whip-toting Ukrainian guards or cold-eyed SS doctors.

Recalling his experiences in Dachau before the war, Bruno Bettelheim wrote of the way in which guilt makes one resent and then loathe the victims of misfortune or persecution, and how both guilt and physical revulsion hardened the hearts of the guards in his camp: and I think of how I resent and refuse to look at the pallid, whining, drug-addicted beggars who jump on the train at Vauxhall and process up the aisles, asking for small change to pay for a bed for the night, wishing us an unctuous and unappreciated 'God bless' while we stare stonily at our *Evening Standards* or gaze firmly out of the window. It's a relief to escape into the bright midday sun, and to spot the party of Orthodox Jews heading purposefully back along the railway line, towards the gatehouse and the summery world beyond.

Up against the outer fence, with its gravel no-man's-land beyond and porcelain electricity conductors and wooden look-outs on stilts, are ten latrine huts. Shaped like a dormitory hut but without the windows, each contains a long, seat-high concrete bench with two rows of holes, back to back and hung over a trough: like a hellish version of the two-holer lavatories one used to find in country places, perched above a pit and made of warm faded wood rather than abrasive concrete. In the middle of the roof is a stumpy, louvred wooden tower, to let the light in and the stench out. On one wall are stencilled more instructions to keep calm, with exclamation marks attached. Peering into the holes, I notice that an arc of carefully shaped and fitted wood has been set into the front quarter of each, running for some eight inches along the edge of the bench and round a small section of the hole before giving way to the concrete. Petra and I are both baffled by this: the user's thighs would have been on the concrete anyway – not that comfort would have been a consideration – and the wooden section was best placed to be rotted or fouled by drips.

Wandering back towards the railway line, we cup our hands to peer through the mullioned windows of a grander and more substantial hut than those we've inspected so far. I assume it must have been used by guards or trusties, since I can make out some washbasins and what must be lavatories behind a row of greenish-grey half-doors. Elsewhere are bare wooden floors and dusty panelled walls; outside, under a lean-to shed, is a ponderous wooden horse-drawn vehicle with two large wheels at the back, two small ones at the front, and an elaborate turning mechanism. It looks like something from the Keystone Kops, and I wonder what dreadful use it was put to.

By now Petra is exhausted and sets off, slowly, in the direction of the main gate, while I dart about looking at things. Left alone among the huts and the banging doors and the steppe-like sea of waving grass, my courage ebbs away. I want to look at a hut in which, according to the notice, Mengele carried out some of his experiments: but at the sight of the black front door flapping in the wind, my nerve cracks and I stay outside, peering in through the windows. I'm relieved to catch up with Petra near the front gate. Time is running out if we're to catch the hourly bus back to the main camp; four Germans hurry towards it, talking loudly and laden with cameras. I dart into one of the men's huts, wish I had time to take in the Commandant's house, and take a last look at Birkenau from a room over the main gate. Looking in the opposite direction, away from the camp, I'm struck by how close a nearby village is, and how small, mediaeval-looking fields come up against the camp, with only a narrow road separating them from the outer wire fence.

Despite the horrors perpetrated there, Auschwitz seems almost everyday after the bleakness of Birkenau. Grim as they are, the three-storey blocks in which the prisoners lived are recognisably those of a barracks or prison, albeit of a particularly poisonous variety; and whereas Birkenau has been left as it was, Auschwitz is much more like a museum, with photographs and exhibits on display and guided tours briskly moving about, like amoeba forming and reforming. After a quick meal in a cafeteria we walk though the souvenir shop, the information desk and the lavatories, and up a gravel path to the entrance gate, with its wrought-iron promise that 'Arbeit Macht Frei' still framed above it. To the left is a wooden hut where new arrivals were booked in and, in theory, went to collect their post. I gawp through the glass into dusty, greenish, wood-panelled rooms: in the warm early summer sun it smells pleasantly of pine and creosote, like a well-kept garden shed or the prep school cricket pavilions of my childhood.

We pass under the entrance arch into the camp proper. It seems tiny after the vastness of Birkenau. There are some thirty-odd buildings within the oblong perimeter of the wire, with gravel paths between them, and the ubiquitous pale green poplars rattling and sighing in the wind; every now and then the wind picks up the yellow dust and sends it spiralling between the liver-coloured buildings like a miniature tornado. To the right of the entrance is a particularly grim-looking set of buildings, low-browed and heavy-eaved, with huge and heavy chimneys up above: these turn out to have been the camp kitchens, and – to my disappointment – a sign informs us that entry is reserved to 'Staff Only'. To one side of the kitchens is a patch of gravel on which the camp orchestra serenaded prisoners as they made their way to and from Birkenau, where they worked as slave labourers for IG Farben and other firms; in front was the gallows, like a metal washing-line. The dark brick and grey or black wood and metalwork suggest a monochrome world, at variance with the bright blue sky, the scudding white clouds and the reassuring greenness of the trees.

Guide book in hand, we set out at a brisk pace on a tour of the buildings, which are lined up in serried ranks. Unlike the huts at Birkenau, these are solidly built affairs, with stone-flagged floors highly polished by generations of feet, and broad, handsome stone staircases with metal banister rails, reminiscent of those in a Thirties block of flats or a department store like Peter Jones. Several buildings are given over to 'national' exhibitions, dedicated to the sufferings of the Jews, the Poles, the Russians, the French and other peoples of occupied Europe; others have been turned into more general museums. Particularly frustrating are those which are closed to the public, including – just outside the wire – the Commandant's house and SS headquarters. I long to know what there is to see in their grey, deserted rooms. Has anything changed since they were hurriedly abandoned back in 1945, when the Russians liberated the camp? Might one still find discarded uniforms hung up in cupboards, or pictures on the walls, or cutlery untouched for half a lifetime or more?

Gripped, as ever, by small domestic details, I peer through a wall of glass at rows of sludge-coloured porcelain washbasins: they're more like troughs than free-standing basins, and at regular intervals the smooth flow of the orangey-green china is interrupted by a built-in soap rack. Each of the three walls visible from the doorway is painted cream, and carries a sentimental frieze, weirdly at variance with everything one associates with this place, yet horribly consistent with the glutinous Viennese or South German liking for *schmaltz* and sickly cream cakes: painted in shades of brown, one depicts two furry, beribboned kittens licking each other, another two nymphs cavorting, the third barebacked horsemen riding their steeds through the waves. I'm struck once again by the way in which sentimentality and hatred, kitsch and brutality, often go together, and the fascist liking for excremental hues. Mud-coloured lavatories are on display beyond the hideous-coloured washroom: lacking seats, doors and partition walls, and flushed with a stiff wire rod attached to the cistern, they look almost civilised after Birkenau's hundred-holers.

We peer into a dormitory, in which well-made wooden bunks, three tiers high, are crammed tightly together: the bedding has an austere and faded look, but at first glance it doesn't look that different to the youth hostels I visited while hitching round Europe in the early Sixties. Moving down the corridor towards the front door – the afternoon sun aslant on the steps, the dust motes dancing in the bright white light of Central Europe – we inspect a room that had once belonged to a capo or trusty: he was allowed a bed and a table, and his blue-and-white-striped uniform is suspended from a hanger. On the other side of the corridor is a room once occupied by an SS guard: it contains a bare pine table, an upright office chair, a bakelite telephone and, behind the desk, one of those multi-tiered metal racks in which office workers used to leave their cards after punching in for work first thing in the morning. Jamming my nose against the glass, I try to read what's written on the cards, but my eyes aren't up to it. Were prisoners booked in and out, like guests at a devil's hotel?

In one corner of the camp is the Death Block, where prisoners were tried by the Gestapo: they were shot in an alley alongside, and the windows of the neighbouring block had black shutters to prevent its inmates from watching the proceedings. This seems curiously squeamish, even genteel, given the horrors that were taking place all round – just as, in the curious hierarchies of death and horror, being shot against a wall seems oddly old-fashioned, almost gentlemanly, compared to being hacked to death with a spade, or drowned in a vat of excrement, or herded naked into the gas chamber at the other end of the camp. Executions by shooting and mention of the Gestapo remind us of Auschwitz's origins as a camp for Polish political prisoners: their photographs line the corridors, each snapped in triplicate – from the right, the left, and face-on – and wearing a striped jacket.

Later we realise that we failed to visit the basement of Death Block, where prisoners were held in cells so tiny that it was impossible to lie down straight or stand up to one's full height. I'm a tall man, and the thought of this gives me instant claustrophobia: I kick myself for not reading the guide book carefully enough, but am half-relieved as well. Instead we hurry on to the 'museum' blocks, with their notorious freights of human hair, spectacles, artificial limbs, suitcases and children's clothes. Banked up against the glass, the hair, like the luggage, occupies half a large room: it looks dusty and grey and fibrous, lacking the lustre of living hair. The suitcases are piled up to the ceiling, each carrying the owner's name and home town painted in white on one side, and so are the discarded shoes: many of the women must have arrived in summer, teetering along in sling-backed, open-toed shoes more suitable for a cocktail party than the mud and slime of Auschwitz. Another glass case is crammed with combs, hairbrushes and toothbrushes made of wood, and a small cabinet contains tins of shoe polish: a battered tin of 'Nigger' polish, made in England, strikes a homely and oddly reassuring note. We linger longest over a cabinet filled with children's clothes, all hand-made, the dresses carefully stitched and embroidered in cheerful colours, the tiny cardigans knitted from thick blue wool. These mementoes of children are particularly affecting: I remember, in Yad Vashem, the Holocaust Museum in Jerusalem, being stunned by a blown-up reproduction of a famous photograph of a child hiding behind its parent as a German soldier advances on them, rifle raised to shoot, and of emerging into the sunlight unable to speak, my eyes awash with tears.

Time is beginning to run out, and I glance at my watch, wondering how much more we can face or fit in. Many of the photographs on display have become all too familiar, so we make our way down the camp and through the wire to the gas chamber. A low, almost subterranean building with a chimney to one side, it looks like the lair of some troglodytic monster. Inside, it's crammed with people, with rival guides battling to be heard. The gas chamber itself is smaller than I'd imagined: a mud-coloured room with white-streaked walls and a coved ceiling, in the middle of which is a square hole through which the Zyklon B was dropped. Next door are the ovens – identical, I imagine, to those of a modern crematorium. Given the press of people, it's hard to move without tripping over the rails along which corpses were shunted to the ovens, and we make our way out as soon as we can.

We still have twenty minutes or so before the bus leaves. I wonder about revisiting the Death Hut to inspect the cellars, but decide against: better, perhaps, to wander slowly back to where the bus will pick us up, and try to get a place near the front of the queue. As we leave the reception area, with its shops and cinema and *bureau de change* and the café in which we ate a waterlogged hot dog after our return from Birkenau, another party of schoolchildren surges past us, all identically clad in navy-blue tracksuits with three white stripes down each leg and trainers underneath. They look blonde and healthy and jolly, giggling and nudging and joshing one another: it may be that, in generations to come, when the last survivors are all long dead, the twentieth century is a fading memory and other horrors have been perpetrated by people battling for air, food, water and somewhere to live, this vile place will come to seem like a cross between the Tower of London and the Chamber of Horrors at Madame Tussaud's, and the terrible things that happened here as remote as mediaeval instruments of torture or the Massacre of the Innocents; but as they vanish in the direction of the gatehouse, these children seem to embody the temporary triumph of life over death.

My father, I suspect, was greatly affected by what he had seen on the other side of what had been the Third Reich. V.S. Pritchett said of the hyper-sensitive Smollett that he suffered the anguish of a 'man who has a skin too few'; the same could be said of my father, and his wartime experiences may have made him even more unwilling and unable than he already was to cope with a career, and to live up to the high hopes that had been vested in him. As a doctor, he was unusually kind and conscientious, but I often felt he would have been happier as a sheltered academic, dealing with test tubes and abstractions rather than difficult and demanding human beings. He had a poor opinion of mankind in general, but although he became, in due course, so detached and so reserved that he had very little contact with the world at large, he was loved by those who knew him; he indulged in rhetorical violence ('Shoot the lot of them!'), but wouldn't hurt a fly.

In the meantime, though, he had a family to keep; and even if his instincts were those of a recluse, he was not without ambition. He returned from Germany laden with looted carpets, brassware, surgical implements and a left-hand-drive Opel car; we moved to London in the freezing winter of 1947, and he went to work in a fashionable private clinic in Queen's Gate. He had, after St Thomas's, qualified as a surgeon, and as a urologist he specialised in illnesses of the bladder and the kidneys; the mantelpiece of our flat in Prince of Wales Drive was littered with grey bladder stones, like marble-sized balls of pumice or Maltesers after one has sucked off the chocolate. When not at work he was a dear, affectionate father, adept at pinning us to the bed by our arms and making us hysterical with laughter as we waited to be tickled. He worried about the moles on my back and round my waist, and from time to time I would lie face-down on the scrubbed deal kitchen table while he cut one out. But for all the tickling and jokes we were, as a family, stiff, self-conscious and undemonstrative, never given to kissing or overt displays of affection.

But all was not well. In later years my mother told me that, even as a young man, he had to have a drink before he could face a party or a social gathering of any kind; they had all drunk like fishes in that carefree pre-war world, but as he moved into his thirties and forties the drink became a problem. It began to affect his standing, if not his performance, at the Queen's Gate Clinic, which may explain why, in the mid-1950s, he decided to start afresh in the Canadian prairies. Regina, Saskatchewan, could hardly have been more different from South Kensington, geographically or in terms of its clientele, and it proved a disaster. He had a total nervous breakdown, exacerbated by a cocktail of drink and phenobarbitone, and we limped home after six months.

By now his days as a surgeon were over. He worked for eighteen months as a doctor on a cable ship, tossing between Mombasa, Bombay and Cape Town, and the drink was cheap and in steady supply; he went out to Sudan as a doctor, but had to be flown home after only six weeks away. We had led a peripatetic life since returning from Canada, moving from one London flat to another, from Iver to Wadhurst and back to London, but eventually my mother bought a windswept, wave-lashed cottage on the seafront at Seaford for £1,000, and we lived there for the next ten years: we had no particular reason to be there, but she had spent part of the war in Seaford to be near some old aunts, and at least it was familiar. My father eventually joined us, and in due course he set up as a GP. His patients adored him, and he took endless trouble on their behalf, but he found the whole thing an intolerable strain and once again took refuge in the bottle; and after a few years he had to give up his practice. He was never aggressive or unpleasant when drinking, but one knew at once, from the tone of his voice and an unwonted (and unwanted) jocularity, when he'd been at the gin bottle.

He spent the last thirty-odd years of his life as a virtual recluse, going for long, solitary walks over the Downs, doing carpentry in his garden shed (his tools immaculate and in prime condition, as if he were still a surgeon), peeling and preparing the vegetables for lunch. He and my mother smoked incessantly – the front room of their cottage was kippered orange – and did the *Times* crossword together at disconcerting speed. He never wanted to visit other people, or meet anyone new, and happily spent long hours rereading Dickens and Trollope, two authors into whose worlds it is so easy and tempting to escape. He felt, I think, a terrible sense of failure, and longed to pass retirement age, when people would no longer ask 'And what do *you* do?' His drinking and his sense of failure put up barriers between us, and he found it impossible to articulate interest in what my sister and I were doing, let alone encourage or advise, however proud he may have been deep down. I was in my early fifties when he died, but he still treated my sister and me as if we were children: intentionally or not, he always made me feel intellectually inadequate, possessed as I was of little Latin and no Greek, and no understanding whatsoever of the sciences. If I have deluged my own daughters with affection and encouragement and embarrassing emanations of paternal pride, and like nothing better than helping other people with their writing, this may to some extent reflect my own awkward dealings with my father.

He died in the autumn of 1994, not long before his eightieth birthday. He had a stroke just as he was about to pull some ivy from the front of their cottage, and was rushed to hospital in Eastbourne. Summoned from London, we gathered round his bedside later that day. Bare-chested and with various tubes taped to parts of his body, he was lying on his back, breathing heavily but incapable of speech or movement: the doctor thought it unlikely that he was aware of anything that was going on around him, but we took turns to talk to him, and stroke his arms and head, and hold his beautiful prehensile hands. My mother struck up a joshing friendship with a jovial Cypriot greengrocer who was a couple of beds away, and every now and then they would vanish into the corridor for a fag. Towards midnight she suggested that we should all go back to Seaford to get some sleep, and we crept out of the now darkened ward.

He died in the night, and I have always regretted, terribly, that we left him alone to set out on the most dreadful journey of all. I didn't cry over his death, as I did for Alan Ross, but for several nights after his death I found my eyes brimming over with tears, like a tap that wouldn't turn off, just as they had when I came out into the sunlight in Jerusalem after visiting Yad Vashem. There was so much I wanted to tell him and to ask him, not least about what he had seen in Germany in the closing weeks of the war; but now it was too late.

# ABSENT FRIENDS

## TWENTY-ONE

# *De Mortuis*

Most of us, in our teens and early twenties, have an almost neurotic need to keep in continuous touch with our closest friends, including those whom we saw yesterday and will almost certainly see again tomorrow. As schoolgirls, my daughters were never off the phone to friends they had left ten minutes before; as an undergraduate, I spent a sizeable slice of my vacations pounding out letters on my portable typewriter, hurrying down the road to catch the last post lest my musings on the human condition should fail to arrive by the first post; were I young today, I would stride about with my mobile clamped to my ear, and fire off even more emails a day than I do in my mid-sixties. I remember being faintly outraged by the casual attitude of my parents *vis-à-vis* their contemporaries: they spoke of them with fondness, and almost certainly remembered them as glamorous young people in Cambridge or South Ken in the 1930s, but they made little effort to keep in touch, or to make more than the most cursory visit; and when, in due course, they learned that So-and-so had died – unseen and unspoken to for a good twenty years – they continued to talk about him or her in the present tense, and with the same amusement and affection as before. This seemed unnatural, almost callous, to my warm-hearted, romantic younger self; but now that I'm their age, I see this blurring of the barrier between the dead and the living as a benign business, a means whereby, albeit unconsciously, we adapt to our own deaths, and those of the people we love. Or, as an ailing Allen Lane wrote to his brother Dick in Australia, 'Our old pals are popping off like flies, and I realise that I now know more people on the other side than I do here.'

Two ways in which one can pay tribute to old friends are by speaking at their funeral and memorial services, and by writing their obituaries. To make a speech assumes a degree of closeness and fondness for the subject, and the speaker is half expected to be moved to tears, or at least to suffer from a frog in the throat, as much by his own eloquence and nimble turns of phrase as by the death of his much-loved friend. Obituary writing is a cooler, more ruthless trade, so much so that I have sometimes felt half ashamed of my part-time calling, as if I were a professional mourner or a branch of the undertaking business: still more so when, as is so often the case, one is asked to write an obituary while the subject is still alive, on the understanding that one's words will be put 'on ice' and warmed up when required, much like a TV dinner. One tries to tell oneself that one is doing a last kind service for a friend, but it's hard to tamp down the feeling of being an amalgam of traitor, voyeur and spy – the sort of character who might riffle through someone else's underwear, or steam open letters on the sly.

Even when one has never met the person, obit writing is a riveting business, like writing a miniature biography in a day rather than over three or four years. Much time is spent scouring the pages of *Who's Who*, leafing through yellowing press cuttings, ringing assorted friends and relations, and – if the subject has recently died – begging the obituary editor for an extra hour or two, knowing all the time that even if one meets the deadline, the chances are that, with rival candidates for the obituary page's space raining down to left and right in an unstoppable flow, weeks may go by before one sees one's words in print. Gripped and touched by the minutiae of his subjects' existence, the obituarist sleuth-hound becomes, for a brief instant, an expert on someone else's life, crammed with knowledge which, unless he is writing about a friend, will almost certainly be forgotten within a matter of days – in itself a neat metaphor for the transience of earthly fame. Since I was thought to know about publishers, literary agents and the like, I was asked to write literary obits, mostly, but not exclusively, for the *Daily Telegraph*.

Among the friends I was asked to put 'on ice', some time in the early Nineties, was my old boss, André Deutsch. To describe him as a friend would have seemed, for much of the time I knew him, extremely presumptuous: I admired him as a publisher, and looked back on my brief spell as a junior editor at his firm in the late Sixties with pride and nostalgia; but, a quarter of a century on, I still thought of him as a likeable but alarming figure, to claim intimacy with whom might have excited Bateman-like seizures of pop-eyed indignation, rather as if someone from the sergeants' mess (or lower) had presumed to address a brigadier by his Christian name.

Small, volatile and dapper, Deutsch was one of that extraordinary influx of Jewish immigrants who had come to this country before or immediately after the war: his coevals included his good friend Paul Hamlyn, his rival George Weidenfeld and Robert Maxwell, with whom, in the days before his disgrace, Deutsch would sometimes enjoy conversations at our editorial meetings, with the teak-lined speaking box on his desk turned up loud. Unlike George Weidenfeld, who kept his distance from clubbish, convivial London publishers, far preferring to mix with newspaper proprietors, Cabinet Ministers, film moguls and literary socialites than with booksellers, printers, paper-makers, literary agents and suchlike riff-raff, Deutsch was popular with his fellow practitioners; no doubt he suffered from the genteel anti-Semitism endemic among the English middle classes of my parents' generation, but before long he came to exemplify the prevailing ideal of the publisher as a kind of superior tradesman, nimble and sure-footed in the pursuit of both profit and excellence, but without the social, literary and political pretensions of their American and European equivalents, who were more likely to see themselves as important public figures, arbiters of taste and scholarship, and pillars of whatever Estate publishers belong to.

I left the firm in 1970, and I don't remember clapping eyes on André – as we called him, bravely, behind his back – for nearly twenty years. One day, towards the end of my time at Chatto, I was heading up Tottenham Court Road, en route for the office in Bedford Square, when I spotted a familiar figure in front of me, made even smaller than remembered by the fact that he was walking in the gutter rather than on the pavement, and recognisable at once by his wavy silver hair and square-shaped head, like that of a diminutive Roman emperor. As I drew level, I did what I would never have contemplated doing all those years before: I reached down, and tapped him on the shoulder of his silver-grey lightweight suit. 'My dear boy,' he said, 'how very nice to see you. Come back to the office and tell me what you've been up to.' He had recently sold his firm, and as we made our way along Great Russell Street – André clutching my upper arm as he spoke, while I looked down from a height – he told me of the alleged iniquities perpetrated by his new partner; and I found myself amazed, not for the last time, by the way in which otherwise shrewd and level-headed businessmen can sell their companies, pocket the proceeds and expect to continue running the business as before. Over the next few years André spent a good deal of time and energy complaining to the world at large about how badly he had been treated, and since he was a well-liked figure in the publishing world, he received a sympathetic hearing: but, fond as I was of André, I couldn't help feeling that Tom Rosenthal – himself a fine and distinguished publisher, but transmogrified overnight from saviour of the firm to its fearful nemesis – was getting rather a raw deal.

A few years later I was asked by the *Daily Telegraph* to write André's obituary: he hadn't died, but he wasn't in good health, and was well into his seventies. I wrote an affectionate and admiring piece, reminding readers that, as an enemy alien, he had been briefly interned in the parrot house at Manchester Zoo, that George Orwell had urged him to publish *Animal Farm* (he had not yet set up on his own, and was in no position to take up the offer), and how, during a sales conference held in his first-floor office overlooking Great Russell Street, he had been unable to resist taking a phone call from New York while Laurie Lee was entertaining the reps with a violin solo: since André insisted on leaving the teak-lined speaker on at full blast, the sound of the fiddle fought for our attention with transatlantic shouting as we craned eagerly forward to listen to a master-negotiator hard at work.

I had just returned from posting off my obit in the pillarbox on the corner of the street when the phone rang, and a familiar Hungarian accent rang out. 'My dear boy,' it said, 'will you do me a great favour?' I was reluctant to commit myself sight unseen (as we used to say in the publishing business, though I could never quite understand the logic of the phrase), but before I could utter a word André was pressing home his advantage. 'I have greatly enjoyed the profiles you have been writing in the *Sunday Telegraph*,' he said – Selina Hastings, then employed by the paper, had asked me to do some extended interviews with literary types – 'and I will die happy if you will write my obituary. I know the man on the *Independent*, and I'm sure I could fix it for you.' I couldn't bear to tell him that I had just polished him off for the *Telegraph*, but made low burbling noises to the effect that I was hugely flattered to be asked, and that of course I would see what I could do.

To do nothing would, I knew, provoke another phone call, so I decided to come clean. I wrote André a card, and told him that I had posted off his obituary that very day. I had an uneasy feeling that it wasn't the done thing to show subjects their obituaries, and that I could be jeopardising my career as obituarist to the book trade, but I offered him a choice: would he like to read it now, or would he rather read it on a cloud? Next day André was on the phone. What would I do if I were in his position? I told him that curiosity would almost certainly get the better of me, and that I would want to read it. We agreed that I would send him a copy, and I sat back and waited for the worst.

Two days later André was on the phone again. It was a marvellous piece, he said, but he had one or two tiny corrections to make: could we discuss them over lunch? He had always been famed for his cheese-paring ways – his recycled envelopes and low-watt lightbulbs loomed large in publishing folklore, and he was rumoured to have lost one of his most distinguished authors, famed for his love of vintage wines, by his insistence on serving the cheapest plonk on the market – so an invitation to lunch was not to be spurned. In the event, my obituary earned me three lunches at an extremely expensive restaurant on the Fulham Road.

André's editorial changes were of the footling variety, much concerned with his mother's racial origins – a dash of Turkish blood was somehow involved – and where his father had trained as a dentist: but he had finally, and unhappily, severed all connections with the firm he had founded soon after the war, and wanted to talk about the old days, and to suggest ideas for books I might write. For my part, I was thrilled to find myself talking man-to-man with someone I had always admired, albeit from a worm's-eye point of view. Like all the best publishers, André in his prime had been both monomaniacal and workaholic, moving at speed from one detail to another and never wasting time on pleasantries or ruminations, but now he had the time to gossip and digress, and very entertaining it was. Every now and then he would pause and ask, in rhetorical vein, why he had let me go: but, despite our new-found intimacy, I wasn't brave enough to tell him that I had only accepted a job with A.P. Watt, the literary agents – a type of work for which I was utterly unsuited – because I couldn't screw up my courage to ask him for a rise, and knew very well that if I didn't move away I would still be earning £850 a year at the age of sixty-five.

I noticed, during our last lunch, that André was becoming much vaguer and more forgetful, scrabbling around in his mind to remember names and dates, looking panic-stricken when nothing floated to the surface, and losing the sharpness and quickness of mind that had been among his most obvious qualities; and from now until his death he slowly deteriorated. One manifestation of this was his moving out of his elegant house in Selwood Terrace in South Kensington. André had never married, but since the beginning of time, it seemed, he had had a girlfriend called Gwen. She was, during my days with the firm, a remote and mysterious figure, who never came into the office or turned up at publishing parties, but was occasionally spotted out of the corner of someone else's eye, like a snow leopard or the abominable snowman. She was rumoured to be extremely rich, married, some years older than her diminutive admirer, and, as a devout Catholic, unable (or reluctant) to obtain a divorce. As he grew frailer and more forgetful, André moved into Gwen's palatial first-floor flat on Chelsea Embankment, bang next-door to George Weidenfeld's equally palatial apartment: had André equipped himself with a Black & Decker, he could have drilled through the partition wall and surprised his old rival drinking tea from a tall glass in a filigree metal holder and smoking a large cigar while entertaining a concert pianist, a minor royal or a Labour Party peer. The two men had known each other since shortly after the war, when they had co-founded *Contact* magazine, and though they had drifted apart, they were invariably linked together in the minds of their fellow-publishers; although he never mentioned it, their proximity had a cruel irony, in that whereas André had lost control of his firm and his health, and had ended his publishing career amidst bitterness and recriminations, largely self-induced, George Weidenfeld was still intimately linked with the firm that bore his name, went into the office several times a week, had recently remarried, and seemed as bright and alert as ever.

By now I was going into the Chelsea Harbour offices of the literary agents Peters, Fraser & Dunlop (formerly A.D. Peters) once a week to read manuscripts, and when André learned of this he insisted that we must meet. One day he rang to ask me round during my lunch hour. That would be very nice, I said, but since I had never been to Gwen's flat, I needed to know the address. '*I* don't know,' said André, sounding surprised by the question. He put the receiver down, and I could hear him shouting 'Gwen, Gwen, where [pronounced "vair"] do we live?' '*I* don't know,' Gwen shouted back (it turned out that she was becoming equally forgetful). I told André that in that case I probably couldn't come round; but half an hour later he rang back with the address, and all was well.

A couple of months later I called again at Chelsea Embankment. André wanted to gossip about old days and to find out what was going on in the publishing world, so I happily agreed to pop round. I was let in by a goofy-seeming Scandinavian maid, and explained that I had come to see Mr Deutsch. 'Please to follow me,' she said, and led me into a vast bedroom, where André and Gwen were lying side by side on their backs on an enormous double bed, like a pair of Tudor effigies, staring up at a television screen which had somehow been bolted onto the ceiling and was showing a quiz in which the contestants tested their brains to the utmost to the accompaniment of drum rolls and high-pitched squealing. 'Mr Lewis to see you, Mr Deutsch,' said the goofy-seeming Scandinavian, and promptly withdrew. I don't know whether André or I was the more embarrassed; either way, he suggested that I should make my way to the sitting room, on the far side of the corridor, while he climbed into a dressing gown.

A moment or two later he reappeared, looking far removed from his normal dapper self and leaning on a zimmer frame. Lit by at least four full-length french windows overlooking the river and Battersea Park, the sitting room was replete with velvet-covered sofas of the kind that, once sunk into, are almost impossible to climb out of; two chairs were positioned on either side of a gigantic marble fireplace, one of which André took for himself while waving me into the other. A few minutes into our conversation, the door was flung open, and a wild-looking woman appeared before us, clad in a dressing gown, her white hair waving in the non-existent wind, a walking stick wagging in one hand. 'That's *my* chair,' Gwen shouted in my direction, waving her stick under my face, 'and no one is allowed to sit in it.' I made my apologies, removed myself at once, and took my place on an equally sumptuous sofa opposite the fireplace.

No sooner had Gwen sat down in her chair than she started shouting. 'I want my tea,' she cried; and then, when the goofy maid failed to materialise, 'I want my tea,' only louder. 'Gwen, will you *please* be quiet,' André said, cutting across the barking of orders. 'I'm trying to talk to Mr Lewis.' Eventually the maid produced a cup of tea, but still the shouting continued. 'I want to drink it from a spoon,' Gwen cried, overriding André's pleas for silence; and then, 'This tea is too hot. Please make it cooler.' 'Gwen,' said André, trying to be masterful, and slipping into an untruth, 'Mr Lewis and I are trying to have a business conversation, and we can't hear ourselves above the noise.' 'Well,' said Gwen, in the same stentorian tones, 'this is *my* house, and if I can't shout in my own house I don't know where I can.' This seemed entirely reasonable to me, so I made my excuses and left; they were still arguing as I saw myself out. I never saw André again, and he died a few weeks later. It was not the happiest of endings, to a life or a friendship; but he remains one of the heroes of my working life, an exemplary publisher who kept afloat, often by the skin of his teeth, and published only the books and authors he believed in.

It's just as well I wasn't asked to write an obituary of the eminent Bengali writer Nirad C. Chaudhuri, since although I edited his last and longest book for Chatto, I know very little about Indian history, politics and culture; and because Mr Chaudhuri was over a hundred when he died, and had been a controversial figure in the literary world since he published his first, much-admired book, *The Autobiography of an Unknown Indian*, in his fifties, he may well have been put 'on ice' long before I started work as a part-time obituary writer. In *Kindred Spirits* I described how, digging in his front garden in a dhoti and sandals, Mr Chaudhuri sliced through a telephone cable, temporarily disconnecting all the houses in Lathbury Road, in north Oxford, and how, on our first meeting, he subjected me to a musical and literary quiz which, to his delight, I miserably failed. He died a few years later: here are some concluding memories of the great man.

The last time I saw Mr Chaudhuri alive was on his hundredth birthday. Hugo Brunner, who had published him years before at Chatto, and had remained a keen admirer, arranged a celebratory party in Trinity College, Oxford. Mr Chaudhuri was now living with an Indian manservant in the same North Oxford house I remembered so well from earlier visits. The long-suffering Mrs Chaudhuri had predeceased him, worn out by cooking enormous meals for his admirers and pandering to his every whim; and as we sipped our champagne and waited for the arrival of the sage, I recalled my first visit to Lathbury Road.

Since Mr Chaudhuri was then writing in English – he was hard at work on Volume Two of his autobiography, the 950-page *Thy Hand, Great Anarch*, the successor to *The Autobiography of an Unknown Indian* – he was wearing a dapper three-piece suit, with cuffs on the wristbands and lapels on the waistcoat, and

Mrs Chaudhuri had been ordered to cook an English meal: had he been writing in Bengali, he would have been wearing a dhoti, and she would have been preparing a curry. Mr Chaudhuri and I sat in the dining room at the back of the house; he lectured me on the wines we were about to sample, springing from his chair with the agility of a ten-year-old, pointing out details on the labels and telling me how to hold my glass to the best effect, while Mrs Chaudhuri lumbered to and fro from the kitchen carrying steaming vats of steak and kidney pudding, carrots, mashed potatoes and cabbage. Some years younger than her tiny, hyperactive spouse, who must have been in his late eighties by then, she had recently had a heart attack, and was worryingly overweight. Every time I saw Mrs Chaudhuri bearing down on us, her features obscured by steam, sweat beading her brow, I leapt to my feet and offered to help, but was waved back to my seat by Mr Chaudhuri, who made plain his irritation at being interrupted in mid-flow while lecturing me on seventeenth-century weaponry or etiquette in England at the time of Jane Austen.

After we had eaten our three courses, all of them hot, I sprang to my feet once more, and offered to clear the table and do the washing up. 'No, no,' cried Mr Chaudhuri, in mid-peroration on the works of Hector Berlioz, 'I have a servant to do that.' I dutifully followed him back to the sitting room, where the monologue resumed. At some point I excused myself to go to the lavatory, and made my way towards the back of the house; and there, in the tiny, overcrowded kitchen, stood the hapless Mrs Chaudhuri, a crutch under each armpit, sweating heavily and working her way through a mountain of washing up, very slowly and with ponderous circular motions of the brush. I was far too fearful to defy Mr Chaudhuri's wrath and seize a drying-up cloth, but I wasn't surprised when, a few months later, Mrs Chaudhuri burst into tears while talking to Petra in the garden, and told her that her husband, marvellous as he was, was going to kill her off by his insistence on her cooking three-course meals for his literary friends.

Ten years later, here we all were, minus Mrs Chaudhuri, celebrating his centenary. Suddenly the door of the common room was flung open, and Mr Chaudhuri appeared. As always, he was impeccably turned out, in a suit rather than a dhoti; he was in a wheelchair, which had to be negotiated down a short flight of steps by his manservant. After Mr Chaudhuri had been handed a drink, the business of the day could begin. Hugo clapped his hands for our attention, made some complimentary remarks about the great man, and then, in his capacity as Lord Lieutenant of Oxfordshire, proceeded to read in Latin a birthday telegram from the Queen. Barely a sentence had passed his lips before Mr Chaudhuri interrupted from his wheelchair, correcting Hugo's pronunciation of every other word with much wagging of an index finger. Somehow the reading of the telegram was completed; Mr Chaudhuri, looking very satisfied with his day's work, was wheeled out and made his way back to North Oxford, and the rest of us could relax.

Mr Chaudhuri was not known for his tact, nor did he try to disguise his contempt for large swathes of the population. Despite his love of England, he regarded most of its inhabitants as degenerate, and a sad falling off from the men who had once ruled India; he considered the Pakistanis and Bangladeshis who ran corner shops or garages as the lowest of the low, and had no time at all for Africans. Years earlier, Alan Ross went to hear Mr Chaudhuri give a talk at Sussex University, and found it a mortifying affair. Always something of a dandy, Mr Chaudhuri believed, very sensibly, that our clothes influence the way we think and behave – hence his interest in uniforms, and the way he changed his clothes to suit the language in which he was thinking and writing. He had taken particular trouble with his clothes on this occasion, and was wearing (among other garments) a white lawn shirt with frills and filigree down the front. Quite how this affected his thinking was not clear, but at some stage in the proceedings he launched a fierce attack on Africa and Africans. It was, Alan remembered, fairly abusive stuff, and some African students began to barrack Mr Chaudhuri and demand his removal from the podium. 'What is all this nonsense?' he cried. 'Why are you great big fellows picking on a little chap like me?'

Some years later Mr Chaudhuri himself fell victim to the English tendency to lump together all dark-skinned non-Europeans as 'blacks'. Dennis Enright was working late one summer evening in the ramshackle old Chatto & Windus offices at the bottom of St Martin's Lane, when an elderly temp appeared, looking distraught and wild-eyed, and with her hair standing on end. 'Oh, Mr Enright,' she said, 'I'm so glad to find you. There's a *black man* in the office, and I don't know what to do about it.' Fearful of encountering a drug-crazed Rasta intent on raiding the petty cash, Dennis armed himself with a ruler and, with the temp tiptoeing tremulously behind him, set out to investigate. In reception he found Mr Chaudhuri holding a small grandchild by the hand: they were up in London for the day, she was bursting to go to the lavatory, and he wondered whether they could make use of the Chatto amenities? Lavatories loomed large in Mr Chaudhuri's thinking: he disapproved of the European variety, believing that squatting to defecate was healthier and more effective, and I remember him springing onto one of the Chatto lavatories to demonstrate how, making the best of a bad job, he always squatted rather than sat in the firing position.

Mr Chaudhuri died in 1999, aged 101. I was one of four people asked to speak at his funeral, for which a double session was booked at Oxford Crematorium. Looking very small and pale, Mr Chaudhuri lay in an open coffin in the middle of the chapel, and as the mourners filed past we sprinkled rose petals over him. I have no idea what I said or how it went down, but the last speaker turned out to be a menace. He had only met

Mr Chaudhuri twice, but admired him to distraction; and we knew trouble was in store when he strode up to the podium clutching a copy of *Thy Hand, Great Anarch* bristling with yellow post-it stickers, marking the passages he wanted to read out and comment on. We were obviously in for a full-length lecture, and after a couple of stickers had been discarded a member of the family asked him, in the kindest possible way, to desist.

When it was all over we gathered in a nearby church hall for tea and cupcakes. Petra and I found ourselves talking to Mr Chaudhuri's manservant. He spoke of his late employer with reverence and admiration, but had found him a demanding taskmaster. Towards the end of their time together (or so he told us) he had incurred Mr Chaudhuri's wrath by refusing to obey an order. At some stage in his wanderings, Mr Chaudhuri had acquired an enormous scimitar of the Arabian Nights variety; frustrated by belated physical decrepitude, he decided to end his days, and insisted that his manservant should cut his head off. The manservant refused, claiming that if he did so he would almost certainly spend the rest of his life in prison; Mr Chaudhuri accused him of gross insubordination; the manservant was adamant, and – for the first time in his very long life, perhaps – his master was forced to climb down. All this confirmed me in my opinion that Mr Chaudhuri was the most extraordinary man I had ever met: selfish and self-absorbed, yet curiously lovable as well.

Most literary men are brave enough when perched at the keyboard, but – in the post-war years at least – have lacked the opportunities as well as the inclination to match action to rhetoric. Best remembered for being condemned to death by Idi Amin after describing him as a 'village tyrant', and for being the subject of a mercy dash to Kampala by the then Foreign Secretary, Jim Callaghan, Denis Hills was brave in person and in print. As a young officer in Italy at the end of the war, he had defied orders by refusing to return captured Russian soldiers to Stalin's mercies, urging them to make a dash for it while his superior officers were otherwise engaged; at a more parochial level, I remember him telling us, with glee, how he had spotted a couple of yobs vandalising a phone box in Twickenham and, stealing up behind them to catch them unawares, had seized them both by the scruff of the neck, kneed them in the buttocks, one after the other, and sent them on their way. He was then in his early eighties; knowing what a tough old bird he was, I saw no reason to disbelieve him.

I first met Denis in the early eighties, when Hugo Brunner, then still at Chatto, took on a book he had written about his adventures in Southern Africa. Richard Cobb, another of Hugo's authors, was a keen admirer, as was my old friend Michael Wharton, best remembered as the *Daily Telegraph*'s 'Peter Simple'. They had been in the same college at Oxford; I don't think they had met for years, but each asked after the other with affection and admiration. 'How *is* old Michael Nathan?' Denis would ask, with a wicked glimmer in his eye, before regaling us with the story of how, in a drunken frenzy, Michael had dismembered a sofa in his rooms in Lincoln and hurled the pieces into the quad. (At some point in his career Michael had changed his surname from Nathan to Wharton: he liked the notion of being the scion of an English country house, whereas his father's family were Jewish-German immigrants who had settled in Bradford.) Denis had recently come back from a return trip to his beloved Poland – he had not been there since before the war, and had been expelled by the authorities – and was living in the rusty white camper-van he had brought back with him from his time as a teacher in Africa. Like André Deutsch, he had the head of a Roman emperor; but whereas André would have been a domestic emperor, much involved with the intrigues and minutiae of imperial life in Rome itself, Denis was of the conquering, martial variety, never happier than when slaughtering obscure Germanic tribesmen. As a young man he must have caused havoc among the ladies: even in old age he remained a strong, fit-looking character, with broad shoulders, a muscular torso and not an inch of surplus flesh; he had a resolute, aquiline nose, a firm jaw, cold sea-green eyes, and thick grey hair brushed back from his forehead. He had the yellow, faintly kippered look of the heavy smoker; he liked flirting and exchanging cigarettes with my mother, and his eyes lit up when my daughter Hattie came home from Poland with a large supply of vodka.

Clever, good-looking and a keen games-player, the young Denis must have been disconcertingly self-confident and a bit of a bully. Shunning the left-wing views of most of his contemporaries, he went to Germany after leaving Oxford in the mid-1930s, working there as a labourer for several years before moving on to Poland, and soon coming to loathe the Nazis as much as he liked the German people. Less endearing is an account in his autobiography of how he and some muscular, games-loving school friends debagged a clerklike figure on a train, painting a face on the victim's buttocks, inserting a mock cigar between the cheeks, and holding the wretched fellow out of the window for the amusement of passers-by.

I saw this side of him in evidence at the *Spectator*'s summer party one year. He had been at school in Birmingham with Enoch Powell, whom he had derided and persecuted as a pallid swot who spent his days in the library instead of on the games field. Denis and I were among the first to arrive, and we made our way out into the garden. At the far end stood Enoch Powell, clad in a black serge three-piece suit despite the sweltering summer heat, his face the colour of ash. 'There's old Enoch,' said Denis, his face lighting up with demonic glee. 'Let's give him some sport.' We advanced on our victim, who seemed to cringe before us, seeking refuge in the shrubbery. 'Here, Enoch, catch!' cried Denis, passing an imaginary rugger ball in Powell's direction with a sideways, swerving motion – a gesture I remembered with dread from my own games-loathing schooldays. A look of terror and panic shot across Powell's face, as though sixty years had dropped away and he was once again the inky, despised school swot facing his tormentors; but then the professional politician reasserted himself, the years intervened once more, and 'Ah, Denis,' he said, 'how *very* nice to see you again.'

Denis had, I suspect, been equally ruthless in his marital and domestic relations. I never asked, and never quite sorted them out, but it seemed that he had deserted two wives, one Polish-Jewish, and one German; for all his charm and geniality, he would have been hell to live with, utterly uninterested in domesticity, regular employment, pensions and the duties of fatherhood as he moved about the world, from Poland to Turkey to Africa to the Balkans, teaching and writing to make ends meet, climbing mountains, mastering innumerable languages, and suiting only himself. Not surprisingly, he had earned very little, and saved even less. Shortly after I got to know him he sold the rusty white camper-van, and went to live in digs in a small suburban house in Twickenham; and it was here that the man who had refused to give the Hitler salute at frenzied pre-war rallies, and fought the length of Italy with the Polish Division, and defied Idi Amin, and kneed two shaven-headed yobs in the buttocks, finally met his match. His landlady, he told us in a theatrical whisper, made his life an absolute hell: she insisted on his weeding the garden and mowing the lawn, made him read the memoirs of her dog, and – worst of all – stole into his room when he wasn't there and drank his supplies of vodka.

More often than not these had been provided by his daughter, Gillian. She had been – and still is – famously beautiful; at some stage she had been discovered by Roger Vadim, and is best remembered for rolling round in the nude in Antonioni's *Blow Up*. She and her husband, Stewart, a friendly, bear-like music impresario, had a large house on the Thames near Maidenhead, and spent much of the year rushing between New York, London,

Moscow and various European cities. She was understandably proud of her improvident, feckless parent, and was keen, whenever in England, to take him to expensive restaurants and invite him to dinner in Taplow; but he seemed as baffled by their opulence and their kindly goodwill as they were by his insistence on remaining with his landlady, who seemed to grow madder and more demanding with every day that passed.

To provide some respite from mowing the lawn, hacking at the brambles which seemed to infest his landlady's garden, and reading fresh instalments of the dog's autobiography, I did what I could to add some variety to Denis's life. I introduced him to Alan Ross, and got him to review for the *London Magazine* and, later, for the *Oldie*; and I took him along to meet Peter Kemp, who had lived an equally adventurous life and, like Denis, lent support to my theory that soldiers and men of action often write far better prose than their more literary and desk-bound contemporaries. After leaving Cambridge, Peter had disgraced himself in the eyes of *bien pensants* by fighting for the Carlists during the Spanish Civil War, during which he took part in a cavalry charge against a flock of sheep. Enrolled in the SOE when war broke out, he had been parachuted into Albania, fighting alongside my old hero David Smiley, Julian Amery and Billy McLean before moving on to Poland, where he had found himself trapped between the Germans and the Russians, and spent time in a KGB prison. Since the war he had kept himself as a freelance insurance salesman, breaking off every now and then to report on some far-flung conflict. He had covered the Hungarian Rising of 1956 for the *Tablet*, and the wars in Indo-China; according to the journalist Dick West he had been parachuted into Southern Rhodesia at a pensionable age, his walking stick clutched firmly in one hand, and a few years later I received a card from Dick and Peter in Nicaragua, on which Peter celebrated the recent death of his old enemy, Enver Hoxha, the Communist dictator of Albania ('Stoke Well the Fires of Hell,' he wrote, in jubilant vein). I don't remember what the two old warhorses said to one another, but was struck by the physical contrast between Peter – frail-looking, leaning on a stick, and with one eye shooting out an angle, like Jean Paul Sartre – and Denis's sturdy, muscular frame.

When Peter died a year or two later, Denis and I went to his memorial service in Chelsea Old Church. Julian Amery gave the address, and the church was full of fine-looking Englishmen with red faces and white hair neatly combed back from the forehead, clad in chalk-striped suits and highly polished black brogues or chestnut-coloured suede shoes – a vanishing breed who had been in their twenties and early thirties when I was a boy, and were now in their eighties and beyond. After it was all over, Dick West and I took Denis to Daquise, the miraculous Polish restaurant in South Kensington which has remained unchanged since the early 1950s, and was traditionally the haunt of gloomy, black-clad Polish commissionaires who had come to this country in 1939 and remained here ever since. After several vodkas had been drained, Denis suddenly said, *à propos* one of the gloomy commissionaires, 'Good God! There's my commanding officer from the Polish Division! I haven't seen him since 1944.' Denis had been living in Warsaw when the Germans invaded, and had made his way via Romania, Turkey and Iraq to Egypt, where he had enlisted: he hurried over to join the commissionaires, addressing them in fluent Polish, and downing glass after glass of vodka amidst a flurry of backslapping; and so we left him to it.

Denis was never quite the same after he finally gave notice to his landlady – so proving, perhaps, that a little adversity does one good. He moved into sheltered housing in Richmond; he fell and broke a leg, and was sent to a hospital in Isleworth, where he addressed the African nurses in their native tongues. Gillian got him a room at the Star and Garter Home, at the top of Richmond Hill. I loved visiting him there, and fully expected him to share my liking for the polished brass and gleaming parquet floors and fading regimental photographs and over-bright oil paintings of Spitfires engaged in dogfights over the orchards and oast-houses of the Weald. But Denis was far too much of a loner to relish institutional life of any kind. He complained – wrongly – that his fellow inmates were all 'other ranks', and that there was no one of any intelligence to talk to; as we tucked into steak and kidney pie and chips, followed by apple crumble, in the huge dining room, he kept up a running commentary on the other veterans as they shot past us in their wheelchairs or hobbled up to join us at the large institutional tables ('Poor old boy, he's absolutely had it,' or 'This one's completely gaga'). At his funeral service, one of the speakers revealed that Denis had happily involved himself in the social life of the Star and Garter, and had helped to run the library; but that wasn't how he liked to see himself portrayed.

For all his mockery, Denis himself was beginning to fail. I brought him books to review, but he could only read a page or two; Petra found him the sort of wireless he wanted, but he couldn't remember how to work it; he complained that the nurses were half-witted, and seldom ventured out of his room. Death must have come as a relief for the old adventurer.

Books that make one laugh out loud are far rarer than one likes to think, and the subject of endless and often heated debate. P.G. Wodehouse usually comes out top, but although I loved him in my twenties, I have lost the appetite in late middle age: comicality needs to be combined with sadness, a sense of the absurd with a countervailing melancholy, and Wodehouse's genial socialites seem too lacking in humanity, too short in Chaplinesque pathos, to engage me as much as they did. One of my candidates for the funniest book ever written – battling it out with Mr Pooter, James Lees-Milne's *Another Self*, and Evelyn Waugh's *Black Mischief* – is H.F. Ellis's *The Papers of*

*A.J. Wentworth BA*, a work that is all too redolent of familiar human frailties.

A.J. Wentworth is an old-fashioned prep schoolmaster of the pompous, bustling, self-important variety. Utterly ineffectual at controlling his pupils but much given to ferocious rhetoric and the consoling saws of his trade, he has been teaching maths at the school for most of his life, and the end of his career is in sight. Written, like *The Diary of a Nobody*, in diary form, the book begins on a note of crisis. Enraged beyond endurance by a pestilential boy called Mason, Wentworth has hurled a copy of Hall and Knight at the wretched youth, but misaimed and brought down another pupil instead. 'It has been suggested that it was intended to hit Hopgood II. This is false. I never wake up sleeping boys by throwing books at them, as hundreds of old Burgrove boys will be able to testify,' he tells us. Unmoved by his teacher's fury, Mason continues to distract and defy with loathsome insouciance. 'I never overlook impertinence, and I gave Mason a talking to which he will, I think, remember as long as he lives,' Wentworth would have us believe after he has failed to quell yet another act of defiance.

Regarded as an incompetent buffoon by pupils and colleagues alike – these include Matron and the Headmaster, the Reverend Gregory Saunders MA – Wentworth blunders from one humiliation to another. A pigeon is concealed in his desk and flutters out when the lid is opened (the boy responsible 'will soon learn, whoever he is, that it is a bad mistake to underrate your enemy'), paper pellets fly about the classroom ('This sort of thing has to be put down with a firm hand or work becomes impossible'), and a case of mass insubordination provokes threats of terrible retribution ('It can be imagined that I was in no mood after this to stand any nonsense from anybody, and IIIa found that they had a very different person to deal with this morning from their usual good-natured master'). He topples into a shoe basket, snagging his gown on the wickerwork, gets tangled up in a fishing rod, and becomes wedged in a drain while out walking with the boys. A new source of irritation is provided by the arrival of Major Faggot, a Terry-Thomas lookalike with bristling moustache and yellowing teeth who maddens Wentworth by smoking his pipe in the corridor, reading to the boys with his feet on the desk and handing out the pink blotting paper reserved for Common Room use only.

And yet, for all his absurdity, Wentworth is an extraordinarily lovable character: unlike Bertie Wooster, he is recognisably one of us, as endearing, absurd and touching as Mr Pickwick, another disaster-prone bachelor of advancing years. Like Mr Pooter, whom he so closely resembles, he made his first appearance in *Punch*, in November 1938, and was published in book form eleven years later – at about the same time that Nigel Molesworth of St Custard's was starting his own career in *Punch*. Comparisons with *The Diary of a Nobody* were inevitable, and deeply resented by Wentworth's amiable creator: but whereas Pooter was restricted to a single volume, the old schoolmaster resurfaced in *A.J. Wentworth BA (Ret'd)*. Published in 1962, it describes how Wentworth, now living in retirement on the south coast, suffers at the hands of WI ladies and jocular vicars: it has its moments, but *The Swansong of A.J. Wentworth*, published in 1982, is regarded by those in the know as an altogether inferior work.

Wentworth's creator, H.F. Ellis, was a veteran of both *Punch* and prep school life. Born in 1907, he was educated at Tonbridge and Magdalen College, Oxford. 'You think you're funny,' his fellow undergraduate John Betjeman once told him. 'Well, you are.' Between school and Oxford he had taught at his old prep school near Liphook, and after leaving Oxford he taught for a term at Marlborough. But he found the work uncongenial, and abandoned teaching for the more hazardous life of a writer. A cheque from *Punch* arrived just as he was about to propose to his future wife, and had an emboldening effect.

Sir Owen Seaman, the editor of *Punch*, encouraged Ellis to become a regular contributor; his successor, E.V. Knox, appointed him assistant editor in 1933, in charge of an editorial staff of four. The Ellises' house in Roehampton became a rendezvous for fellow contributors like A.P. Herbert, Bernard Partridge, E.H. Shepard and A.A. Milne; congenial ingredients of *Punch* life included long lunches at the Garrick and country house weekends with a cricket match thrown in. After spending the war in the Royal Artillery, Ellis returned to *Punch* under the editorship of Malcolm Muggeridge and Bernard Hollowood, serving spells as literary and deputy editor. He took an instant dislike to William Davis, who became editor in 1968, and severed all connections with the magazine. Salvation was at hand in the form of S.J. Perelman, who urged him to become a regular contributor to the *New Yorker*.

Ellis had been an enthusiastic rugger player and cricketer at Oxford, and whereas *The Papers of A.J. Wentworth* has remained only fitfully in print, surging back onto the bookshelves when an enthusiastic publisher takes up the cause before sinking back into oblivion, his account of the rules of rugger, *Why the Whistle Went*, was endlessly reprinted and translated into innumerable languages, including Japanese. He also edited *The Royal Artillery Commemoration Handbook* and co-edited *The Manual of Rugby Football*.

Although I wrote Ellis's obituary for the *Telegraph*, and his entry in the new *DNB*, I only met him once. Not long before his death in 2000, I decided to interview him for the *Oldie*. He and his wife lived in a remote corner of the Quantocks, and since we were spending the weekend in Somerset they very kindly invited us to lunch. We soon got lost in a maze of tiny lanes, and arrived at least forty minutes late, gasping and panic-stricken. As we screeched into the drive of a pleasant red-brick house, a tall, distinguished-looking man with hawk-like features came out of the front door to greet us. I knew from the back of my Penguin Wentworth that Ellis was a chubby-looking cove with moonlike features and a quiff of white hair. 'That's not him,' I told my wife. 'We've obviously come to the wrong house.' She let off the brake, and was just about to rev off down more country lanes when the Duke of Wellington tapped on the window, introduced himself as H.F. Ellis, and invited us in. Penguin, he told me a few minutes later over a stiff gin-and-tonic, had muddled his photograph with that of some eminent child psychologist, albeit of the moon-faced variety. It seemed a very Wentworthian state of affairs.

I first met James Lees-Milne – or 'Jim', as I was eventually emboldened to call him, in letters if never face-to-face – when I was working at Chatto in the early Eighties. Although he ended his days where he should have begun them, with his old school friend Jock Murray in Albemarle Street, Jim was a peripatetic author, being published by Hamish Hamilton, Collins, Faber and Sidgwick & Jackson; as well as publishing a novel and a biography of his old friend Harold Nicolson, Chatto had launched the first two volumes of his diaries, in which he described how, after being invalided out of the army in September 1941, he had rejoined the National Trust, and spent the war years trundling up and down the country in his baby Austin interviewing the owners of remote and dilapidated country houses, many of which were saved for the nation as a result of his endeavours. Some of the country-house owners were eccentric to the point of lunacy, and Lees-Milne had a keen eye for their foibles; I thought his diaries far and away the most entertaining I had ever read, relishing their combination of self-deprecation, comicality and – back in London between forays – feline literary and social gossip, much of it to do with Ivy Compton-Burnett and her companion, Margaret Jourdain, and the satanic publisher Charles Fry, who appears elsewhere in this book. Mr Lees-Milne was a close friend of the then boss of Chatto, the terrifying Norah Smallwood, and since she was extremely proprietorial about her authors, like a lioness with her cubs, it seemed unlikely that I would ever meet my hero in the flesh; nor was I sure that I wanted to, since writers are often best encountered in print rather than in person.

Jim decided to leave Chatto after Norah retired – the new regime was too feminist, left-wing and strident for his tastes – but in the aftermath of her departure I found myself acting, briefly, as his editor, working with him on *The Last Stuarts*, a study of the Old and Young Pretenders' melancholy lives in exile, and *Caves of Ice*, Volume Three of the diaries, which took his perambulations on into the post-war years. He was a model author: quick, efficient, open to advice (not that much was called for), and unlikely to take offence at one's suggestions, unless too obviously half-baked. What I particularly enjoyed about him – and here he differed greatly from the pompous, self-important sort of writer – was the great gulf set between the way in which he presented himself, and what he actually achieved. He had spent his life as a hard-working, highly professional author who wrote to length and delivered on time, and whose scholarship, however lightly worn, was entirely genuine; yet he liked to present himself as a bumbling, ineffectual fellow, bordering on senility at times, whose reputation as an authority on architecture and country houses, and talents as a biographer, were almost certainly undeserved. 'Oh dear, no, I'm far too gaga, quite gone in the head,' I can hear him saying as I urged him to bring out another volume of diaries, a further nine of which would eventually be published. I found Jim's modesty and self-deprecation entirely congenial, but suspect that those who so indulge do themselves a disservice: the world is a literal-minded place in which those who shout loudest attract the most attention, and the self-effacing are taken at their own estimation.

Encountered in the gloomy, labyrinthine, lino-floored corridors of the old Chatto building in William IV Street, so reminiscent of a prep school or an old-fashioned lunatic asylum, or over lunch at Brooks's, or in his honey-coloured home by the gates of Badminton House, Jim proved nothing like as alarming as Norah would have had us believe. A willowy, rather dandified figure, clad in unusual jackets and wearing a multi-coloured silk foulard at the neck, he had a long, humorous face, not unlike that of a kindly camel, wavy white hair, and a soft, hesitant voice: a slight suggestion of a stammer added to the import, and comicality, of what he had to say. Like many of the best writers, he had a gift for the embellished or suitably heightened anecdote, delivered in an appropriately deadpan voice; despite the occasional outbursts of fury or revenge recorded in the diaries and in *Another Self*, his manners were impeccable. I met him far less often than I would have wished, but there was no one whose good opinion I valued more.

After Jim left Chatto, he published the next volume of the diaries with Faber before moving to John Murray, who brought out a further eight volumes. Murray's office in Albemarle Street was his spiritual home, and Jock Murray – clad, invariably, in a bow tie, a lovat corduroy jacket and flannel bags held up by scarlet braces – had been his contemporary at Eton and Magdalen. Towards the end of Jim's life, John Murray decided to reissue his memoir *Another Self*: running true to form, Jim said he felt too tired and gaga to write an Introduction, and suggested that I should do it for him.

Originally published in 1970, *Another Self* is a brief, episodic and highly charged piece of work which – ostensibly – takes us from his childhood in Worcestershire to his wartime experiences, at which point the diaries take up the story. It is almost certainly the funniest autobiography ever written, but readers with too literal a cast of mind should probably give it a miss. Indeed, I have often used *Another Self*, along with Patrick Leigh Fermor's two magical books about his pre-war walk from Rotterdam to Istanbul, as a litmus test, designed to smoke out kindred spirits with tastes similar to my own; and just as, very occasionally, one comes across some unromantic soul who objects to Leigh Fermor on the prosaic ground that he couldn't possibly remember in quite such persuasive detail the interiors of ochre-coloured East European country houses glimpsed sixty years before, so some dim spirits grumble about the implausibility of *Another Self*, with particular reference to Lees-Milne's account of how he short-sightedly marched a platoon of Guards over the cliffs of Dover, leaving them clinging to outcrops of chalk or tufts of grass, or how the bottom fell out of the clapped-out horse-drawn carriage in which he and his mother arrived at his prep school, so forcing them to run round and round the circular drive, while the headmaster looked on, until the cabby could bring his vehicle to a halt. Most literary memoirs and a good many travel books tend to the hyperbolical, merging invention with recollection: quite why I am happy to go along with Lees-Milne and Leigh Fermor, but am irritated by Bruce Chatwin, or by Laurie Lee's tales of his heroics during the Spanish Civil War, is something I have never quite worked out.

The finest set-piece of all describes Lees-Milne's unhappy dealings with that wasp-like martinet Sir Roderick Jones, husband to Enid Bagnold and the then Chairman of Reuters: office-workers who have suffered under the tyrant's lash will scarce forbear to cheer as Sir Roderick's former secretary takes his revenge on the pompous little monster. Like all the best comedy, though, *Another Self* is tinged with sadness: some of its most poignant moments deal, with a kind of rueful regret, with lost or unrequited love; and the jokes and the self-deprecation are combined with a hatred of the modern world, and a terrible anger at the way in which so many beautiful things, from country houses to the Roman Mass, have been abandoned or destroyed.

In an appalling scene, Lees-Milne describes how, as a generally unhappy undergraduate at Magdalen, he visited Rousham, a beautiful eighteenth-century house on the Cherwell, and stood impotently by while its then tenant, a rich, half-mad philistine, flicked at the paintings with a riding crop and took potshots at the statues in the garden: from that moment, he tells us, he decided to dedicate his life to preserving the 'infinitely fragile and precious' buildings of England, for they 'meant to me then, and have meant ever since, far more than human lives'. Such sentiments could hardly be less politically correct. They are matched only by his regret that – given his hatred of Communism, and his love for the Catholic Church as it was – he never fought for Franco during the Spanish Civil War. Equally unfashionable was his delight in class distinctions, which he rightly regarded as 'a chief ingredient of the world's greatest fiction'. Class barriers, on the other hand, he found abhorrent, and welcomed their diminution.

Though often accused of being a snob, Jim never seemed remotely pompous, stand-offish or reluctant to have dealings with the unsuccessful or seemingly unimportant; he rushed round the country in his Mini till he was well into his eighties, travelled by tube when in London, and seemed the soul of affability when encountered in the London Library or wandering along St James's Street. As a diarist he combined comicality and self-deprecation with a lethal eye for absurdity, pretension and pomposity, and I suspect that many of those who knew him far better than I ever did must have felt a degree of dread when the latest instalment of the diaries was announced in the Murray list, and looked themselves up in the index with a palpitating heart.

Every time I saw David Hughes, which was all too seldom, we would agree to have lunch. 'My dear fellow,' he would say, 'it's been far too long'; but then we would return to our respective desks, and nothing would happen till our next encounter, usually at a publishing party or at Alan Ross's mews house off Beaufort Street. This failure to convert rhetoric into action reflected no reluctance, on my part at least – the very thought of having lunch with David was a pleasure in itself – but I knew, as he did, that a lunch would almost certainly involve writing off the rest of the afternoon, and a combination of parsimony and puritanism usually prevailed. Every now and then, though, we both succumbed. We would agree to meet, more often than not, in a now-abandoned Spanish restaurant up a flight of steps somewhere near The Oval cricket ground, within walking distance of his house in Kennington; and since David was one of those rare individuals who could make an invitation to lunch in a cavernous, half-empty tapas bar seem both exotic and exciting, I would rush through my quota of work as fast as I could on the morning of the great day, and head down the road to Mortlake station dreaming of a glass of cold white Rioja, the bubbles frosting on the glass.

True to expectation, David would be already installed, the bottle of white Rioja already opened and glinting in its silver bucket. 'My dear fellow,' he would say, rising to his feet, 'how very nice to see you.' He must have been in his mid- to late-fifties when I got to know him, and he was still the tall, elegant figure who had captivated his fellow undergraduates at Oxford in the early 1950s. In those days, I gathered, he had been prone to wearing a cloak and carrying a cane, which I would have found off-putting; but he was still a sartorially striking figure, with an enviable genius for buying olive- or mustard-coloured corduroy suits off the peg from Fortnum's. As often as not we would be joined by another equally natty dresser, Miles Huddleston, a convivial and entertaining mutual friend who had published several of David's novels at Constable back in the 1970s, and was another member of Alan Ross's circle.

Nothing quite lived up to the first swig of ice-cold Rioja – except, perhaps, the moment when a second bottle was called for – but despite the cracked tiles, the dusty warehouse windows with sunlight slanting through the motes, the greasy, leathery food and the incessant strum of gypsy guitars, silenced only when the waiter forgot to change the tape, our lunches never disappointed. David loved literary gossip, with its heady mix of hyperbole and affection spiced with malice, and he had years of experience to draw on. He was the quintessential man of letters, in that he combined writing his own books, articles and reviews with practical experience of the literary world: a condition I both admired and aspired to.

As a young man, newly down from Christ Church, he had worked for John Lehmann on his newly-established *London Magazine*, founded as a successor to *Penguin New Writing* after Allen Lane discontinued his support, and eventually sold on to Alan Ross in 1961. A brilliant editor and a predatory homosexual, Lehmann always sounded a most alarming figure, looking like a blond, bad-tempered eagle, tetchy and parsimonious in equal measure – Christopher Hawtree, who worked for him once, claimed that he would be sent to the nearest newsagent to buy a single stamp and a single cigarette – but David had been devoted to him and was, with Miles and Charles Osborne, one of his literary executors. From there he had moved on to work for Rupert Hart-Davis, another of the great figures of post-war literary London, revered by his contemporaries for his standards of design and his insistence on publishing only the best, but less adept at keeping his firm afloat. David struck up a friendship with Gerald Durrell, one of the more popular authors on the Hart-Davis list: he began, abandoned and, years later, completed a portrait of Durrell, the most memorable moments of which describe – in a manner perfected by Patrick Leigh Fermor and Lawrence Durrell in their books about Greece – long, bibulous, sunlit lunches of the kind we tried to replicate up the flight of steps near Vauxhall station.

After André Deutsch had published his first novel, David became a full-time writer. His first wife, the Swedish actress Mai Zetterling, was a famous beauty of her day, and they lived in Sweden and the South of France; he taught at universities in America, and won the W.H. Smith Prize with his best-known novel, *The Pork Butcher*, published by Constable. He wrote a book about J.B. Priestley, whom he greatly admired, and another about Billy Bunter; he was involved, for a time, with the tawny Australian writer Jill Neville, one of the most beautiful women I have ever seen, and, with his good looks – round neat head, large liquid eyes, slim build – and affable urbanity, he was an understandably popular figure on the London literary scene.

By the time I got to know him David was going through a fallow period, and, as a Committee member, was much involved with the doings of the Royal Literary Society in Hyde Park Gardens. It was, in those days, a magical institution, much frequented by old ladies in cardigans and flowered cotton dresses tuning their hearing aids. There was a large garden overlooking the Bayswater Road, in which parties were held in summer, a long refectory table around which Fellows' lunches were eaten, and a grand assembly hall, complete with podium, where lectures were held and new Fellows introduced. An elaborate stone staircase led up to a handsome first-floor room where David's wife, Elizabeth, and Maggie Parham, who ran the Society between them, typed and telephoned and photocopied among a litter of Roman busts and dusty sarcophagi. Next door was Marie Stopes's library, and beyond it was a tiny, sunlit room in which dying flies buzzed on the window panes and the floor and shelves were piled high with green carbon copies of long-forgotten letters, several of which were given over to a Fellow's missing umbrella. Best of all, though, was the glass-fronted wooden medicine chest screwed to the kitchen wall. I don't imagine it had been replenished since the late 1940s, containing as it did an ancient tube of Veganin, a scroll of yellowing cotton wool, and, most mysteriously of all, an oblong leather pad with long canvas straps on either side: Isabel Quigly, who knew about these things and wrote a short history of the Society, told me that in the event of a Fellow having a fit during a meeting, the pad would be jammed in his mouth and the straps tied behind his head, so preventing him from biting off his tongue or unduly disturbing the proceedings.

At some point it was agreed that the RSL should publish a quarterly magazine, and David was appointed its editor: a slimmer and less lavishly produced precursor of the present-day *RSL*, it provided reports of recent meetings and debates, a diary of forthcoming events, obituaries of recently deceased Fellows, snippets of gossip and the occasional article on some literary matter. Miles Huddleston had, earlier in his career, produced particularly elegant book jackets and publicity material for Constable, so David asked him to design *Letters* and liaise with the printers; I was to be David's deputy on the editorial side of things. Given David's genial nature and convivial ways, Miles and I expected our occasional business meetings to be a riot of laughter, punctuated by the pulling of corks, but we were gravely disappointed. David's father, Fielden Hughes, had been a charismatic schoolmaster, and some of his characteristics must have rubbed off on his son. Once behind the editorial chair, David was a very different man – serious, efficient, barking out orders, with not a joke to be heard and the wine cupboard firmly locked. I don't think we produced more than three or four issues of *Letters*, and I wasn't too sad when it folded.

David eventually broke his novelistic silence with *The Little Book*, but although it was well and widely reviewed, I couldn't work up any enthusiasm for it. Reading books by friends is often an agonising business: one wants to genuinely enjoy and admire, and if one can't one is faced with the embarrassing problem of wondering what to say without giving grave offence or jeopardising a friendship. Dennis Enright and Alan Ross felt as I did about *The Little Book*, and, like Shakespearean conspirators, we huddled together, wondering what to say. The sensible thing is to concentrate one's comments on the book's good points, if any: I told David how much I enjoyed his evocation of Seaview in the Isle of Wight, where we had both spent summer holidays, and where he – and his hero – had gone to recover from a recent operation. No doubt he saw through our various ruses and evasions: in his later years he seemed, at times, an embattled figure who had not received the credit he felt to be his due, and any reservations on the part of his friends, however tactfully disguised, must have contributed to this sense of being undervalued and underrated. When a copy of his last book, *The Hack's Tale*, arrived at the *Oldie*, to which David had become an occasional contributor, I took it home from a sense of duty, and with no intention of reviewing it. To my amazement, I loved it, and said so in print: its thesis was absurd, but its evocation of the pitfalls and pleasures of the freelance life and of long liquid lunches was vivid and contagious, reminding me once again of why he was such a good man with whom to share a meal and a bottle.

I saw David last when he came to see me at the *Literary Review*: I had hoped to persuade him to review for the magazine, but he didn't think much of the book I sent him, and died before I could try him with something else. He was not a well man by then: he was keen to see Bron Waugh's old office in Lexington Street, but climbing the bare wooden stairs to the first floor left him gasping and exhausted. He looked as dapper and well-dressed as ever, a tweed coat flung over his shoulders, the mustard-coloured corduroy suit visible underneath; but he was leaning on a stick, and he looked worryingly pale. We cleared a pile of books from the one available armchair, and he sat down to regain his breath. Once he had recovered, and examined the unusual wallpaper, and the office noticeboard, and the curiosities lined up on the mantelpiece, we tottered next door to the Academy Club. We had a long, gossipy lunch washed down with a couple of bottles of house red, the wintry sun streaming in through the window beside us; after it was over, we shook hands on the pavement outside, and went our separate ways.

When I left university in the mid-1960s, I couldn't decide whether to plump for journalism or publishing. With the arrogance of youth, I assumed that some grateful newspaper or publishing house would hurry forward to offer an important position to someone who had edited two of the three university magazines at Trinity; although I was, in those days, so timid and so tongue-tied that I spoke in a series of gasps and grunts, it never occurred to me that I might be utterly unsuited for both professions, and would be lucky to find the most lowly perch in either. My sister was working at the time for Alastair Hethering-ton, the editor of the *Guardian*, and while I was trying to make up my mind, he suggested that I should help out in the Features Department: if they liked me, and vice versa, something might come of it. Hetherington, who had moved the paper from Manchester to London and defied the government over Suez, was a raw-featured, red-faced Scotsman with a pointed nose and Bugs Bunny teeth; there was something of the scoutmaster about him, and I liked to imagine him in plus-fours, thick woollen socks and hobnailed boots, clambering about the rain-sodden mountains of his native land.

Every now and then he left the final editing of the paper to his deputy, and would visit my parents and my sister in their flat in Ashley Gardens, just by Westminster Cathedral: my parents were invariably in bed, and he would perch on its far end, comparing notes with my father about their wartime experiences. A year or two later, after I had got married, he used to take Petra and me to breakfast in the National Liberal Club before we dispersed to our various offices, and we would eat kippers in a vast, half empty dining room with a dado of brown and white lavatory tiles, and portraits of Liberal statesmen lowering down above them. He came to see us one evening in our tiny rented flat in Barnes. Funds were so low – I was earning £800 a year from Collins, and Petra £50 a year more from A.D. Peters – that we used to eat fish pie made from coley rather than cod; that evening the coley tasted as though it was past its prime, but he was too well-mannered to say so, and I had terrible visions of an ashen-faced Editor vomiting wildly into the printing presses after he had made his way back to Gray's Inn Road to see his paper to bed.

The Features Editor, Christopher Driver, was Hampstead Man made flesh, wearing socks and sandals, a grey Viyella shirt and knitted tie, specs of a kind then fashionable, with horn above the lenses and transparent plastic below, and an Assyrian beard, bushy under and around the chin but with the upper lip clean-shaven. Scholarly and quiet-spoken, he was an expert on food, and years later, at Chatto, I commissioned his history of our national eating habits, *The British at Table*. Every now and then he would take me out to lunch to sample the food in some restaurant he was vetting for a restaurant guide he edited – with his Assyrian beard and socks and sandals, he must have been instantly recognisable, far removed from the anonymous ideal – and he would tell me what to order, and spend much of the meal plundering my plate and masticating thoughtfully: on one occasion he took me to a new West African restaurant in Longacre, where the food was served on thick wooden platters and eaten with the fingers, washed down with palm wine drunk through straws from coconut shells sawn in half; even he was baffled by what to order.

As a dogsbody in the Features Department I was worse than useless. I was happy enough reading proofs – long, curling strips of paper, the ink from which came off on one's fingers – but I gave a convulsive leap whenever the phone rang, and hurried from the room; and because I wasn't a member of the NUJ, I was not supposed to be on the premises, and had to lie low whenever a union official was spotted bustling down the corridor towards us. Despite the officials, I was occasionally allowed into the bowels of the building, where the paper was printed by hot metal. It was like being in a vast submarine – hot, noisy, sweaty and smelly. I have always enjoyed being taken round printing works: I had no idea what was going on, but dutifully nodded my head as one of my colleagues, craning forward and shouting in my ear, pointed out the typesetters clacking away on Linotype machines, enormous typewriters which produced lines of hot metal type; the black-fingered men in aprons who made up the pages from the lines of type, reading everything upside-down and back to front, replacing material as changes or corrections came through from the sub-editors in the quiet, well-lit floors above, and adding half tones and headlines as required; and the stereo machines, which took 'right-reading' papier-mâché moulds of the flat, made-up pages, which were then somehow converted into enormous 'wrong-reading' semi-circular printing plates, two of which we attached to a rotary press to print a 'right-reading' final version of the paper.

One evening, on one of my illicit visits, I was told to take a phone call from one of the leader writers, who wanted to make a last-minute change to his copy. Heart pounding, I picked up the receiver and gave voice to a trembling 'Hullo.' I couldn't hear much above the clanking and pounding of machines, but as far as I could tell his last-minute correction involved either Mr Crosland or Mr Crossman, both of whom were Cabinet members in the current Labour government. I knew the difference between them well enough – Mr Crosland had a purple face and slicked-back hair, was given to red braces and smoking cigars, and had written an influential, unreadable and long-forgotten book called *The Future of Socialism*, whereas Mr Crossman had white hair, wore Arthur Askey specs, and had written an altogether more enjoyable book about Plato as a proto-fascist – but no sooner had I put the phone down than I had no idea which of the two the leader writer had in mind. I didn't know the leader writer's name and couldn't ring him back, so I plumped for Crosland. Of course it was the wrong one, and even Alastair Hetherington was not best pleased.

All in all, it seemed I was not cut out for a journalistic career. I hated the idea of having to ring up people out of the blue, let alone stick my foot in their doors; I had disgraced myself by muddling up Mr Crosland and Mr Crossman; Christopher Driver suggested I might like a job in the Manchester office, and I was outraged at the idea. Not long afterwards he told me about a job in the publicity department at Collins, in St James's Place. My mind was made up: publishing was the job for me. I wouldn't be expected to answer the telephone, life would be an altogether more leisurely affair, and I would spend my days sipping dry sherry with men in bow ties and corduroy jackets. I said my farewells to my overworked, shirtsleeved colleagues in the Features Department, and set forth to claim my inheritance.

I quickly discovered that I knew as little about publishing as journalism. Apart from drawing up review lists of the people and papers to whom copies of new books should be sent and keeping a tally of which reviewers were employed by which papers to review particular subjects – this, like noting which authors were published by whom, soon became second nature, and an essential tool of the trade – my job consisted of designing and writing copy for the advertisements which, in those days, funded the books pages of newspapers and magazines. The advertisements that really mattered, in the *Bookseller* and *Smith's Trade News*, were masterminded by Jilly Cooper in the office next door, but I was happily employed choosing suitable quotes ('incomparable', *Liverpool Post*) and carefully tracing lettering on sheets of greaseproof paper held over manuals of typefaces; after which, with the help of a ruler, I measured out exactly what proportion of an ad a particular book had occupied, converting this from inches into pounds, shillings and pence, and deducting the sum from that title's publicity budget.

Apart from my colleagues in the office, my guides to the world of publishing consisted of the men – mostly middle-aged, and all hard-drinking – who flogged round publishers' publicity departments trying to persuade them to buy advertising space in their papers. At least two of these would call in at St James's Place every week, in time for a liquid lunch. We would hurry round the corner to the nearest pub, and over several pints, given ballast by a pork pie or a sausage on a stick, they would regale me with the gossip endemic to the trade, and the activities of the titanic figures who bestrode the world of publishing. It's unlikely, in retrospect, that any of them had ever met the glamorous whiz-kids Tony Godwin or Tom Maschler, or shaken the hands of George Weidenfeld, André Deutsch or my own boss, Billy Collins, and most of what they told me was probably both inaccurate and third-hand. But they conveyed a sense of awe and excitement that I never quite recaptured in later life, and when they took me to meetings of the Publishers' Publicity Circle, and I found myself talking man to man with such giants of the profession as Tony Colwell of Cape and Jeremy Hadfield of Weidenfeld and Miles Huddleston of Constable and Leo Cooper of Hamish Hamilton (the cricket-loving husband of Jilly) and the octogenarian tipster Eric Hiscock, with his mane of white hair, nutcracker jaw, long black cigarette-holder and mouth so deeply sunk that he looked as though he had forgotten to insert his false teeth, I felt I had made it at last. Hiscock, after all, had worked on the *Evening Standard* with Arnold Bennett and Howard Spring, and so influential was his column in *Smith's Trade News* that he was wooed by the likes of 'Billy' Collins, 'Jamie' Hamilton, 'Bob' Lusty and 'Fred' Warburg.

My particular guide through the labyrinth was Michael Roberts, who looked after publishers' advertising for the *New Statesman*. Puce-faced and watery-eyed, he was well known and much liked in the trade, being both convivial and a bottomless pit of gossip: he spent his days preparing for and recovering from his three- or four-hour pub lunches, during the course of which he garnered fresh gossip and passed on the news from yesterday's port of call, so keeping the system lubricated and in good working order. I looked forward keenly to Michael's visits, though since there were far more publishers then than now – firms like Hamish Hamilton, Michael Joseph, Weidenfeld, Cape, Chatto, The Bodley Head, Hutchinson, Heinemann, Allen & Unwin, Routledge and Secker & Warburg, which have long since been subsumed into conglomerates, were still independent entities, co-existing with long-forgotten imprints like the Cresset Press and Barrie & Jenkins, and all inhabiting ramshackle offices in Covent Garden or Bloomsbury – weeks might go by before his luminescent features could be spotted in the creaking, wood-panelled reception area, where the desk was adorned with a fragrant bowl of flowers, fresh from the Collinses' house in Kent, and a portrait of an earlier member of the dynasty, raffishly puffing on a long cigarette-holder, gazed down on the proceedings; but because Collins was the biggest and most commercially-minded publisher in London, and an important account, we were visited more frequently than most.

I moved from the publicity side of publishing into editorial after a couple of years, and as publishers stopped advertising in the book pages except for the occasional bestseller, Michael had to busy himself rustling up ads from British Gas and the like; but we remained in touch, meeting every now and then for a gossipy pub lunch in Bloomsbury or, later, near his home in Richmond. Like Alastair Hetherington and Christopher Driver, he has been dead for some years now. At his funeral in Mortlake

Crematorium, old veterans of publishers' publicity, sprightly, youthful figures when first encountered nearly forty years ago, now paunchy and grey and red of nose, gathered to recall the old days. One of them gave the address and, as is the custom nowadays, combined jokes and melancholic, affectionate evocation with a résumé of Michael's career. It didn't add up to much in terms of a c.v. – he had been born in Derbyshire, spent most of his working life at the *New Statesman*, was a keen supporter of the Labour Party, and was fond of beer – and, thinking about it afterwards, I couldn't remember a single anecdote or incident I associated with Michael. But the same could be said of most of us: he had been, in his day, the best of company, and that in itself was no mean feat.

I described in *Kindred Spirits* how, as an unhappy office worker longing to escape into a Dickensian past, I discovered the novels of R.S. Surtees, and how, years later, I was elected to the committee of the R.S. Surtees Society, an unusual body devoted to publishing facsimile reprints of the great man's books, and keeping them in print. I bought the old World's Classics edition of *Mr Sponge's Sporting Tour* because of John Leech's gloomy, cross-hatched engravings of apoplectic hunting squires, bottle-nosed butlers and dodgy-looking horse-copers, assuming – rightly – that they were the harbingers of a lurid, highly-charged world, in much the same way as the drawings of Phiz and Cruikshank complemented Dickens's universe. I had no interest in hunting, and I imagined that Surtees would be a poor substitute for my beloved Dickens, but in the half century (almost) since I picked up *Mr Sponge* in Bumpus in Baker Street, my tastes have changed. Although I still have a soft spot for the early Dickens, for *Pickwick* and *Nickleby* and *Chuzzlewit*, I find the sentimentality and the saccharine heroines and the purple prose and the great gulf set between the Good and the Bad too much to be borne, and can only manage a few pages at a time; as a young man I found Trollope dull and thin-blooded, and happily subscribed to the absurd notion that his novels were tedious affairs concerned only with clerical tittle-tattle and the machinations of civil servants, but now he is far and away my favourite English novelist, unmatched in his evocations of love and of women, and utterly unDickensian in seeing the world in shades of grey, peopled by characters who, like most of us, are a mixture of good and bad, strength and weaknesses.

Unlike Dickens, Surtees seems as good as ever. I love his flashy, cigar-puffing, champagne-swigging *demi-mondaines*, his con men and wide boys, mid-Victorian used-car salesmen dealing in spavined nags, his tuft-hunting country gents, his anxious mamas desperate to matchmake for their frumpish daughters, his bleak ancestral homes, his sullen peasantry, his fascination with the minutiae of clothing, his sodden, muddy Northumberland fields with the hunt trailing off in the distance; I relish his hard-boiled, unillusioned account of human nature, his coarse-grained, fast-moving prose, his lack of sentimentality, his boisterous, unsubtle sense of humour, and the way in which, like Dickens, he will seize on some absurdity of speech or behaviour and milk it for all it's worth, on the reasonable grounds that a good joke will bear endless repetition. His tough, cynical view of the world and his reluctance to moralise remind me of my other great hero, Tobias Smollett: though admired by other writers, including George Orwell and V.S. Pritchett, neither Smollett nor Surtees is thought worthy of consideration by the academic world, devoted as it is to the 'canon' of approved authors. The Eng. Lit. industry likes writers who are difficult, like Sterne, or sententious, like Fielding: novelists like Smollett or Surtees, who get on with the job in a brisk and businesslike way, provide no purchase for their critical teeth, and are ignored as a result.

But not by the R.S. Surtees Society. Michael Wharton first came up with the idea of a society devoted to bringing the novels back into print, and Sir Charles Pickthorn and his wife Helen put theory into practice: my fellow Committee members have included Hermione Hobhouse, Lord Charles Cecil, Sir Richard Body, the former MP and erstwhile 'Muckspreader' of *Private Eye*, and, most recently, Alexander Waugh. They were, and are, a fine body of men and women; but the most remarkable of all was a publisher and bookseller called Joe Allen, who died some years ago at a ripe old age. A tiny, upright figure with a grey military moustache and white, swept-back hair, invariably clad in a black three-piece serge suit, white shirt, dark tie and high lace-up boots, briskly polished, he looked and behaved like a survivor from the vanished world of Edwardian tradesmen-publishers, of Grant Richards and John Lane and J.M. Dent and William Heinemann; he was Edwardian too in his raffish demeanour and his liking for champagne and pretty women. As far as the Surtees Society was concerned, he had a knowledge of a particular area of publishing that none of us could claim to rival, and he put it to good effect.

Joe's father was born in 1848: he worked as a sporting journalist in Manchester before coming to London, where he founded and edited a racing paper called *Sporting Luck*. Joe was born, appropriately enough, in Bloomsbury; his mother died when he was two, and he was educated in Ireland and at St Clement Danes Grammar School, which he left at the age of sixteen. His father died shortly after, leaving behind his doctor's bills, a collection of horse books, and a run-down building in Bloomsbury. The building contained a second-hand bookshop, and Joe would remain a bookseller for the rest of his long life. His customers included Bernard Shaw, Max Beerbohm and Virginia Woolf, whom he found 'uppity'. He thought Lady Ottoline Morrell altogether more congenial. She was at least a foot taller than Joe, and one day he found her lying on the floor examining some works by D.H. Lawrence. 'Now we're the same height,' she remarked.

Like his eighteenth-century predecessors, Joe always combined bookselling with publishing. In 1926 he asked Kipling for permission to reprint, in pamphlet form, an essay called 'The Art of Fiction'; and despite his firm belief that 'anything cracked up by the intelligentsia is generally unreadable', he published Lawrence Durrell's first collection of poems, the early work of the Indian writer Mulk Raj Anand, and Eric Gill's *The Lost Child*. But he made his name as a publisher of a very different kind. Just before the outbreak of war he put down a deposit on No. 1 Lower Grosvenor Place, immediately opposite the Royal Mews, where the buses roar past on their way from Hyde Park Corner to Victoria. With its austere black fascia board, enlivened by a royal coat of arms, it became the best-known and most highly regarded equestrian bookshop in London, flogging copies of *Horse and Hound* and, in due course, the publications of the R.S. Surtees Society, as well as new and second-hand books on racing, hunting, horse maintenance and the rest; and although Joe had not sat on a horse since his childhood in Wexford – he was the size of a jockey, but more sturdily built – after he had been demobbed J.A. Allen established himself as Britain's leading equestrian publisher.

Uninterested in money or possessions – he never owned a car, and rented his shop, his Surrey cottage and his flat in a fearful concrete block over the road from the Rubens Hotel – Joe was the quintessential old-style publisher. He knew every aspect of the business, ran the office on a shoestring, worked all hours of the day, paid over royalties if the author happened to ask for them, published only those books he believed in and saw a market for, and used the occasional bestseller to subsidise less profitable works. The bestsellers included Sylvia Stanier's *The Art of Lungeing*, which sold over 100,000 copies in Joe's lifetime. I don't imagine he paid her an advance, but so long as she remembered to ask for her royalties that would have been neither here nor there.

Like many publishers, Joe couldn't resist a title. Hamish Hamilton's last years are said to have been made miserable by his being passed over for the knighthoods granted to Billy Collins and Robert Lusty, let alone the peerage bestowed by Harold Wilson on George Weidenfeld. Joe was far too modest to expect such recognition, and would have ridiculed such a misplaced sense of grievance, but he liked to remind us that the Duke of Edinburgh was among his authors, that he was the proud owner of two Royal Warrants as 'Suppliers of Equine and Equestrian Works', and that he was frequently summoned over the road to do business in the Royal Mews, crammed as it was with keen readers of *Bloodstock Breeding* by Sir Charles Leicester, *Family Tables of Racehorses* by Count Stefan Zamoyski and Captain Kazimierz Bobinski, and, until he sold it to *The Field*, that hardy annual, *Baily's Hunting Directory*.

In the mid-1990s the lease on the shop expired. The rent soared, and much had to be spent on repairs. 'Get a bigger bucket and publish another book,' Joe told his publishing director when she complained about the rain coming through the roof. But old age and hard times for independent publishers were taking their toll. The bookshop closed in 2000, and Joe sold his publishing business to Robert Hale, a still-surviving family firm which, on the outbreak of war, published T.C. Worsley's forgotten master-piece *Behind the Battle*, one of the best books ever written about the Spanish Civil War, and is best remembered for books about English counties, thrillers designed for the rapidly shrinking library market, and a brief, unhappy and improbable spell as Elizabeth David's publisher.

At meetings of the Surtees Society Joe was, rightly, regarded as the resident sage, knowledgeable about every aspect of publishing, hunting and that vanishing race of red-faced countrymen and their raw-boned wives for whom *Mr Facey Romford's Hounds* and *Jorrocks's Jaunts and Jollities* are the finest novels ever written. Every now and then Joe would invite Petra and me to dinner at the Goring Hotel, just round the corner from his erstwhile office. The Goring seemed, like Joe himself, a relic from a vanished age: the staff all knew him and would hurry forward to take his coat and show him to his usual table, where he would talk about publishing between the wars and try, without success, to explain what 'lungeing' was all about. At the end of one such dinner he gave me a rare copy of the Kipling essay he had reprinted three-quarters of a century earlier, patting me on the arm as he handed it over. It was raining when we came out of the hotel, and we made our way, very slowly and under umbrellas, to the horrible concrete block where Joe kept his London flat. A few weeks later Lady Pickthorn rang to say that he had died, at the age of ninety-one.

In the early summer of 1977 I reluctantly traded in a brief, enticing spell of freelance life for a job at OUP. Moving from London to Oxford was a disruptive business, and for the first few weeks in the job I stayed with old friends from Trinity, John and Christine Kelly. He had recently been offered a Fellowship at St John's: since then he has become a Professor of English, and has devoted his life to editing the multi-volume letters of W.B. Yeats for OUP. John Carey once suggested that since Kelly's notes were so much more entertaining than Yeats's letters, in future volumes the notes should be set in the larger text typeface and the letters themselves in that reserved for the footnotes. The Kellys had recently arrived from the University of Kent, and were camping out in a flat in Belsyre Court, a gaunt Thirties block at the bottom end of the Woodstock Road. They were, and still are, unusually convivial, and on my first evening in Oxford they took me round the corner to a pub off Observatory Street called the Gardener's Arms. It was in those days a pleasingly decrepit place, with a rusting bed frame propped against an apple tree in the unkempt back garden, woodwork kippered yellow with cigarette smoke, a lino-covered floor, a pockmarked darts board and a red-nosed, watery-eyed clientele propping up the bar or perched on greasy wine-coloured banquettes, the stuffing of which was bursting out at the seams. It looked like heaven to me, and life became still better when I spotted through the smoke the tousle-haired figure of Tim Hilton, the art historian and future biographer of Ruskin. I had last seen him in the Museum Tavern, opposite the British Museum, where he spent long hours drinking with the publisher Tim O'Keeffe and Michael Roberts; and here he was, clutching a pint, looking redder in the face than anyone else, and wearing, as he always did, a baggy grey tweed overcoat with the collar turned up and the pockets crammed with cigarette stubs and pages torn from magazines. I never really took to Oxford life, loving its component parts but finding the overall effect oppressive, and scuttled back to London as soon as I could, but my first evening in the Gardener's Arms got me off to a flying start.

At some stage in the evening Tim introduced me to a burly, red-faced man who sat full-square in the tiny front bar like a king holding court, swathed in smoke and surrounded by cronies, each with a pint in his hand, which were drained and recharged in ruminative silence. He had a large, solid-looking head, like a cannonball plastered with sweat, with a few wisps of hair still draped across it, protuberant eyes, a wide gash of a mouth and an iron jaw, and he looked like a cross between Trevor Howard and Hermann Goering. His name, I discovered, was Dan Davin; a fellow of Balliol and OUP's Academic Publisher, he had worked for the Clarendon Press, the academic and scholarly arm of OUP, since shortly after the war. I took to him at once, and although I never knew him at all well, I found him a kindred spirit: he said very little, but exuded a benign melancholy and kindly, sardonic wisdom.

I had never heard of Dan Davin before, but I soon discovered that he was a much-revered and well-liked figure within OUP, and was urged to read his best-known book, *Closing Times*, which the Press had published in 1975. In the post-war years, it seemed, Davin had hovered on the fringes of Fitzrovia, and the book consisted of memoirs of his friends from those days, all of them now dead: Julian Maclaren-Ross, to whom he had lent money; Louis MacNeice and the inevitable Dylan Thomas; the Jewish writer Itzik Manger; Enid Starkie, the flamboyant French scholar; and Joyce Cary, who had come to live in Oxford and became a close friend of Davin and his wife Winnie. Davin's pen portraits of his drinking companions were vivid, affectionate and well-made, but the real interest of the book lay in the shadowy figure of the author himself, forever torn between the self-indulgent delights of bohemia and the disciplined constraints of institutional life. He had experienced far too much to indulge that donnish affectation whereby fear and ignorance of the outside world are disguised as lofty disdain, but he had, perhaps, an academic's sense of haunting the antechambers of life; and in his book he portrays himself, with rueful self-knowledge, as a part-time roisterer and writer who keeps a reluctant eye on the clock, hurrying to catch the Oxford train and meeting the demands of an increasingly bureaucratic career while the seemingly free spirits remain behind.

Some years after Davin's death, Alan Ross, another erstwhile habitué of Fitzrovia and pub companion of Maclaren-Ross, asked me to review Keith Ovendon's *A Fighting Withdrawal: The Life of Dan Davin*, published, appropriately enough, by the OUP. Ovendon was a fellow New Zealander, and his biography was sympathetic, informative and suffused with an engaging melancholy: the fact that it was virtually ignored elsewhere – to my amazement, I never saw another review – seemed a poor reflection on the literary and academic worlds. From it I learned that Davin was born in 1913, in the far south of the South Island; his father had emigrated from Galway, and his mother's family from Cork. A good linguist, a classicist and a historian, he underwent a Catholic Irish schooling before going to the

University of Otago. From there he won a Rhodes Scholarship to Balliol in 1936; and although he often returned home, set most of his novels there, and came to be regarded as a kind of godfather-cum-ambassador for innumerable New Zealand writers settled or adrift in England, he spent the rest of his civilian life in Oxford. He was proud of his Irish ancestry, but within OUP he was known as part of a New Zealand mafia that also included Jon Stallworthy, Bob Burchfield the lexicographer, and Burchfield's wife, Elizabeth Knight. Davin's wife, Winnie, was another New Zealander, frequently sighted in the Gardener's Arms or the Victoria Arms in Walton Street: I remember her as a dark-eyed, prune-faced, kindly-seeming figure who invariably had a fag in one hand or in her mouth, and smoked so heavily that her hair and face looked as though they were shrouded in coal dust.

Leaving Winnie to look after the first of their three daughters, Davin joined up as soon as war broke out, serving as an Intelligence Officer with the 'Div' – the 2nd New Zealand – under his hero, General Bernard Freyberg: in the pub, or in the corridors of OUP, he sometimes talked of writing a book about men of action, seeing it as a counterweight or counterblast to the heavy-boozing literary types celebrated in *Closing Times*, and pinning much of the action on the figure of Freyberg, but nothing ever came of it. He lost the manuscript of his second novel in the mud of northern Greece, and was wounded in Crete: years later he wrote the volume dealing with the Cretan campaign for the official history of New Zealand's part in the war. From Crete he made his way to Cairo, where he shared an office with Enoch Powell, who insisted on wearing full regimental uniform, including Sam Browne, whatever the heat: Davin found him a martinet, a 'raging egotist with a bookish twist'. Through Walter and Amy Smart he met Lawrence Durrell, Bernard Spencer, Terence Tiller and G.S. Fraser, who between them had converted Cairo into a Middle Eastern outpost of Fitzrovia. Reggie Smith became a lifelong friend, but Davin never took to Smith's wife Olivia Manning: when he learned of her death, he remarked that she had been 'poisoned, no doubt, by her own venom'. He took part in the battles of Alamein and Monte Cassino, and was demobbed in 1945 with the rank of major. Not long afterwards his first novel was published, on the recommendation of the writer and journalist Walter Allen, by Nicholson & Watson, and sold 10,000 copies in hardback: André Deutsch may well have been the sales manager at the time, and I wish I'd asked him about it.

Back in civvy street, Davin was recommended to OUP, where he was taken under the wing of Kenneth Sisam, another New Zealander, and moved into a tall, gaunt house in Southmoor Road, backing onto the canal. Though devoted to Winnie, whom he had met in Otago, he had a roving eye, and for a time the Davins gave house-room to a flame from his Cairo days, and his daughter by her. Before long he had become an Oxford institution, holding court in his favourite pubs, dining out in college, entertaining visiting Kiwis, supervising publication in seven volumes of the Complete Works of John Locke, winkling works of scholarship from reluctant donnish hands before nudging them into print, and waiting in vain for a collation of John Donne's prose writings which had been commissioned in the 1930s and was still unfinished when its editor died in harness.

From an early age, Davin had alternated between gloom and elation, and as he grew older he became more melancholic. Publishing obscure but important works of scholarship and definitive editions of poets' letters was the Clarendon Press's *raison d'être*, but it was far removed from the literary life Davin had sampled in the Wheatsheaf or the Fitzroy Tavern. He disliked and resented the way his beloved OUP seemed to be sacrificing quality to the demands of accountancy and big business, venturing into areas of publishing best served by the conglomerates that were increasingly dominant in London publishing, or by quick-witted, fast-moving little firms cornering particular aspects of the market. After a spell with Michael Joseph, his novels had ended up being published by Robert Hale, a firm that specialised in short runs of crime and romantic novels aimed at the library market, and whose books were disdained or ignored by the critics. He began to mix anti-depressants with prodigious quantities of drink, and after his retirement in 1978 he spent long hours lying in bed in his and Winnie's cottage in Dorchester, and in a home for alcoholics.

He died in September 1990, and the following January I went to his memorial service in the hall at Balliol with Richard Cobb, a drinking companion of his since before the war. Both Richard and I felt that the speeches did Dan a disservice, in that they combined justifiable affection and regard with ludicrously exaggerated claims for his fame and qualities as a writer and a publisher, and as one fulsome eulogy followed another Cobb writhed on the bench beside me and muttered 'Nonsense' under his breath. Unless they become embittered or resentful, failures – or those who regard themselves as failures – are often more congenial than those who achieve all that they set out to do, if only because they are more like the rest of us: no doubt Dan Davin felt himself to be a failure, and would have ridiculed the overblown compliments paid him in Balliol hall. As a writer, he had failed to make his mark; as a publisher, he was an academic midwife rather than a fully-fledged practitioner, far removed from contemporaries like George Weidenfeld or André Deutsch. But he wrote one very good book, led a more interesting life than most, and was loved and admired by many; and those are no modest achievements.

It must have been soon after Dan Davin's memorial service that Richard Cobb decided that he had had enough of Oxford, and moved, with his family, to Whitby. It was not a success, and in due course he moved back south. I next heard about him from Hugo Brunner, who had published *Still Life* and *A Classical Education* at Chatto, and had later persuaded Richard to move with him to John Murray. Cobb, Hugo told me, was now living in Abingdon, and was at death's door: but he had perked up no end when Hugo suggested that we should make a joint visit, and was keenly awaiting our arrival.

I took the train down to Oxford, and Hugo and I drove over to Abingdon, where the Cobbs were living in a small terrace house on the edge of a housing estate. Richard was sitting in an armchair in the front room when we arrived, with a half-empty bottle of red wine on a table beside him. He was wearing a sleeveless v-necked sweater over an open-necked shirt with the sleeves rolled up, grey worsted trousers and a pair of brown and white Pirelli slippers; and he looked, as he always did, like a freshly skinned rabbit, red and blue all over and faintly clammy to the touch.

Since Hugo had seen him fairly recently, and was regularly in touch, he talked to Margaret Cobb in the back room, leaving me alone with Richard. He poured me a large glass of wine, refreshed his own glass, and immediately started to talk, with passion and indignation, about Oxford academic politics – a subject I knew nothing about. He was particularly keen that Hugo should be appointed the Master of Trinity, and – quite forgetting that I was neither an Oxford graduate nor a member of Trinity, and had as much influence in such matters as the milkman or the lady behind the Post Office counter – hoped that I would lobby vigorously on his behalf. It seemed odd that someone who liked to shock or deride his fellow academics, and had allegedly fled to Whitby to get away from Hebdomadal Councils and the like, should want to talk of nothing but who was going to be appointed to the Chair of this or that, and what folly it had been to allow So-and-So to be elected to a particular post: but I gathered from Richard Ingrams that whenever they met Cobb talked only of Shrewsbury masters past and present, and kept a keen eye on what was going on in his old school. Despite my lack of interest in Oxford politics, I relished his indignation and his passion for gossip, preferably scurrilous, albeit about people of whom I knew little or nothing. Other people's shop talk, if well done, has a curious, almost hypnotic fascination, and I found Richard's obsession with the minutiae of status, dress and the like, and with the vagaries of human behaviour, both sympathetic and familiar.

Despite the revivifying effect of our visit, Richard died not long afterwards. Rereading his letters recently for a proposed selection edited by Tim Heald, I remembered how funny and indiscreet he had been, both in print and in person, and what a tremendous support he'd been when I published my first book of memoirs, even to the extent of reviewing it in two different papers. His own are masterpieces of the genre: colourful, comic, informative, self-aware and full of those precisely observed details that – or so I am told – made him one of the great historians of his day. It seems absurd that *Still Life*, *A Classical Education* and *The End of the Line* have long been out of print, but with luck their time will come round again.

I always enjoyed visiting Frances Partridge in her flat in West Halkin Street, between Belgrave Square and Sloane Street. She must have been well into her eighties when I first went round there, but her quickness of speech and motion and her trim, slight figure were those of someone half her age. She had a face like an animated walnut, brown and lined, with a long upper lip, bright dark eyes, short grey hair and a smiling mouth. Reminders of Bloomsbury were to hand in the shape of items from the Omega Workshop: a Boris Anrep mosaic of a black cat warming itself in front of a fire had been built into the fireplace, like a relic of Byzantium, and on an adjacent wall she had hung a portrait by Carrington of Lytton Strachey, whose long red silky beard cascaded down his chest. But the room I liked best was her kitchen. It made no concessions to modernity in the form of built-in features or labour-saving devices. The walls were painted in shiny cream gloss, and the floor was covered with an equally refulgent dark green lino; an oblong china sink stood on four spindly metal legs, with a wooden draining board to one side; the stove, an antique gas model *circa* 1945, was made of enamel patterned in tiny triangles of black and grey and white, and stood on little curved legs; the fridge, *circa* 1960, was similarly free-standing, isolated on a sea of gleaming lino, as was a white-painted, glass-fronted kitchen cupboard which stood between two tall windows looking onto the street below.

I got to know Frances in my Chatto days. The firm had agreed to publish a selection of her photographs, and we sat side by side on the sofa, with her albums spread out on a low table, drinking tea before moving on to something stronger. In due course I went to see her about Cyril Connolly, but she had written so well about him in her diaries that she had little new to say. While I was researching my book Selina Hastings, then at *Harpers & Queen*, asked me to review a biography of a middle-ranking Bloomsbury figure. Frances had known the book's subject extremely well, and loomed large in the story, so to illustrate my review the magazine reproduced a photograph, taken in the 1920s, of a girl in a bathing costume sitting rather stiffly on a pebbly South Coast beach. According to the caption this was Frances, but it didn't look remotely like her. A day or two later Frances rang me and explained, with a good deal of laughter, that of course it wasn't her, but a prostitute called Winnie, who had not only been a friend of the book's hero but had come into the Connolly story as well. 'You were quite right about X's book – it went off dreadfully towards the end,' she said *à propos* my review – which was rather a relief, as I knew that X was a good friend of hers, and worried she might have taken umbrage on his behalf. In the *Spectator* that week, regular reviewers were asked to choose their book of the season, and Frances – widely regarded as the soul of probity, loved and admired for her austere devotion to the rational and the true – declared X's book to be a masterpiece. This was, perhaps, a final manifestation of Bloomsbury's exaltation of friendship above all else; and, for good and or bad, it seemed to epitomise much of London literary life.

# TWENTY-TWO

# The Loot

I have never been a great admirer of the *New Yorker*, but when in the mid-1990s I was asked to write for it I was tremendously chuffed, and felt I had made it at last. I boasted about it to all my friends, dropping the news casually into my conversation; my reservations about the magazine disappeared overnight, only to resurface when my commission fell through. These had more to do with tone than with content. I always enjoy reading about the goings-on in publishing and newspaper offices, but although I always hurry to read accounts of life on the *New Yorker* by staffers past and present – among them Brendan Gill, Ved Mehta and the less deferential Gardner Botsford – I am invariably irritated by the prevailing smugness and self-regard, and by the reverential way in which they write about Mr Shawn, the mole-like editor who succeeded Harold Ross and kept an array of sharpened pencils in a mug on his desk, poised to strike out redundant adverbs and other infelicities. Alan Ross often told me of their refusal to apologise or admit that the *New Yorker* was capable of error after he had pointed out that long passages of an article about Graham Greene by Penelope Gilliatt, then a regular contributor, had been lifted verbatim from a piece by Michael Mewshaw in the *London Magazine* (the fact that she was almost certainly drunk at the time was neither here nor there); towards the end of my time at Chatto, V.S. Pritchett suggested that there was no need for me to edit two stories in his last collection, since they had been published in the *New Yorker*; I took an ignoble pleasure in pointing out two minor howlers of the kind that were amenable to common sense, if not to the fabled fact-checkers. But all was forgotten and forgiven when I was asked if I would like to write a profile of Stuart Preston, an elderly American then living in Paris.

'Everyone knew Lieutenant Padfield; even Guy, who knew so few people,' Evelyn Waugh wrote in *Unconditional Surrender*, the concluding volume of his 'Sword of Honour' trilogy of novels. 'Twenty-five years old and in England for the first time', 'the Loot' was one of a vast army of American soldiers who had arrived in this country from 1943 to prepare for the D-Day landings and the invasion of France, but whereas many of them seemed homesick, gum-chewing, and ill at ease, he was 'ubiquitous' in bohemian high society. 'Two or three widows survived from the years of hospitality and still tried meagrely to entertain. The Lieutenant was at all their little parties,' Waugh wrote. 'Two or three young married women were staking claims to replace them as hostesses. The Loot knew them all. He was in every picture gallery, every bookshop, every club, every hotel. He was also in every inaccessible castle in Scotland, at the sick bed of every veteran artist and politician, in the dressing room of every leading actress and in every university common room, and he expressed his thanks not with the products of the PX stores but with the publications of Sylvia Beach and sketches by Fuseli.' Stuart Preston was the Loot made flesh, albeit more than fifty years older than in the days of his glory.

The *New Yorker*'s Paris correspondent had suggested that I should pay Preston a visit as soon as possible, so I booked a seat on the Eurostar for a week hence, and prepared to do my homework. The most obvious place to look was in the diaries of James Lees-Milne, who had not only seen a great deal of my subject during the war, but fallen in love with him. He had first met him with Harold Nicolson, who had forecast that 'the next time we see Stuart over here, he will be in uniform'. On the penultimate day of 1942, Lees-Milne learned that Preston had just arrived in England. They met a couple of days later: a lanky, blond, ashen-featured figure, Preston was sleeping under a single blanket on a straw palliasse in a billet in South Audley Street, and feeding himself off 'a plateful of ready-cooked American field rations of meat minced up with beans from a tin', but despite such inauspicious living conditions he 'talked with rapture and awe of his dinner last night with the Duff Coopers', finding his hostess in particular 'wondrously, incredibly flippant, brilliant and witty, but cruel and un-middle-class. He kept on repeating the last phrase, with wide open eyes.' A couple of weeks later Lees-Milne and James Pope-Hennessy accompanied the eager young American to a reception at Argyll House: he drank too much, was reluctant to leave, and 'James and I had some anxious moments with him in the bus. In the restaurant he ate no dinner and talked of lords and ladies in a loud American voice.'

Writing some fifteen years after the end of the war, Evelyn Waugh gave Preston's fictional equivalent a commission denied him in real life: instead of being 'the Loot', he was referred to, behind his back at least, as 'the Sergeant' or, by Nancy Mitford, as 'the Sarge'. His finest moment occurred in February 1943, when he was struck down by jaundice, and was incarcerated in a public ward in St George's Hospital on Hyde Park Corner. 'He is happy there because he is in the centre of London and can see Apsley House from his window,' Lees-Milne noted. 'He is quite a different colour – no longer grey but saffron.' Stephen Spender, in his fireman's uniform, was a particularly attentive visitor, sometimes calling twice a day: the Sergeant complained that he talked of nothing but himself and his writing, 'but I am sure Stuart is very proud of being the recipient of these confidences'.

'The whole of London congregates round the Sergeant's bed,' Lees-Milne reported a fortnight after Preston's arrival in St George's. 'Instead of meeting now in Heywood Hill's shop, the intelligentsia and society gather in public ward No. 3. When I arrived Stephen Spender, looking worn out by his fireman's duties, was sprawled on the end of the bed. Raymond [Mortimer] came for a brief visit. Lady Cunard called at the moment when the entire ward were stripped to the waist and washing.' Five days later Lady Cunard called again, bringing with her the Marquess of Queensberry. 'She frolicked in like a gusty breeze, talking volubly, and quite unconscious of the impression she was making on the other patients, who being rankers must be astounded by the Sergeant's host of society friends.' Lady Cunard then urged the Marquess to recite two of Shakespeare's Sonnets; he obliged, in a 'low and rich tone', and she applauded loudly. On Lees-Milne's next visit, Lady Desborough arrived, followed by a chauffeur carrying her shawl: after her departure, 'Stuart got back into bed, looking tired indeed. He promptly began eating a lobster. Whereupon Harold [Nicolson] arrived . . .' Years later, Nancy Mitford explained to her sister Jessica that Preston was 'so famous in the war that the King once said to somebody who was late, "Never mind, I expect you've been to St George's Hospital to see the Sergeant." '

No sooner had the Sergeant recovered from his attack of jaundice than other problems beset him. A married friend of the MP and diarist Chips Channon fell 'madly in love' with him, but his passion was not returned. Chips – also married, but more homo- than heterosexually inclined – quizzed Lees-Milne about his ungrateful friend. 'Chips was plaintive,' Lees-Milne noted in his diary. 'He had meant to do Stuart a good turn by introducing him to a rich man who would ply him with champagne and load him with jewels. But, said Stuart, "I can buy my own champagne, and I don't like jewels . . ." ' Chips wondered whether the Sergeant might not be an impostor, and told Lees-Milne that everyone was wondering whether the rather tight-fisted young American was very rich or very poor. His infatuated admirer, in the meantime, was 'suffering from a breakdown, being odious to his old mother, cruel to his young wife, and about to commit suicide or else murder the Sergeant . . . '

Another susceptible new friend was Cyril Connolly's old mentor Logan Pearsall Smith, a well-heeled Bostonian long resident in Chelsea, famed for his worldly-sounding aphorisms and his patronage of young men with literary aspirations and sound social connections. 'Stuart seems to be his present preoccupation. He admitted that at first he thought Stuart too good to be true, endeavoured to catch him out, and failed,' Lees-Milne noted in his diary in July 1943. After making enquiries among those in the know, Pearsall Smith 'pronounced him to be aristocratic (according to American social rules), rich and popular'. The waspish sage of St Leonard's Terrace was soon in thrall, 'for Stuart has flattered him not merely by congratulating him on his books (which is easy) but by quoting long passages from them (which is clever)'.

Even Lees-Milne, fond as he was of him, sometimes found the Sergeant too much to be borne. He was rung at two in the morning to be told that his new friend had just been dining with Rex Whistler, Lady Cunard and Duff Cooper, 'and they had talked of love and kissing on the mouth, one of Emerald [Cunard]'s new pet subjects. He was in ecstasy over the evening. Petulantly I asked why this astounding piece of information could not have been withheld until later in the morning.' Lady Cunard may not have been a wholehearted admirer – 'I do wish you'd explain him to me,' she told Harold Acton. 'I can't make out what he does in the army. He is too cultured and well-informed for a sergeant, yet he never says anything memorable' – but when Lees-Milne dined alone with Mrs Belloc Lowndes, 'she began dinner with "I am told there is a most charming, handsome and clever American over here, a Mr Sergeant. Do tell me all about him." Oh Lord, I thought, the same old subject.' The Sergeant accused Lees-Milne of being self-absorbed, yet he himself 'lacks sensibility, and has no inkling of the meaning of love or the mysteries. He is a feather on the stream of life . . . But he is a very clever feather all the same. He also quivers with sensitivity, if not sensibility.' But Lees-Milne was horrified when the Sergeant, 'intellectual and sensitive', was 'treated like a Spartan slave, and made to undergo a Commando course, for which he is totally unfitted, among plebeian thugs'. He met him on Swindon station – a 'tall, smiling figure wearing a long gas cape' – and was won over by 'his charitable and sunny disposition'.

The Sergeant may have been disappointed by Vita Sackville-West on a visit to Sissinghurst – 'she was not as Spanish, masculine and hirsute as he had pictured her' – but his assault on the English upper classes continued remorselessly. He told Lees-Milne about a weekend with Lord Berners at Faringdon with 'a sort of ecstasy which blinded me with its fatuity'. Lady Desborough was not best pleased when he 'forced his way' into her room when she was feeling poorly and insisted on reading poetry aloud. 'Have you ever heard of such a cruel thing?' she asked the diarist afterwards. 'It is like the worst Polish atrocity.' Over tea at the Travellers Club, he informed Lees-Milne that 'he is no longer to be called the Sergeant, and gets fretful when addressed by that term of endearment'. Preston accused Lees-Milne of repeating gossip and making wounding remarks: they agreed not to meet again after a blazing row in Brooks's, but on learning that the Sergeant was on leave from France, Lees-Milne confessed that 'I can see further temptation looming.' They met at Aylsham railway station, in Norfolk, and 'He was in his sergeant's uniform, unchanged in figure and face, though a little red like a porcupine without quills – the suns of Normandy.'

The war over, Stuart Preston seems to have shunted between New York, Paris and London. He came to stay with Nancy Mitford in the rue Bonaparte in November 1946, and she reported that he 'had brought no money but a blue overcoat which he hopes to sell – I believe he expects me to wheel it round on a barrow for him'. In the summer of 1948 he surfaced in London, where Lees-Milne noted that 'he looks well, is brown, not fat but stalwart, and has become very bald, with a tonsure.' In 1949 he was appointed the art critic of the *New York Times*, a post he held until 1965: he wrote books on Vuillard and Titian, but his successor on the paper, John Russell, a former protégé of Logan Pearsall Smith, told me that 'I never met anyone who remembered (or spoke of) a word he wrote. Those were very dull days on the *NYT* art pages.'

No doubt they were, but it's hard to imagine that the Sarge had much time for the work of Jackson Pollock and the other abstract expressionists being vigorously promoted at the time by the influential New York art critic Clement Greenberg. Harold Acton remembered how, as a prominent art critic, Preston was consulted about pictures, and how 'he cultivated the younger painters, most of whom were more agreeable than their productions, which had to be seen through a metaphysical mist to be understood. On our visits to the modern galleries that were cropping up like mushrooms I was disarmed by his kindly tolerance, his readiness to detect virtues in what were mere daubs to me.'

But the post-war Sergeant comes across as a melancholy figure. James Lees-Milne found him, in later life, a fearful bore; on a visit to New York in the autumn of 1949, Evelyn Waugh reported him as being 'very lonely and disregarded by all', and a year later, on another trip to the States, he told Nancy Mitford that 'Sergeant Preston is as bald as an egg and very watery-eyed. I suspect he drinks.' He weekended on Fire Island, a well known homosexual hangout, but after he left the *New York Times* he settled in Paris; he was treated for alcoholism, consorted with well-heeled expatriates, most of them homosexual, and became in due course an avuncular, benign, almost Jamesian figure, a relic of a vanished era, sought out by people much younger than himself who longed to learn more about it.

By the end of a week I had done a modest amount of homework, and arranged to have lunch with the Sergeant and look up various old friends of his in Paris. On the day before I was due to leave I spoke to his godson, James Fox, the author of *White Mischief*, who had earlier been helpful in providing names and addresses. But now, it seemed, everything had changed. James urged me, very strongly, not to try to see Stuart Preston. My journey would be a complete waste of time: the Sergeant hated to disappoint me, since he'd greatly enjoyed my biography of Cyril Connolly, but he didn't want to be interviewed, or to be written about in the *New Yorker* or anywhere else. Of course I was disappointed to lose my trip to Paris and my *New Yorker* commission all at once, but my overwhelming feelings were of relief and sympathy. The Sergeant's moment of glory had been so brief, and so absurd: he was, in his public persona at least, a figure of fun, a butterfly caught in flight for a few seconds only by Waugh and Lees-Milne, and of no interest to the world at large once he had fluttered out of their range of vision. He must have known that to have been the case, and I could see exactly why he flinched from public exposure.

I realised too that I could never have been a successful journalist: had I been a real sleuth, rather than a book pages amateur, I would have ignored James's warning, taken the train anyhow, tracked down the Sergeant in his lair near Les Invalides, and pointed out – politely, but with steely insistence – that if he didn't talk to me he might find himself lumbered with someone even worse. As it was, I wrote an apologetic note to my editor at the *New Yorker*, and abandoned my quest.

A few months later, James Fox invited Petra and me for dinner to meet the Sergeant, who had come over to London for James Lees-Milne's memorial service, and was staying at Brooks's. I don't remember anything he said, but I liked him at once, and found him a most touching figure. He was, as Waugh and Lees-Milne had mentioned all those years before, very bald, and his head seemed to balance on his neck like a poppy on its stem. His shirt was several sizes too large, so emphasising the scrawniness of his neck; his fawn lightweight suit, on the other hand, was several sizes too small, riding up on his sleeves, exposing long stretches of black sock and drawing one's attention to his feet, which were shod with those huge, boat-shaped, kidney-coloured lace-up shoes one associates with East Coast Americans of the old school. The knot of his tie seemed larger than most, with the result that the two ends were out of synch, with the wider, kipper-shaped one at the front far shorter than the skinnier one at the back. I couldn't decide whether he looked more like a very old, bleached-looking tortoise or a gangly prep-school boy who had grown out of his suit but not into his shirt. Either way, I was glad I hadn't written about him; but now he's no longer with us, it's hard to resist.

# TWENTY-THREE

# Peter Gunn

I first met the writer Peter Gunn in the early Seventies, when I was trying, without success, to make my mark as a tyro literary agent with A.P. Watt. My predecessor, David Machin, had gone off to be the editorial director of Jonathan Cape, then the most stylish and well-regarded publisher in London, and his authors – who had included Michael Holroyd, Paul Bailey, Mordecai Richler, Nell Dunn and Frederic Raphael – had left or been distributed between the two remaining partners: it was up to me to build up a list of my own from scratch, and I had been presented, as new agents always are, with an empty desk and a *tabula rasa*, on the understanding that I would scour the literary magazines, read the newspapers with unusual care, and trawl though publishers' catalogues, keeping a keen eye out for apparently unagented authors. This proved, as it always does, a slow and dispiriting business, and I filled in the long hours very slowly typing out permission letters and reading the pink carbons of the office's outgoing letters, which were circulated every day in a battered buff folder, in the hope that I would pick up tips from my more experienced senior colleagues. So I was relieved and grateful when the more forceful and flamboyant of the two partners, Hilary Rubinstein, breezed into my room one morning to say that he was passing on to me a published author who had approached the firm in search of an agent. 'Over to you, my friend,' Hilary said, passing me the applicant's letter between the tips of his first two fingers, before hurrying back to his orange-painted office in pursuit of more important matters.

Written in a tiny, upright hand on a small sheet of what looked like airmail paper embossed in black with a self-evidently remote address in Yorkshire, the letter revealed that its sender's name was Peter Gunn, and that he had several topographical and biographical works to his credit. He was hard at work on a study of the fifteenth-century Dukes of Urbino in which Christopher Maclehose, then at Barrie & Jenkins, had expressed an interest, and had recently parted from his agent. He would be down in London the following week, and would like to call at our office in Bedford Row to discuss the possibility of our representing him. The Dukes of Urbino, admirable as no doubt they were, seemed unlikely to make the firm's fortune, or to establish my reputation as a thrusting new agent guiding the destinies of the nation's top young writers: but the days stretched emptily ahead and my desk was still distressingly unencumbered with type-scripts, contracts, book proofs, incoming and outgoing mail and other reassuring evidence of professional progress being made, so I wrote a warm letter to Mr Gunn to say how much I looked forward to meeting him and learning more about the Dukes, pencilled the suggested date in my otherwise empty diary, and strolled across to the Holborn Public Library in my lunch hour to look up my new client in *Who's Who* and discover which, if any, of his books were in print.

He had been born in Australia in 1914, the son of Frank Lindsay Gunn CBE and Adele Margaret (*née* Dunphy), and educated in Melbourne and at Trinity College, Cambridge. He had served in the Rifle Brigade during the war and been taken prisoner in Italy. He had taught at Sandhurst for five years before becoming a full-time writer: his books included lives of the critic Vernon Lee and, confusingly, Byron's half-sister Augusta Leigh, neither of whom rang bells, as well as the *Companion Guide to Southern Italy*, a short history of Italy for Thames & Hudson, and, for the Penguin English Library, a selection of Byron's prose. The only book of his I could find on the shelves was his first, *Naples: A Palimpsest*. I couldn't remember the meaning of 'palimpsest', but it carried a laudatory preface by Harold Acton: Mr Gunn was, he assured us, 'eminently *simpatico*' and something of a 'life-enhancer', as well as being a 'master-observer, a man drunk with the fact of being alive'. This sounded more like it, so although I felt uneasy about giving avuncular advice to a man of exactly my father's age, and a former prisoner-of-war at that, I sauntered back to the office with a paper bag of sandwiches in one hand and *Naples* in the other, feeling rather more cheerful than before.

My office was separated from the reception area by a long sheet of frosted lavatory glass, enabling me to pick out visitors like ghostly grey silhouettes, and a few days after my trip to the Holborn Public Library I noticed, at exactly the appointed time, a tall, thin, rather stooped figure, with a tonsure of white hair, bending low over the lady on the switchboard to announce his arrival. Eager to create a keen impression, I sprang from behind my desk, flung open my grey metal door (which had its own pane of lavatory glass), and ushered the newcomer into my office before the receptionist had time to dial my number. After waving him into an armchair, I scuttled back behind my desk and tried to assume the grave, responsible look of an old-fashioned bank manager or friendly family doctor. The first things I noticed about my visitor were his bright blue eyes, and his elegance of dress and manner. His head was more egg-shaped than most, bald on top, and his complexion mottled rather than uniformly red; he was clad in a well-cut olive-green tweed jacket with a faint orange over-check and leather patches on the elbows, well ironed mustard-coloured cords, highly polished chestnut brogues, a Tattersall-check Viyella shirt, and a black silk knitted tie;

a monocle, unused, hung from a black cord, and he carried in one hand a brown and white tweed cap more suited to the race-course than literary London. With his ruddy face and blackish brows, he looked like a choleric gentleman farmer who had strayed from the pages of Evelyn Waugh and should be out touring his acres, walking stick in hand.

He spoke in an angry staccato, stammering at times like a pneumatic drill; although, as I learned later, he had left Australia for good after taking his degree in classics at Melbourne, he retained a barely perceptible twang, a give-away clipping of vowels that went, somehow, with the country clothes and the shimmering brogues. He seemed, on first acquaintance, to be angry about everything, from publishers in particular to the world at large, and even more beleaguered than most in his profession; and as he described, in a low monotone, his unhappy dealing with The Bodley Head over Augusta Leigh – never the most worldly of men, he had failed to clear some crucial copyrights, the effect of which had proved disastrous – I felt, with a sinking of the spirit, that this was probably the kind of author I could do without. Anxious to lighten the gloom, but fearing the worst, I made some jocular remark, intended to be funny. The diatribe suddenly ceased; a terrible silence fell, and I waited for the awful moment when he picked up his brown and white tweed cap and the bag containing the Dukes of Urbino and stalked angrily out of the office, protesting as he went that he refused to be represented by a young man who was not only patently ignorant about Renaissance Italy, but facetious and flippant as well: but then, quite suddenly, his face split open in a huge, crescent-shaped grin, like a watermelon dropped on a flagstone, his blue eyes began to twinkle over his chiselled, cubist cheekbones, and I knew that everything would be all right. And so it was, for despite his forbidding exterior Peter was – unless very drunk, or so I was warned – the mildest and kindest and gentlest of men. For all his mutinous mutterings he was surprisingly

reticent and diffident when it came to advancing his own
interests, and since I soon proved to be an unusually ineffectual
literary agent, we were perfectly matched, in human if not
professional terms.

Peter's diffidence and modesty extended to his writing as well.
Scrupulous, scholarly, and too rarefied ever to become a popular
or well-known writer, he was the antithesis of someone like Cyril
Connolly, in that whereas everything Connolly wrote was covert
(or not so covert) autobiography, Peter's writing was impersonal
and self-effacing to an equal and opposite degree. Though
tending to the Connollyesque end of the spectrum myself,
I found Peter's lawyer-like reticence and reserve oddly attractive.
Much to his disappointment, the Dukes of Urbino never found
a home – Christopher Maclehose moved on to Chatto, who
weren't persuaded of their saleability, and other publishers felt
the same – but before long Livia Gollancz was commissioning
books on Normandy and Burgundy in which Peter could
combine his finely tuned sense of place with his knowledge of
history and architecture. I felt, to my relief, that I was beginning
to earn my keep, at least as far as Peter was concerned: I could
relax, and enjoy his company as well.

Before long Peter had introduced me to his wife, Diana. A tall,
nervy, fine-boned woman with elegant, hawk-like features, she
wore her fair hair pinned up on her head: wisps and strands
kept coming loose, and she would twist them absent-mindedly
round her fingers before patting them fiercely back into place.
While still in her teens she had been discovered by Herbert
Read, then an editorial director at Routledge, who had published a book of her poems. Chatto and then Hamish Hamilton
published her novels, and she wrote a life of Dorothy
Wordsworth. She and Peter had first met when he was at
Cambridge immediately after the war, reading Moral Sciences
under the supervision of John Wisdom. Though drunk for
most of his three years at Trinity, Peter found time between

drinks to go for long country walks, sometimes in the company of Ludwig Wittgenstein, and on one of these he encountered Diana James, then barely twenty and extremely beautiful. He was, she remembered, a startlingly handsome man, with his elegant figure and bright blue eyes, and together they must have made – as they always did – an unusually stylish couple: but Peter was in love with an Italian girl – he had learned fluent Italian as a prisoner-of-war – while Diana was already married to a young man reading Agriculture. Eight years later they met again, by which time the Italian girl had been long forgotten, and Diana was divorced: they got married, and Peter found himself the stepfather of four, with one of his own on the way. By the time I met them, the stepchildren were all grown up, and Peter's son was nearing the end of his time at Eton.

I became extremely fond of the Gunns, and when, one early autumn day, they asked us if we'd like to come to stay in Yorkshire, we were quick to accept. For most of their married life they had lived in Great Shelford, near Cambridge, where David Garnett was a friend and nearish neighbour. Garnett had a cottage in Swaledale, and when in due course the Gunns decided that the Cambridgeshire countryside was too heavily populated for their liking, and that the time had come for a move, they followed his example and moved up north. Hunt House was, they warned us, very high up, at the end of a long and bumpy track: warm clothes were advisable, so we hurled some extra jerseys into the back of the car before we started out, adding for good measure the sheepskin-collared American jeep coat which my father had worn while serving with the Guards Armoured Division. We turned left off the A1 at Richmond, which blocks the open end of Swaledale like a cork in a bottle, and began to pick our way in a westerly direction.

A few miles out of the town we passed through Marske, where Rupert Hart-Davis lived, far removed from the London literary scene he had once adorned: he and David Garnett had founded the firm that bore his name, but had later fallen out. The dale was still open and green as we passed by the publisher's house, the afternoon light filtering through a few surviving elms and glinting off eighteenth-century windows, but as we trundled slowly on, steadily climbing as we went, the road grew narrower between its drystone walls, and the country bleaker and more grand. Swaledale is a great U-shaped valley gouged out by a glacier millions of years ago. The River Swale and a broken ribbon of grey stone cottages ran along its bottom, and its vertiginous slopes were criss-crossed with a rectangular pattern of drystone walls; as we moved west the colouring changed from green to russet and grey, and when, from time to time, we stopped to look at the map or admire the view, the only sounds we heard were the baaing of sheep, the cawing of rooks, and the ripple of the river.

At Low Row we turned left, as instructed, and began an apparently perpendicular climb up one side of the valley. Two-thirds of the way up we opened a gate held shut with a twist of wire, and began to bump along a track made of diamond-shaped splinters of rock, the pointed ends uppermost; and then, to our relief, what could only be the Gunns' homestead loomed before us, and behind it the bare, bald countryside rolled away to the valley bottom. Built from gigantic slabs of stone punctured, on the windward side, by tiny lancet windows, the house looked as though it might have been built a thousand years before to repel Viking invaders. The wind never stopped blowing, buffeting us about as we pulled our cases from the boot: but no sooner had the Gunns flung open their front door – a mediaeval-looking affair of rectangular bolts and giant hinges – than we found ourselves, by contrast, in an almost Italianate world. The walls were white, the huge flagstones on the floor covered with overlapping Turkish rugs, and the air seemed to be warmed by the olive and maroon of early-nineteenth-century portraits: I had an impression of mirrors and pictures in heavy gold frames, of marble-topped tables and bottles of claret and barleysugar spirals like miniature versions of those that support the *baldacchino* in St Peter's; books overflowed their shelves and were piled up on the floor and the marble-topped tables and around the ingeniously hinged, lyre-shaped lectern from which Peter would read while stretched out on a velvet *chaise longue*, cigarette in his mouth or smouldering in a loosely draped hand. The windows on the leeward side of the house afforded panoramic views; by now it was late afternoon, and the dusk was closing in, but it was still light enough to see how the country fell away, like a rollercoaster, to the thin grey ribbon of houses and the fuzz of green trees in the valley below.

The part of the house in which Petra and I were staying was self-contained, with its own kitchen and marble-topped table off which we could eat our breakfast, and a rose-papered bedroom almost completely filled by a brass-framed double bed with a rose-patterned pot thoughtfully placed beneath, and on the walls gold-framed Victorian portrait drawings by Richmond, the highlights on cheeks and foreheads accentuated by chalky streaks of white. We were to entertain ourselves by day – going for long walks, squatting in the shelter of drystone walls, avoiding the local bulls, eating lunch in a pub in the valley, wondering how and whether we'd ever make our way up again – while our hosts got on with their writing; in the evening, after a bath and a change of clothes, we joined them for dinner, with Diana profusely apologetic about some delicious stew while Peter – no longer in any way alarming, despite some blackening of the brows and an occasional splenetic stammer – held forth about the iniquities of the book trade as he tugged open another bottle of claret. It was, I think, the first time either of us had seen the life of full-time writers at first hand, and very alluring it seemed.

One afternoon we drove back down the valley for tea with Rupert Hart-Davis in his grey Georgian rectory, the rooks wheeling in the trees about. He was very affable: with his grey moustache and his expensive tweed jacket and his blue-and-white-striped shirt and military tie and his pipe at the ready, he looked more like a retired brigadier than a publisher revered by his contemporaries for the elegance of his books and his flawless editorial judgement. I particularly admired his well-organised, tightly-packed bookshelves, sage-green on one floor, salmon-pink on another, and the way in which new books were set out in fan-like formation on a circular Regency table. He lectured me on the importance of printing a book's title and the names of the author and publisher across the spine and the jacket, and deplored the vulgar modern practice of running them up and down: he had, he explained, had great trouble in persuading OUP to follow the correct practice with his Selected Letters of Oscar Wilde, but had somehow won them round. He was, he reminded me, the literary executor of old friends like Siegfried Sassoon, Edmund Blunden and Arthur Ransome, all of whom respected him as a scholar and a safe pair of hands, who could be relied upon to act wisely and well on their behalf. Years later I was told that Hart-Davis had to be dissuaded from setting fire to documents which showed close friends like Duff Cooper in an unflattering or over-amorous light: in the concluding volume of his memoirs much space is devoted to the problems of keeping the Aga alight, but there is no evidence that incriminating diaries or letters were used to stoke the flames. Either way, pyromania is hardly what one expects from a scholarly publisher and man of letters who had edited a much-revered edition of Oscar Wilde's letters.

Not long after my Connolly biography was published, Hart-Davis's son Duff rang to ask if I would be interested in writing his father's biography. I was attracted in principle: unlike most of its reviewers, I had found his multi-volume correspondence with his old schoolmaster, George Lyttelton, unbearably whimsical, pompous, smug and condescending, but I thought his biography of Hugh Walpole one of the best I had ever read, relishing in particular the sleight of hand whereby he made no explicit mention of Walpole's homosexuality, which might have upset the large army of elderly ladies who enjoyed his novels, but made it apparent to those in the know via references to Turkish baths and the like; I loved the look of the books he had published and the care he took with their design and production, and I remembered the awe and admiration he excited among fellow publishers like Norah Smallwood and André Deutsch.

'That's marvellous, but don't breathe a word of it to anyone,' Duff said when I told him I liked the idea. 'If he gets wind of it, he'll set fire to his papers, and you'll have nothing to go on.' I dutifully kept my lips sealed, and began, in a desultory way, to do some background reading. A few years later, I bumped into Duff as we gathered on the church steps after James Lees-Milne's memorial service in South Audley Street. Duff has a loud, commanding voice at the best of times, and – making no apparent effort to modify his tones – he boomed out, 'I hope you're still interested in writing my father's life? Mind you, not a word about it to a living soul.' Speaking in little more than a whisper, I swore myself to silence once again, but no sooner had Duff moved away than Hugh Massingberd tapped me on the shoulder. 'Duff tells me he wants you to write Rupert's biography,' he said. 'That seems a very good idea.' It was all rather confusing.

When, not long afterwards, I read in the paper that Sir Rupert had died, I turned to Petra and said, 'Well, at least I know what I'll be doing for the next couple of years.' This pleasant feeling was short-lived: an hour or so later I received an apologetic letter in which Duff explained that, without telling him, his father had appointed Philip Ziegler to be his biographer. Now that I've read Philip's biography, I'm glad my proposed involvement in the project fell through. Few publishers merit or can stand a full-length life, and, rather to my surprise, Hart-Davis proved to be no exception. With their bevelled buckram boards and Reynolds Stone engraving of a fox on the wrappers, the classics he published in his Reynard Library are, like their equivalents in Francis Meynell's Nonesuch editions, among the most beautiful books to be published in the last century, and I admired the way in which he balanced his bibliographical and scholarly publications with bestsellers like *Elephant Bill*, *My Family and Other Animals* and *Seven Years in Tibet*; but, like all good literary publishers, he found it hard to remain both solvent and independent, and for the last forty-odd years of his life he lived like a recluse, far removed from the world in which he had played so distinguished a part. I'm afraid Duff was understandably annoyed when, in my review of the Ziegler biography, I described his father as a pompous curmudgeon ('I was knighted in 1967, but clearly the news hasn't filtered through to you yet,' he thundered, after a young editor at Faber had dared to address him as 'Mr').

For some reason the Gunns were not on good terms with the Hart-Davises, but that evening they quizzed us eagerly about our visit over the pre-dinner drinks. The following day, very reluctantly, we packed our cases for the long journey back to London and the dreary wastes of office life. We stayed only twice in their windswept eyrie, but it remained in my mind as one of those rare, magic houses in which the passing of time and the tedium of every day seem somehow suspended, and its inhabitants enviably if misleadingly exempted from the wearisome routines of work and domestic life. But, like all romantics, the Gunns were seized with a fatal restlessness, a sense that somewhere else an even more perfect house could be found, and the ideal life awaited; and because, like old-fashioned *rentier* writers, they had just enough money to scrape by on, and because, with their children grown up, they wanted only to be with one another, working on their separate books and fretting about the other's state of health and mind, they were able, far more than most, to divorce themselves from the humdrum and indulge their romantic yearnings.

The urge to move on was, inevitably, combined with terrible regrets: according to Diana, Peter 'wept all the way down the lane' when they left their Great Shelford house for the last time. Neither of them liked London, but for a time they divided their days between Swaledale and an elegant, box-shaped barge, painted maroon and gold and white and formerly the property of New College, Oxford, with mullioned windows and wooden pineapples running along the balustrade, which was, and still is, moored off Cheyne Row; but then they sold Swaledale, and their restlessness was given full rein. They sampled Lewes, but found it too noisy and too busy; a farmhouse in mid-Wales had the advantage of remoteness, but seemed a poor substitute for Swaledale; they tried Cambridgeshire again, but there were too many people and cars – and it was, no doubt, haunted by the shades of old friends like David Garnett and John Davenport, the hard-drinking literary bruiser and friend of Dylan Thomas who was said to have hoisted a pompous, undersized judge onto a mantelpiece in the Garrick, leaving him there to splutter in stranded fury.

The last time we saw them together they were back in Swaledale, only this time down on the valley floor, hundreds of feet below their lost eyrie. They were contemplating a return, and were camping out in a rented house, with not a gold-framed mirror or marble-topped table in sight. Peter met us at the door, tweed cap in one hand, walking stick in the other, and explained in a low, conspiratorial mutter, with much shaking of the head and raising of the eyes to heaven, that Diana was in a poor way, very low, and that we might do better to let her rest while we went to the local pub. It was raining, and the pub was full of bearded Pennine walkers in anoraks and chunky Norwegian sweaters and knee-length woollen socks and buckled moleskin trousers and boots with hooked eyes and interminable laces, and we had to pick our way over their rucksacks *en route* to the bar; but as Peter gave us his gloomy tidings over several pints of bitter – money was in short supply, Diana's health was not good, her mother was a constant source of worry and aggravation – his face lit up with that contagious watermelon grin and his eyes twinkled like the Mediterranean in summer.

Later, over a glass or two of wine in the rented house, Diana drew us aside while Peter was drawing another cork in the kitchen and explained, *sotto voce*, that poor old Peter was in a very bad way, and in dreadfully low spirits for much of the time. By now we had learned that this mutual anxiety, though strongly felt, was endemic, a persistent *leitmotif*. Nor was it restricted to the Gunns themselves: whenever we saw them, after six months or a year or more, Diana would greet us with a cry of, 'My dears, Peter and I have been so worried about you both: are you sure you're all right?' and we would worry what terrible things they had heard, or whether news of some fatal illness or imminent bankruptcy was being withheld from us by kindly, well-meaning friends. Though absorbed in each other, they took a passionate interest in the doing of their friends, asking eagerly after our daughters, revelling in one's rare success, and convulsing with sympathetic shudders when, after A.P. Watt and I had gone our separate ways and I had reverted to being a publisher, I described the travails of working at Chatto & Windus under Norah Smallwood and her equally alarming successor.

For months, sometimes years on end, we would hear nothing from the Gunns beyond an occasional frenzied scrawl from Diana, prophesying doom – her writing, energetic and impulsive and pouring over the edge of the paper, was the antithesis of Peter's cramped, impeccable hand – and then they would resurface in London, longing for news and as worried as ever about how they (and we) were going to survive. And then, in the summer of 1995, Diana rang to say that Peter had just died. She was struggling to write his obituary, and wondered if I knew anything about that sort of thing. I told her I'd write something for the *Telegraph*, and got down to work.

As is so often the case, I realised how little one really knows about people one instinctively likes, and thinks of as friends, but only sees from time to time. I found myself rereading *Naples: A Palimpsest* – my agent, Gillon Aitken, told me that it was the first book he worked on as a young editor at Chapman & Hall, back in the 1950s – and poring once again over Peter's entry in *Who's Who*, like a Kremlinologist hunting for clues. His list of publications was longer than before, with a study of the Acton family, a life of the Duchess of Abrantes (that really rang no bells) and a lavish volume for Weidenfeld on the churches of Rome added to those I knew of already, but even within the telegraphic restraints imposed by the publishers, it remained a typically reticent entry.

From Diana I learned that Peter's father, a remote figure whom he hero-worshipped, had made a fortune in the timber trade in Tasmania and then committed suicide; that Peter had spent a year in Paris after leaving Melbourne, and had walked from there to Yugoslavia, sleeping in haystacks; that he had been stranded in Dieppe with John Davenport on the day war broke out, and had served as a firefighter with assorted literary men before joining the Rifle Brigade. An implausible soldier, he had been captured in North Africa while out on patrol; his Italian captors had plied him with brandy before despatching him to a prisoner-of-war camp in northern Italy, where his companions had included Eric Newby and the future literary editor Rivers Scott. He and a friend had escaped, and holed up in a cave in the Abruzzi before being recaptured by a German patrol and sent to a camp in Germany itself. She told me how, on their honeymoon in Athens, as later on their travels in France and Italy, he had displayed the topographer's instinctive sense of place and direction, disdaining the use of maps and guide books: I found this entirely sympathetic and wished, once again, that I'd known him better. Two years ago, she went on, they had moved to an eighteenth-century house outside Dieppe. Peter had loved living there, but in the end he was brought down by bronchitis and heart trouble. It was time, once more, to be moving on; but this time he would be travelling alone.

# TWENTY-FOUR

# Closing Time

One of the great perks of literary life was lunch with Alan Ross.
It was never wise to arrive too early – novices or the over-eager
might be told, via the buzzer at the front door, to fill in the next
half-hour in the pub next door, or over the road at the V&A –
but, assuming punctuality, one would climb the stone steps of a
white, stuccoed building in Thurloe Place, just round the corner
from South Ken tube station, walk through the flagged floor of
a solicitor's office, let oneself out through the back door, pick
one's way down a precipitous iron staircase into the garden at
the back, and push open the door of the superior garden shed
which housed the magazine. Alan would rise from behind his
paper-strewn desk – clad, it may be, in faded pink corduroy
trousers, a v-necked cricket jersey, an open-necked blue-and-
white-striped shirt, rather frayed at the neck, and a battered
suede jacket – and greet one with some jocular remark; we would
look through the teetering pile of review copies stacked up
behind the door to see if anything appealed, I would help myself
to the latest issue of the magazine and do a quick survey of the
office to see what new pictures or postcards had been pinned to
the walls, jostling for space among the nudes, Indian gods,
literary men and views of Sussex; after which Alan would switch
off the electric fire and lock the glass front door, and we would
wander out.

'Indian or Italian?' Alan would ask, both being on offer immediately opposite, on the far side of Thurloe Place. More often than not we headed for the Italian, where Alan immediately ordered a bottle of Lambrusco, a sweet pink Italian sparkling wine: it didn't seem to go with any of the food that followed, and tasted faintly like Lucozade, but he must have discovered it on visits to Italy in the 1950s, and never wanted to sample anything else. He was not particularly interested in or knowledgeable about food, but he liked well-ironed pink tablecloths, low lighting, gold-plated pudding trolleys heavily laden with thick slabs of *tiramisu* and sliced oranges floating in Grand Marnier, and a bowing, beaming *maître d'* rubbing his hands together and saying, 'Good morning, Mr Ross, and how are *you* today?' At the end of the meal Alan made a point of asking for '*Il conto, per favore*': as the erstwhile author of a book about Sardinia he may well have had more Italian at his command, but that was as far as it went, over the lunch table at least. I once took him and Mordecai Richler, who had similar tastes, to an Italian restaurant in Soho where the food was far superior to that on offer in Thurloe Place but the tables were formica-topped, the salt and pepper dispensers were of moulded glass with silver-plated screw-on tops, and a fat housewife in an apron dished out the steaming bowls of pasta: it wasn't a success.

Once the pleasantries had been exchanged with the *maître d'* and the food had been ordered – Alan usually had a first course and a pudding, followed by a glass of *grappa* and a cigar – we would get down to the business of the day. He shared my liking for hyperbolical gossip, whereby a nugget of truth is embellished by the elimination of such qualifications as might have diluted or contradicted the main thrust of the story, and the punchline polished and refined by endless repetition: and since he forgot much of what he was told, and liked to repeat old favourites in a low, conspiratorial mutter, the same anecdotes or items of gossip would be recycled again and again, with Alan exclaiming

'*Really?*' in tones of amazement when on the receiving end, his round Armenian eyes bulging like those of a lemur caught in the beam of a torch. He was always the best of company – funny, affectionate and well-informed, as devoted to the *London Magazine* and its writers, and as keen to discover new talent, as he had been when he took over as editor from John Lehmann in 1961. 'He's a good fellow,' was his highest term of praise, 'He's no good, is he?' the moment of damnation.

One day in the summer of 1988 I called by on the dot of a quarter past one, but instead of heading over the road we made for the Rembrandt Hotel, a couple of hundred yards up the Brompton Road. Alan didn't seem his usual jocular self, and when we got there he slumped in his chair and peered out at me through dead, coal-black eyes. Every trace of animation had drained from his face, as if all the lights had been turned out in a skyscraper that was, under normal circumstances, more dazzling than its neighbours. As he toyed with a sandwich and looked askance at his glass of wine, I tried to engage him in conversation, and regale him with the kind of literary tittle-tattle he normally enjoyed, but I could get no response beyond a reluctant 'yes' or 'no'. After a while he told me that he was feeling so utterly depressed that there was no point in our trying to talk; we spent the rest of the lunch sitting in silence, after which I walked him back to the office. On the steps he turned and, as always, gave me a friendly pat on the shoulder before vanishing back into the garden shed.

He had, I later discovered, suffered a severe bout of depression shortly after becoming editor of the *London Magazine* – brought about, in part, by John Lehmann's grouchy and resentful behaviour as he reluctantly let go of the magazine he had founded seven years before. It had been treated with blasts of ECT, a form of shock treatment then in its infancy, and compared by patients to being plugged into the mains. Melancholia had been kept at bay since then, but now it had returned with a vengeance,

prompted by his split with his long-time girlfriend, who had
become fed up with his refusal to commit himself to a more
permanent relationship, and by the death of his old English
sheepdog, Boppa, who had walked with him to and from the
office every day from their mews house in Elm Park Gardens,
greeted visitors as they picked their way down the vertiginous
metal staircase, and held the fort when his master was lunching
over the road. He was put on lithium, several doses of which
were flushed down the lavatory; he went, for a time, to stay with
his son Jonathan in his large house in Clapham, from where he
wrote to say that he thought he would never recover or be happy
again, and that he sat for hours in the garden, rocking to and fro
like a Jew before the Wailing Wall.

Eventually the black tide receded, and normal life resumed:
but his nerve had gone, and when, a year later, the depression
returned in a still more scouring form, he seemed resigned to
his fate. He talked of how Scott Fitzgerald had compared the
depressive to a cracked plate, doomed eventually to shatter in
the heat; depression was, he assured us, a matter of chemistry
rather than psychology, and there was nothing he could do about
it except to take his pills and try to weather the storm. I wasn't so
sure, and waxed eloquent with amateur psychoanalysis, albeit
behind the scenes and never to his face. It seemed to me that one
of the ways in which Alan was different from other people –
apart from his brilliance as poet, autobiographer and editor, his
prowess as a cricketer and squash player (he had represented
Oxford at both sports), his knowledge of modern painting and
horse-racing, his amorous reputation, his passion for India, where
he had spent his earliest years, and his enviable elegance and
sense of style – was a curious quality of amused detachment. He
spoke of friends and lovers alike with a kind of loving derision;
he had remained on good terms with almost all the women in
his life, and would mock them, fondly, behind their backs in
exactly the same way as he mocked even his closest men friends.

Many women, I imagine, hoped and believed that they would be the one to pin down this elusive and exotic butterfly, but none of them quite succeeded.

He was, in the modern parlance, an 'enabler', and not only in a literary sense: he had a Mephistophelian quality which led those who knew him well to try, in vain, to emulate his own good-humoured insouciance over matters of love and sex. He was selfless in the time, energy and enthusiasm he devoted to discovering and promoting the work of others, selfish only in the sense of ordering his life exactly as he wanted, combining work and travel with enviable dexterity, and taking friends out to lunch or dinner several days a week.

On the surface at least, he treated everything as a joke, spluttering with laughter as he told us, once again, of how 'Lord Flipper' had been arrested in a public lavatory wearing a frogman's uniform, or a clergyman had farted in a railway carriage, or recalled some amorous misadventure, like a scene from a Feydeau farce. And yet, for all his apparent frivolity, he took certain aspects of life, and the whole business of writing and editing, very seriously indeed. Because he only seemed to read modern books, and tended, like so many of the best editors, to work on hunch, 'sniffing' or sampling books rather than reading them all the way through, one was amazed by those rare occasions when, looking rather embarrassed as he did so, he referred to Tennyson, Dickens or – here he might remind us that he had read Modern Languages at Oxford – Baudelaire or Lamartine. Exceptionally quick and efficient, he couldn't quite understand why other people made heavy weather of writing reviews, or why magazines like *Encounter* had employed secretaries, advertising managers, assistant editors and receptionists to do the work he did on his own. His apparent levity, and the breadth of his talents and interests, may have counted against him among those puritan spirits who regard the all-rounder as being, by definition, amateur and lightweight: his wonderfully neat and well-made poems, with their strikingly original similes, seem wretchedly undervalued.

Generous, companionable, funny, mischievous and affectionate, Alan appeared to carry little emotional baggage, to order certain aspects of his life with a lightness and a fleetness of foot that could only be envied by the more committed or conventionally well behaved, weighed down as they were by the ties of love, guilt and obligation. Yet he seemed, at the same time, exceptionally vulnerable and thin-skinned, lacking the camel's hump of emotional and psychological reserves possessed by his more ponderous and admiring friends. Such, at any rate, was my version of events: whatever the truth of the matter, Alan's depression in the winter of 1989 seemed endless and ever-deepening.

In all this, he was lucky in his friends, and Digby Durrant and David Hughes in particular. A benign, kindly character with amused hangdog features, invariably sporting a bow tie and as dapper in his dress as Alan himself, Digby had been, in an earlier incarnation, both a novelist and a top executive at J. Walter Thompson in the days when advertising agencies employed writers like Gavin Ewart, Peter Porter, William Trevor, John Mellors and Jonathan Gathorne-Hardy; by the time I got to know him he had put all that that behind him, and was writing reviews for the *London Magazine*, helping out in Thurloe Place when Alan was too low to take an interest, and entertaining his friends to lunch in the basement of his house in Selwood Terrace, halfway between the *London Magazine* office and Alan's house off the Fulham Road. Living in the suburbs, I was too far removed to be of much immediate use; they both lived closer to hand, and, as Alan's conditions worsened, were ready to drop everything to rush round with words of advice and comfort. Since Alan rejected any suggestion that he should be temporarily institutionalised, their visits to Elm Park Gardens were increasingly frequent.

Throughout all this, Alan remained friendly and grateful for any attention or comfort one could give, however ineffectual or far-removed: although his voice sounded flat and dead, like something on a recording machine, and although it was impossible to engage his interest or enthusiasm, he always thanked one for ringing, asked after the family and made the usual polite noises. One day, shortly after Christmas, I rang to see how he was, and got a very different reception. 'Will you please leave me alone,' he said, and put the phone down. Since he sounded so unlike himself, I immediately rang Digby, who said he'd go round, see how he was, and ring me back. Three-quarters of an hour later he was on the phone again. Alan didn't seem too bad, he said; he was heavily sedated, and was almost certainly asleep by the time he left. Were we on for a very late lunch, he wondered: he and his wife Judy had the remains of a turkey and lashings of booze, and they'd love to see us. It sounded a good idea, and within half an hour we were happily installed in Digby's basement, swilling down the first of several glasses of claret. Just as Judy was handing round the stuffing, the phone rang upstairs: I wondered whether it might be Alan, but Digby was sure he was asleep, and if he needed us he could always leave a message on the answering machine. Not long after, the phone rang again, and Digby stomped upstairs to answer it. He came down looking a good deal less cheerful: the unanswered call had been from Alan, who had left a message to say that he had tried to kill himself; this had been followed up by another message, warning us of what to expect.

Far from being dynamic or resourceful, I rushed about the room, lamenting loudly and wondering what to do about it, while Judy went upstairs to fetch her car keys and Petra rang for an ambulance, something quite beyond my powers of initiative and enterprise. We raced down the Fulham Road, Judy at the wheel, and screeched to a halt in front of Alan's house. While I banged on the doors and windows, Digby, who had a set of keys, wrestled with the lock – which, Alan had warned him, was never easy to operate. It proved immovable, so Petra knocked on a neighbour's door, asked if she could use the telephone, and rang the police. They arrived within a matter of minutes, bashed the door down, and went in to investigate while we hovered on the doorstep.

We stood aside as an ambulance drove up, siren wailing, and a few moments later Alan was carried out on a stretcher. He looked terrified and distraught, utterly unlike his usual self: his face was the colour of suet, his glance swivelled wildly from left to right, and his thick pelt of black hair, normally so well groomed, was ruffled and unkempt. The ambulance revved off with siren wailing, and we drove thoughtfully back to Digby's house to finish our Christmas lunch.

The following day I went to see him in the Churchill Clinic, opposite the Imperial War Museum. He was sitting up in bed, his wrists heavily bandaged, looking bright-eyed and far more alert and cheerful than he'd seemed for many weeks. He couldn't remember why or how he'd tried to kill himself, but he wanted to know exactly what had happened, and how he had looked when he was carried out of his house. He told us that he'd been taken to the Charing Cross Hospital, and had come round to find himself in a public ward; he'd had a terrible night, since another patient had done the goosestep up and down the ward all night, carrying an imaginary rifle over his shoulder and barking out orders to himself when he reached the far end and needed to perform an about-turn. This was just the sort of story he enjoyed, suitably embellished, and it had done him a power of good. I can't remember how long he stayed in the Churchill, but he was still there when David Hughes and I took him the pasted-up proofs of the next issue of the magazine. For some reason David had got it into his head that this had to be done by starting at the end and working to the front, which involved reading the magazine backwards.

'You *are* a couple of chumps,' Alan said as we presented him with our handiwork.

Alan asked me if I would hold the fort at the *London Magazine* while he was recovering, and although I knew nothing about editing magazines I happily agreed: I admired the *London Magazine* more than any other, and was flattered to be associated with it. I loved working in the garden shed, and still more so after Alan returned on a regular basis, clocking in at about 11.30, leaving for lunch at 1.15, and setting off for home at 4.30, taking with him as he went a sackful of letters and parcels, the stamps for which were attached in an entirely arbitrary way, with Alan guessing the postage of each and almost certainly underestimating by 100 per cent or more. I stayed with the magazine until 1993, by which time Cyril Connolly was taking up most of my time, and my place was taken by Jane Rye, who eventually became Alan's second wife.

He was, as an editor, enviably quick and decisive, confident in his own judgement and deciding whether or not to publish something at ten times the speed of ditherers like myself, rejecting or accepting new submissions almost by return, and dealing with proofs, jacket artwork, the sending out of review copies and wooing the occasional new subscriber with his familiar mixture of efficiency and apparent frivolity. One of the few things that drove him wild with rage was the success of *Granta* under Bill Buford's editorship. Alan's great quality as an editor was his ability to spot and encourage new talent – Paul Theroux, Jonathan Raban, Graham Swift, William Boyd, Derek Walcott, Peter Carey, Tony Harrison and Hilary Mantel were among those who had started out in the *London Magazine* – and as such he had done more for young writers than any other editor of his time: rightly or wrongly, he couldn't take *Granta* seriously as a literary magazine, claiming that it never took risks with new authors, but simply promoted modish writers who had already made their reputations or been taken up by fashionable publishers; yet at the same time he resented the enormous sales – at least twenty times those of the *London Magazine* – it notched up as a result of being sold and distributed by, in those days, Penguin Books. One day I suggested that rather than simmer in silence, we should challenge *Granta*'s sales supremacy by persuading another paperback publisher to carry the *London Magazine*: given Alan's passion for publishing unknown if promising writers – a recent issue had contained two pieces by hairdressers, neither of whom, as far as I know, has gone on to make a name – it was unlikely that we'd achieve a comparable circulation, but at least we could narrow the gap; and improved sales might reduce our dependence on an Arts Council subsidy, filling in the forms for which prompted Alan to elaborate flights of fancy and splutterings of mirth.

Alan affected indifference to the idea, but seemed happy for me to trawl round the paperback publishers; and eventually I found a taker in the form of Peter Straus, then the editorial director of Picador. Peter brimmed over with enthusiasm: he suggested an American-style editorial board, made up of famous names – not a suggestion that went down well with Alan, who was used to operating as a solo performer, with occasional help from, over the years, Charles Osborne, Hugo Williams, Christopher Hawtree and me – and insisted on four-colour jackets rather than the monochrome or two-tones that had hitherto prevailed. He also, very sensibly, saw the magazine as a means of attracting to the Picador list bright young writers for whom the *London Magazine* was one of the very few outlets prepared to accept short stories, poems, essays or travel pieces. William Boyd, a long-time admirer who was always happy to give Alan credit for starting him out as a published writer, donated a short story, free of charge; the Pan reps bustled eagerly around, flashing the four-colour jacket in booksellers' faces; the print run was increased from 1,750 or 2,000 to 6,000: in terms of circulation, *Granta* still inhabited a different universe, but at least we were getting through to a larger and younger market. (One of the paradoxes of the *London Magazine* was that although its readership, and its subscribers, tended to be elderly or institutional, it always carried young writers, benefiting from its editor's enthusiasm for new talent, as well as old friends and regular contributors like Julian Symons, Roy Fuller, Frank Tuohy, Gavin Ewart, Stephen Spender, William Trevor, Peter Vansittart, Digby Durrant, Peter Bland and Bertie Lomas).

The honeymoon was short-lived. Alan had, over the years, published quite a few books under the London Magazine Editions imprint – among them Julian Maclaren-Ross's *Memoirs of the Forties*, T.C. Worsley's *Flannelled Fool*, the memoirs of Roy Fuller and Tony Harrison's poems – but he had done so very much as a one-man band, dispensing with contracts, royalties and all the other paraphernalia of the business: he derided, and was made uncomfortable by, the disciplines of formal publishing, ridiculing editorial boards and meetings, and turning up his nose at Picador's jacket designs. The sales force, keen to keep up the momentum, tried to insist that each issue should carry something by a 'big name' like William Boyd, to which Alan replied that although he had been proud to publish early work by Graham Swift, Paul Theroux, Hilary Mantel and Jonathan Raban, he could neither afford the fees they would now command nor expect them to donate their services for nothing, and that his job was to discover new talent which would, in due course, make its way into the literary bloodstream. It was a collision between two different views of the publishing world; after six issues, Picador withdrew its support, and the *London Magazine*'s circulation returned to its former level. Alan seemed mightily relieved, and life could continue as before.

For the rest of his life Alan dreaded a further bout of depression, and only weeks before his death in February 2001 he spent some time in the Priory – prompted, he claimed, by the sinking of a Russian submarine, the *Kursk*, off Murmansk, which brought back dreadful memories of his own wartime experiences on the Arctic convoys. Like many depressives, he hated holidays and weekends, and dreaded being alone: before Jane was there to go with him to functions and on his travels, he used to ask me to accompany him to parties, and stuck closely to me all the time we were there, like an anxious child on an outing: I found this both touching and surprising, given his sophistication, his long experience of the literary world, and the esteem and affection in which he was held. At one such party we came face to face with Sidney Nolan, a large painting by whom hung halfway up the stairs in Alan's house, depicting a moth-eaten lion with one large white fang curled over its lower lip. Alan looked particularly demonic, his black Armenian eyes bulging more than ever and his lower lip trembling as he tried not to laugh. 'You remember that lion you sold me, Sidney?' he asked. 'It's only got one tooth. Could you come round one day and paint in another?' Nolan seemed unamused, and moved briskly away.

Alan was a long-standing member of the Literary Society, a dining club which had been founded in the early nineteenth century, met once a month for dinner in the Garrick, and restricted its membership to around seventy: most were writers, but they also included publishers, politicians and grandees. One day he asked me if I'd like him to put me up for membership, while warning me that I could well be blackballed, and that he'd have to find other members willing to support me. I was thrilled to be asked, since I always enjoyed his descriptions of Lit. Soc. dinners, of the bores whom no one wanted to sit next to, and who had said what about whom. A few weeks later he rang to say that I'd been elected, but his pleasure in getting his candidate through was blighted by the fact that women had been allowed to join for the first time, and constituted three of the five new members. Despite his love of women and his generally liberal views, Alan had led the opposition, but the old guard had been routed, and nothing would be the same again.

We agreed that we would go together to the next monthly dinner. It was hard to know in advance how many members would turn up – it might be as many as thirty, or as few as five – but there was a reasonable quota there that night, several of whom I knew already. Alan had complained of feeling exhausted before he left home, and he wasn't his genial, mocking self that evening: defeat over the women seemed to have made him querulous and irritable. We left the Garrick at about half-past ten, and walked through Leicester Square and on down Piccadilly. Outside Green Park tube station he suggested, to my amazement, that we should hop on a number 14 bus to the Fulham Road. Jane tells me that he was devoted to his Freedom Pass, and spent a good deal of time clambering onto buses and burrowing into the tube, but I had never known him to take public transport of any kind, and always expected him to hail a taxi.

Looking back, it seemed like an omen: next morning Digby rang me to say that Alan had died of a heart attack. He was shaving at the time. 'I think this may be it,' he told Jane, and within minutes he was dead. It was a good way to go, but a terrible shock for his family and his huge army of friends and admirers. Next day I opened his *Coastwise Lights*, with some letters from him tucked inside, and found myself crying like an abandoned child.

By the end of the following year Dennis Enright too was dead, but whereas Alan was suddenly struck down, Dennis endured a slow and wretched death from cancer. Since we lived fairly near, Petra and I would sometimes do his and Madeleine's heavy shopping at Waitrose on Saturdays, which gave us an excuse for a lunchtime drink in their light and airy first-floor flat in Southfields, opposite a playing field. Madeleine opened a bottle of French white wine for her and Petra, which stood waiting on a table alongside a whisky bottle for Dennis and me, an opened box of cheese straws, and a plate containing at least a dozen curried eggs, almost all of which I ate; Dennis would shuffle into the sitting room in his socks and sandals, his rubbery, putty-coloured face lit up by a crooked smile of welcome, his hair shooting off the top of his head like a coil of smoke in the wind. He remained as funny and wise and affectionate as ever, but was fuelled by rage and resentment as his existence became ever more painful and curtailed. He went on writing to the end: on the day before he died in the Trinity Hospice on Clapham Common, his daughter Dominique and her husband Toby Buchan took him the proofs of his last book, *Injury Time*. Dennis and Alan had been my mentors and my friends, the two men I loved and admired more than any others in the literary world, father figures standing in for the one I had lost.